The King's Hussar

The King's Hussar
The Recollections of a 14th (King's)
Hussar During the Victorian Era

Edwin Mole

edited by

Herbert Compton

The King's Hussar: the Recollections of a 14th (King's) Hussar During the Victorian Era
by Edwin Mole
edited by Herbert Compton

Published by Leonaur Ltd

Text in this form and material original to this edition
copyright © 2008 Leonaur Ltd

ISBN: 978-1-84677-452-2 (hardcover)
ISBN: 978-1-84677-451-5 (softcover)

http://www.leonaur.com

Publisher's Notes

The opinions expressed in this book are those of the author and are not necessarily those of the publisher.

Contents

Introduction	9
School Days	11
The Queen's Shilling	23
Regimental Life	34
Hounslow	44
A Long March	55
Scotland and Ireland	66
An Irish Election	76
An Irish Informer	88
I Get My Sergeant's Stripes	100
Kálapoosh	111
Cantonment Life	122
Soldiers' Pets and Pastimes	133
Pallida Mors	144
Court-Martialled	155
Promoted to Troop-Sergeant-Major	166
South Africa	177
To the Front!	188
The Story of Majuba	199
A Stampede	210
Kálapoosh Again	221
Harry	231
"Home, Sweet Home"	241
Depôt Life	252
The Queen's Shilling is Worked Out	263

To

GENERAL LORD ROBERTS
OF KANDAHAR AND WATERFORD

This story of a soldier's circumstances
at home and abroad is, by his lordship's kind
permission, gratefully inscribed

Introduction

Chance brought me into contact with the pensioned cavalry soldier whose fortunes are sketched in the following pages. Many of his anecdotes and adventures I heard long before there was any intention of collecting them for publication. Then the idea occurred to jot down some of his stories in black and white, and this was eventually elaborated until it assumed the form of a memoir.

A military modesty has kept the narrator's name off the title-page; but there is no reason why this reserve should be adopted in the seclusion of the introduction. The name of this King's Hussar is Troop-Sergeant-Major Edwin Mole.

H.C.

CHAPTER 1

School Days

My father was formerly a small farmer at Dudley, in Worcestershire, but in 1852, when I was about seven years old, he left the country and came up to London, and after looking about him for a bit, settled down in Hammersmith, which was then a village, with wheat-fields and gardens all around it.

Here I was sent to learn my ABC at a dame's school till I was eleven years old, when, through the influence of some friends, I was elected to a vacancy in the Latimer School: a fine old foundation, where the sons of tradesmen received a sound education. The only drawback—or what my mother and the parents of the boys considered a drawback—was the strict obligation for all the scholars to wear the Latimer uniform whether attending school or not, and in the holidays as well as term-time. It consisted of a blue swallow-tailed coat with large brass buttons, a high collar, corduroy breeches, grey worsted stockings, a flat-topped cap of blue cloth, and a clean white linen band round the neck; on the right arm of the coat was embroidered a badge, representing a cross in a circle, with the date 1624.

Besides the boys' school, there was another for girls, and a charity for certain old men and women, decayed tradesmen of the place or their widows. The men were obliged to wear the same uniform as the scholars, but without the badge, and twice a year they attended the school to receive a dole. A few of them had been in the army, and we boys always longed for the day to come when they turned out in their best, so that we might see their medals: some being Peninsula ones, with as many as four and five clasps.

One of the parade days was Holy Thursday, when all on the foundation marched in procession to "beat the bounds" of the property belonging to the school. On these occasions the boys led the way in high glee, and the old men hobbled after until a boundary pillar was reached, when the first passer-by or spectator was seized, and, in spite of his protestations, given a good bump on the pillar, and so on from stone to stone.

Very soon after I joined the Latimer School, the building of the new Church of St. John was begun, the site being chosen in the corner of a wheat-field at the top of Cambridge Road. As soon as it was ready, a choir was wanted, and as I could pipe a bit, I was one of the boys selected. There were several privileges connected with choir singing, such as being asked to assist at weddings, christenings, and funerals, and also social entertainments, when we frequently received handsome presents. My great chum, a boy named Bill Thompson, was also in the choir, and I shall have a good bit to say about him later on as well as now.

Underneath the new church was a large vault, where the heating apparatus stood, with a great heap of coke by it. The stoke-hole, as we called it, served as a fine place for us choir boys to lark in when we were waiting about for service or had finished practice. It was under the charge of a verger, a very savage old man, whose delight was in chasing us out with a cane whenever he found us playing down there. But this did not deter us from making it our regular place of *rendezvous,* or refuge, when we were playing some of our games, such as "Thieves and Robbers," or were attacked in force by the boys of the Godolphin School, which stood just behind our school; and between them and us frequent fights took place, we regarding them as enemies and interlopers.

In the days I am writing about the Crimean War was just ended, and one of our favourite games after evening service was "English and Russians." At the top of the stoke-hole was a small parapet wall, protecting the flight of steps that led down to it, and this afforded a sort of battlement, which we named the Redan. Here we had our greatest fights; and I remember one evening in particular ringing the church bell to sound the alarm, which it did properly, for it roused the whole of Hammersmith, and brought the local fire-engine to the spot to see if the church was on fire. There was a great to-do over this, and the next day we choir boys were court-martialled and the old verger, much to his delight, was ordered to give us a good thwacking, which he did till his arms ached.

But this did not quench our spirits, for not long afterwards we arranged for a grand night performance at the same place. The idea occurred to me of blowing up the Redan—a real explosion, with gunpowder and names, and smoke and stones, in the air, all regular and complete. The choir boys tumbled to it at once, and we saved our pocket-money to buy gunpowder in ha'porths and pen'norths, until we had purchased what we thought sufficient. Then a night was fixed for us all to meet at the stoke-hole after evening service. For some time previously we had collected all the stones, bricks, and building material we could find, and stowed them away under the coke, not forgetting an old quart milk-can, and a piece of rag for tinder.

Having chosen a spot in the grass close to the stoke-hole door, and within five feet of the church wall, we began building the stones in a circle, leaving a hollow place in the centre. We then poured our powder into the milk-can, and, there being over twenty of us, there was a good bit of it altogether. The cloth being rubbed with powder, one end of it was laid in the milk-can, whilst the other trailed out on to the ground, and from this we laid a long train of gunpowder almost to the end of the church. Last of all, we heaped stones and bricks and pieces of coke around and over the can to the height of three feet.

We now tossed for sides, I being captain of one, and Bill Thompson of the other. As I had invented the game, the honour of firing the train fell to my lot. Having divided ourselves into Stormers and Besieged, the former retired to the bottom of a grassy slope a few yards off, and I took my garrison to the Redan.

The signal being given, Bill Thompson and his forlorn hope came roaring and shouting up the slope. We met them valiantly and rolled them down it. Then they rallied and came back to the assault with a cheer, whereupon I gave the order to retreat, and as we fell back behind the end of the church, set fire to the train.

There was a great fizz and splutter, with lots of flame and smoke, and a lovely smell, but that was all; for, to our surprise and disgust, no explosion followed. "Why hasn't it gone off?" asked someone; and then two or three, more daring than the rest, began to creep towards the fort.

"Pooh!" cried Bill Thompson, who led them, "it has gone out;" and, stooping down, he began picking off some of the stones till he came to the milk-can, which he lifted out, with the rag still dangling over its side. By this time all the boys had gathered round, and I heard him say, "I wonder why it didn't act?" At that instant my eye caught sight of the glow of a live spark on the rag, but before I had time to utter a word there was an explosion, and the next second every one of us were blown down on the flat of our backs round the Redan.

At first I thought I was blinded, if not killed, and felt sure I was deaf for ever. But after a little while my power of sight and hearing returned, and I saw all the boys stretched on the ground, "Are you hurt?" I asked; whereupon one sat up and said "Not much," and then another and another; but a good many continued to lie where they were.

"Battle-fields and corpses! Here's a many of them for the asking!" thought I to myself, as I wiped my eyes with my cuff and rose to my feet. By degrees a good many followed my example, excepting three, who lay there like logs.

"They are dead!" whispered someone in a trembling voice, and then a sudden horror seized us all, and we shrank away, afraid to touch them At the same time a number of the Godolphin boys came running up, having heard the explosion; but instead of being enemies now, they proved good friends, for some ran for a doctor, and some for water, and others helped to prop up poor Bill and the two who were hurt.

We did what we could to revive them, calling them by their names and imploring them to speak to us—if it was only a groan, to show they were not dead. But they could not, and it was not until the doctor came that we were reassured. Under his directions we carried them to their homes, through a great crowd of townspeople who had collected, and who kept asking what had happened, and if anyone was killed, and whether "them devils of choir boys" had not blown up the new church.

Poor Bill Thompson was put to bed, and all the upper part of his body, as well as his head and face, swathed in bandages, and he remained like this for some weeks. We received a proper punishment; and I remember one part of it well enough, for it lasted the longest. Every Sunday afternoon, when service was over, we were marched from church to Bill Thompson's house. Going down the street, all the townspeople brought their children to see us as we shuffled along, like so many malefactors on their way to be hung, and they would point the finger of scorn at us and call us names. This was all very well from the grown-up folk, but when the kiddies and babies took to making faces at us we felt it very much indeed.

At Bill Thompson's house we were made to sit in a circle round his bed, and the bandages being removed a little from his ears, we read several chapters of the Bible aloud to him, verse and verse about, finishing up with the service for Gunpowder Plot Day. But after the parson had gone Mrs. Thompson used to give us a slice of cake each and a glass of home-made wine, so, except for the faces the children made at us—which we never could get over—we did not mind this part of our punishment very much.

I am glad to say Bill Thompson completely recovered and returned to school, where he and I became greater chums than ever. We had the same way of thinking, and were always talking of soldiering and sailoring in foreign parts. In the school library was a copy of *Mungo Park's Travels,* which I was so much given to reading that my schoolfellow gave me the nickname of Mungo Park. The book was full of fine things about Africa, and lions, and black men, which made me hanker to see them, and feel sorry I was too young to start right away.

In 1859 my school days came to an end, and I was apprenticed to a builder. This line of life did not suit me at all. About the same time Bill Thompson was bound to another tradesman in the town, and as we lived and worked close together, we kept up our old friendship. We used often to meet, and our conversation always ran upon fighting for our queen and country, instead of doing tinkering jobs for Hammersmith masters. But we were both too young to enlist, and sooner than wait till we grew up, we determined to go to sea for a bit. So we began swing up our wages and taking trips on Sundays down the river to Gravesend, where we made inquiries as to the best way to become sailors. Our first intention was to enter the Royal Navy, but we found we should want our parents' consent, which put it out of the question, and obliged us to decide for the merchant service.

We were in a measure reconciled to this by some information we obtained from an old sailor who used to come round begging in the streets. After giving him a few coppers, we began to ask him questions as to how he went to sea. I suppose he saw our drift, for he pitched us a wonderful yarn, saying that when he was a lad he tramped it from London to Portsmouth, which was easily done in a couple of days, and that once arrived there, everything was plain sailing, as lots of lads were wanted for powder-monkeys, which was how he had commenced life in the merchant service. As he had a wooden leg, a patch on one eye, and a battered-in face, all complete, we were satisfied he was speaking the truth. Only Bill Thompson made bold to say he had always held the idea that merchant ships only carried cargo, and never did any fighting. "Ah!" retorted the old salt, "you has to be careful, and see you ship aboard a Fighting Merchantman."

We considered this information highly valuable, and as by this time I had saved thirteen shillings, and Bill Thompson nearly a pound, we decided to put our scheme into execution, and made an appointment to meet early on a certain morning, with our sticks and bundles, and commence our tramp to Portsmouth.

It was dawn of a lovely cold October day when we left Hammersmith, and set out for Guildford. We began our journey at a brisk rate, and covered some miles before we ventured any inquiries, fearing that, in spite of all our secrecy and precautions, our parents might miss us and overtake us. After skirting all the villages on the way, we drew near to Guildford late in the afternoon, but although footsore and weary, we did not think it prudent to enter the town by daylight, and sat down on the roadside to wait for nightfall, and fell fast asleep.

It was dusk when we were aroused from our slumber by someone shaking us, and I shall never forget my feelings as I opened my eyes and saw a policeman standing over me. He asked who we were, and what we were doing. Neither of us knew what to answer, and felt more inclined to cry than anything else; whereupon the policeman repeated the question, and Bill mustered courage to say that we were on our way from London to Guildford to see some friends, and being tired, had sat down and fallen asleep. This seemed to satisfy the bobby, for he pointed out the town to us, which was quite close, and then asked us whom we were going to see, remarking that he knew every one in Guildford, and where they lived. This gave us a terrible turn, and not knowing what answer to make, we remained silent. The policeman seemed puzzled at our strange conduct, and finding he could get nothing out of us, told us we had better move on, and that he suspected we were not up to much good. "But," he added, "before I let you go, just open them bundles of yours, and let me see what you've got in them." We obeyed at once, assuring him very earnestly we had nothing but what belonged to us; and as he only found a little linen, a prayer-book, and a few birthday cards, he had no excuse to apprehend us. "Go along," he said, after overhauling our kit, "and take you care, for it's my opinion you are deserters from the Navy, and I've half a mind to lock you up;" with which he let us depart, and we sneaked down the road.

When the policeman was out of sight we turned into some fields and loitered about, not liking to chance any further danger by entering Guildford. At last we heard the church bells striking half-past nine, and made up our minds to approach a row of cottages, and ask where we could get a respectable night's lodging. The first person we saw was a labouring man, but when we accosted him we found he was thick in liquor.

After listening to our story, he asked if we had any money, and on our saying "Yes," replied that was all right, as we could stand him a drink. In return, he would get us a good lodging. That seemed a fair bargain, and so we gave him sixpence, and accompanied him to a beer-shop, which he rolled into while we waited outside. We kicked our heels about for some time, for he did not come out till he was chucked out. Going up to him, we reminded him of his bargain. "Oh—ah—yes," he hiccoughed. "It's you, is it? All right; come along. I'd forgot about you." He then staggered towards a neighbouring cottage, swearing horribly as he went at the landlord of the beer-shop, whose vitals he promised himself the pleasure of kicking out in the morning.

When we reached his home, we found an elderly woman waiting at the door, whom I took to be his wife by the free way she abused him. He told her to shut up, and that he had brought two young gentlemen to lodge with her, and with that shoved her aside and took us in.

There was a sort of supper spread on the table, and he told us to fall to. We sat down, the woman looking at us all the time as we ate, but not speaking a word. Presently the husband called her out of the room, and we were left alone. I looked at Bill, and he looked at me, and we wished ourselves at home, and no mistake about it. After a few minutes the woman returned, and said she would make us as comfortable as she could, and we would be "quite safe"—a remark that only roused our fears—only we must not mind sleeping on the floor, as her best room was occupied. The charge would be two shillings each; and this we agreed to pay, and asked her to show us up to our room. Whereupon she led us up a rickety flight of stairs to an attic with a sloping roof, very low and dark, and no furniture, and no door in the door frame! We now paid her the money for our lodging, and when she saw we had more in our pockets she said we had not settled for our supper. Bill Thompson asked if we could have breakfast very early in the morning, and she said "Yes"; so Bill promised to pay her in one lump for both meals. "Oh no," she answered; "we don't give credit to strangers. You must pay now." There was nothing to be done but to give the money (especially as we heard the man stumbling about downstairs,) and she eased us of four shillings and then went away, taking the candle with her, and leaving us in the dark. We took off our boots, our feet being very sore, and lay down on the floor without undressing, so that we might be ready to make a bolt for it, if necessary. But there being no pillows, we were obliged to take off our trousers to serve as such.

And now we began to compare ideas in whispers, and found we were both of the same opinion: namely, that the man below meant us no good. So we determined that one should watch whilst the other slept, and the first watch falling to me, I propped my back against the wall, whilst Bill lay down and snored.

It is a difficult thing to look into pitch darkness and keep your eyes open. I considered I was doing it well enough, until I woke up and found the daylight streaming through the windows. I roused Bill, and told him I thought it was time to get up, and we slipped into our trousers; but when our hands went into the pockets, they were empty.

This distressed us greatly, and we began to accuse each other of falling asleep, and I suppose made some noise, for we soon heard the man's voice shouting to us: "Now then, young gentlemen, it's time you were getting on the road if you want to reach London today." So we bundled downstairs, and when the man asked us how we had slept, told him very soundly, for someone had stolen our money during the night.

"What do you mean?" he asked in a threatening tone. "Do you think *I* have?"

Of course we lost no time in declaring that such a thought had never entered our heads, but our protestations failed to satisfy him.

"If that's your artful way of getting off paying for your bed and the good supper you had last night," he said, "I'm just blowed if I don't give you a good hiding."

"We paid your wife everything," said Bill, very scared.

"Paid her?" answered the man, professing great astonishment. "You paid her? Just listen! Ah—I see now the sort of young cocks you are; and I tell you what, if you're not out of this house under a minute you'll be sorry."

He opened the door and pointed to the road. "Out you go!" said he; and out we went.

Our feet were still very sore, and at first we could only hobble along; but we covered a mile before the sun rose, when we met some men who directed us to the Portsmouth Road, along which we tramped till mid-day, hardly speaking, and feeling hungry and unhappy.

About one o'clock we came to a field where two labourers were carting turnips, and one or two dropping out as the waggon jolted, we picked them up and ate them, this being the first mouthful we had munched since supper overnight. Soon after that we reached a country inn, outside which some waggons were standing, with the owners' names and "Portsmouth" painted on them, and when the drivers came out, we begged for a lift, which they good-naturedly gave us, and we rode the rest of the journey, arriving at Portsmouth at five o'clock.

We had no difficulty in finding the docks, but instead of leisurely selecting a smart Fighting Merchantman, we were only too glad to walk aboard the first craft we came across, which happened to be a little coasting brig. Stepping up to a man whom we took to be a sailor officer, we asked him if he wanted any powder-monkeys. He gave a hearty laugh, and after eyeing us curiously, asked where we had come from, and we told him London.

"You look as though you had," he remarked. "Do your parents know it?"

Bill Thompson replied that his parents were dead: which was a cruel lie; and I said my mother had run away from home, and my father had kicked me out: which was a worse one.

"That's a bad job for both of you, any way," said the sailor officer. "have you eaten anything to-day?"

"Only turnips," I answered.

"Well, come and see the captain;" and he led the way down some steps into a low dark cabin, where we saw a man who did not look at all like the commander of a Fighting Merchantman, but more like a very dirty coal-hewer.

"Here, Captain," said the sailor officer, with a wink, "I've brought you two new hands."

The captain looked up, and when he saw us standing meekly in front of him, caps in hand, and covered with dust from head to foot, he laughed out loud.

After a few questions, the sailor officer chimed in, "Better let them pull their boots off here tonight, for they look footsore; and give the little beggars something to eat, for they've only had turnips?"

"Very well," answered the captain. "Come along here, youngsters," he called out to us, as he went down two or three steps into an inner cabin, where he gave us some bread and cold meat to eat, and told us we might stop the night

When we awoke the next morning, and found we were actually on board ship, our spirits began to revive, and we congratulated ourselves on having done it all so cleverly. But when we tried to go on deck, we found the door locked. And locked it remained all that day and all the next day, the captain only coming in to give us meals: which hurt our feelings a good deal, for we had no thoughts of deserting the ship.

On the morning of the third day the captain poked his head into the cabin, and cried, "Now then, youngsters, tumble up! Here's the skipper come who's going to ship you."

Out we tumbled, full of hope, and the first thing our eyes fell on were our two fathers and a policeman.

My father came up to me first, and planting himself in front of me—"Well, boy," says he, "you're come to be a sailor, have you? And I kicked you out of home, did I? You wait till your mother hears she ran away from Hammersmith. She'll want to know more about that, she will." And all the time he kept lifting his hand as if to strike me, and I kept wincing and trying to dodge it, until at last I fairly burst out crying, not so much from fright as from bitter disappointment.

Then came Bill Thompson's turn. Up steps his father and says: "Well, my little orphan lad, your father has come to life again, and you was mistook when you thought him a dead 'un. And your mother, too, she's pretty burly. Wait till I get you home! I'll give you something for bringing me out this journey." Poor Bill was so taken aback that he could not have looked worse if his father had really died and come to life again.

We were marched ashore and taken home by train. I learnt afterwards how we had been tracked. As soon as we were missed, my father had begun making inquiries, and first of all heard from my sister, with whom I had quarrelled the previous day, that I said she would be sorry for treating me as she did .when I was a sailor. "*You* a sailor!" she jeered. "You'll soon want to be home again." "Not I," replied I. "Wait till you come down to Portsmouth, and see me in my sailor clothes!" Having learnt this, my father went to the police-station, where he found out that one of the constables had seen Bill and I starting off with our bundles, but supposed we were going blackberrying. Putting two and two together, my father guessed where we had gone, and got the police to telegraph to Portsmouth, and, as it happened, our description was known and circulated round the shipping some hours before we reached the port.

This failure of my attempt to go sailoring put an end to all my ideas of leaving home, and I settled down to work with the builder to whom I was apprenticed and for the next three years kept steadily at it. But all the same I never lost the old hankering for a soldier's life, but determined as soon as I was my own master to follow the profession of my choice.

Chapter 2

The Queen's Shilling

In 1862 the master builder to whom I was apprenticed, died, and my indentures were cancelled. Being now free I engaged with a Mr. Stark, and after a time, chance brought us to work on the Charing Cross Hotel, which was just being completed.

Whilst employed here I often noticed the great number of recruiting sergeants in different army uniforms who hung about the locality and with some of them I scraped an acquaintance. One day in June, 1863, I had a few words with Mr. Stark, and losing my temper, left off work with the intention of going home to my lodgings; but just as I got outside the hotel, I met a Sergeant Hudson, of the 60th Rifles, whom I knew pretty well.

He asked me where I was going at that time of day, and I told him there had been a bit of a row, and I was clearing out. Whereupon he invited me to have a glass of ale with him, and we went to a public-house in Charles Street, Westminster, much frequented by recruiting sergeants. Here he introduced me to several other men in his line of business, amongst them one with whom I was particularly struck, both on account of his pleasant face and his fine uniform. His name was Gibbs, and he belonged to the 14th Hussars, and was a chum of Hudson's. Glasses were called for, and I remained there for the best part of the afternoon, Sergeant Gibbs being very liberal in standing treat and filling my glass as soon as it was empty. But having no liking for liquor I soon refused to drink any more, and he then suggested we should go to his quarters for a cup of tea.

Hudson said he would join us presently, and I followed Gibbs to the place where he was lodging.

To pass the time he began showing me several pictures of soldiers in different army uniforms, which hung upon the walls. Then pointing to his own rig-out he observed:

"But after all, there's none to beat this one in the Service! And, do you know?" he added, looking me up and down, "I think you'd look a rare treat in stable dress."

I asked him what stable dress was, and he said the walking-out costume, consisting of a dark blue shell jacket, overalls cut tight to show off the figure to advantage, Wellington boots with jingling spurs, a small cap "on three hairs," and a whip. As he reeled off the description I could not help comparing it with the clothes I was wearing, and he spoke in such a friendly, fascinating way that I blurted out: "I've often thought of enlisting."

"I knew you had," he said, "by the smart way you hold yourself." This was pretty thick but I swallowed it all. "See here," he went on, "just step under this and I'll take your height."

He pushed up the slide of a measuring machine that stood in a corner of the room, and waited for me to get under it; but I held back, having a silly idea it might commit me in some way.

"Don't be afraid," he laughed; and all in such a jolly off-hand manner, that I had no power to refuse. He found I was just the proper height, and then began telling me about himself, and what he had seen away in *Kálapoosh*[1] (which was army slang for India), describing his battles in the Mutiny and the marches he had made in the Central India Campaign under Sir Hugh Rose.

"Look at me, lad," he wound up; "I've done sixteen years of it, and the best part of them in *Kálapoosh;* but I don't seem any the worse, do I? I tell you, it's the finest life out."

"I don't doubt that," I answered; "but I'm earning good money, and I've no mind to 'list just now. At least, not without a chum of mine." Meaning Bill Thompson.

"Why, lad, you've only to list, and once your chum claps

---

1. *Kaläh-posh,* Anglice "hat-wearers"; the word is applied to Europeans by the Persian author of the History of Hydur Nark (Or: Tr: Fund 8⁰, 1842).

eyes on you in the Hussar uniform there's nothing 'll stop him from coming after you. As for your earning good money, see the mucking work you have to do for it. And you'll never want money in the 14th Hussars. If you only keep yourself smart and your eyes purling, you'll get your fun and plenty to drink free gratis; for the girls will fight for you, and you'll always find a Christian ready to stand treat. The Fourteenth," he added, with a wink of his eye and a cock of his head, " get the pick of the girls wherever they go."

All this sounded very tempting, but I was determined to do nothing off-hand, and told Gibbs it was no good that day; but that if ever I did enlist I should like to wear the same uniform as he did.

"Well, then, take the bob, and have done with it," ' he suggested suddenly.

But this I declined, and just then Sergeant Hudson came in, and we sat down to tea. Nothing more was said about enlisting; but it was arranged we should go to a theatre, and on the way there I asked Hudson several questions about the army, and at last put it straight to him: "Tell me, Sergeant, do you really like the Service?"

"What a question to ask!" he responded. "I have only one wish, and that is that I had entered it four years sooner; and a man can't say more than that, can he?"

I took his reply at the moment as being the highest compliment he could pay to the charms of a soldier's life, and was satisfied accordingly. But, as Sergeant Hudson had seventeen years' service, and four more would have completed his time, there were two ways of interpreting his reply.

I then asked him if he knew anything about the 14th Hussars.

"They have not been home long," he answered, "but they are a smart corps, and will always get first-class stations. A young fellow like you, if he only keeps himself clean and on the right side of the booze, is bound to get on in the Fourteenth."

This pretty well decided me, though I determined to sleep over it and do nothing till the next day, when I determined to go down and see Bill Thompson and persuade him to enlist with me. When the theatre was over, Sergeant Gibbs said he had a spare bed in his quarters, and I might as well use it. So we returned to Charles Street, where drinks were called for, and what with one thing and what with another, I was enticed into taking a drop too much, and never rightly remember what happened that night or how I got to bed.

Next morning, when I awoke, my head was very lumpy. The first thing I saw was Sergeant Gibbs, sitting up in bed, smoking.

"Hello!" he cried. "You've woke up, have you? Could you do a drop of beer?"

"No beer for me," I answered, "but I'd like some tea or coffee."

"Coffee you shall have and that directly, for you'll have to go before the doctor this morning, and as it's rather late I think you had better get up at once."

"What have I to go before the doctor for?"

"Why, because you 'listed last night, of course; and there's the medical to pass. You're a soldier now. If you feel in your pocket you'll find the bob, and if you want any luck you'd better come downstairs and break it, for that's the custom and according to the Articles of War."

This information staggered me, for I had no recollection of taking any shilling. Thinking Sergeant Gibbs was only joking, I said: "Don't talk silly. If I had 'listed last night I should have remembered it."

"Not by the way you looked when you went to bed," he replied. "Why, you drank me and Hudson blind, toasting your new regiment; and it was as much as we could do to carry you upstairs and sling you on to your cot. But just look in your pocket."

I had my trousers on, and I slipped my hand into my pocket and pulled out what there was there. All my money, I found, was gone, except a few coppers and—

"The Queen's Shilling," put in Sergeant Gibbs, with a knowing nod of his head, as I picked out a solitary one and held it in front of me, between finger and thumb.

It was just the same as any other shilling—yet I could not

help looking at it with a bit of awe, and wondering if I had gone and 'prenticed myself to twelve years' soldiering for this little bit of silver.

"Come on, my tulip, buck about," cried the sergeant, breaking into my reflections; "you've done it now and Parliament itself can't undo it. Get on your clothes or we shall be all behindhand."

I felt in no mood to argue, and after all, it was a relief to me to know I had "gone and done it," and that it was all over. So I jumped out of bed, and began to dress, making up my mind to go right through with it as though I liked it.

After a hurried breakfast we started for the house where the doctor examined recruits, and after a bath I was soon passed as medically fit, with a brief, "You'll do." I was then taken before a military officer, who asked me several questions, including my age, which I said was eighteen, although I was under. After this I fell in with a squad of recruits, and we were marched to Bow Street Station, where we each nipped a thumbful of prayer book, and took the oath of allegiance to Her Majesty.

I spent the rest of the day with Sergeant Gibbs, and in the evening he took me to the house where the recruits were accommodated previous to being sent off to their different regiments. Here we entered a large room with from fifteen to twenty beds in it, and as many young fellows, all about my own age, but mostly cockneys. They were engaged in a free fight, and on seeing me called out: "Here comes another 'cruity. What are you for, chum?" but catching sight of the sergeant, they all stood back in a moment and became quiet. I must say their appearance rather upset me, for I did not expect to begin soldiering with such a queer squad as this, Gibbs having many times impressed on me that all the men in the 14th Hussars were gentlemen, and I believed (though wrongly) that these recruits had been enlisted for the same regiment as myself. What made matters worse was that, before leaving, Sergeant Gibbs said if I had anything of value about my person I had better give it him to take care of till morning. This seemed pretty strong, but I took out my watch and purse and put them in his hands, and he then left, locking the door behind him.

I need not describe the night in detail, but I was heartily glad when morning came, and an old army pensioner, unlocking the door, called out my name, and ordered me to follow him, as he had been told off to take me to Manchester where the 14th Hussars were stationed. On the way to Euston he asked me a number of questions, as to how and why I had enlisted, and so on, to which I gave straightforward answers, telling him, truthfully enough, it had always been my intention to go for a soldier, and all I wanted now was to get into my uniform. When we arrived at the station, he took a ticket for me, and then explained he ought by rights to travel with me, but his wife being ill, he did not like to leave her, and thought he could trust me to go to Manchester by myself.

"But," said he, "if you fail to join your regiment, you'll get us both into trouble, for when they catch you they'll shoot you as a deserter; and as for me, they'll try me by court-martial, and I'll lose my pension, which I am sure you would not like to feel you were the cause of."

I assured him he need have no fear, and, wishing me luck, he went off. I reached Manchester that evening and reported myself at the guard-room at the front gate of the barracks. The sergeant on duty was very surprised at my being sent there, as the Fourteenth had just left for Aldershot, and there was only a dismounted party of women and children and a few soldiers in the place. However, he took me to a barrack-room, and made me over to a man-in-charge, telling him to see I was comfortable.

The next day I went before the regimental doctor and the officer in command. The latter gave me a few words of advice, and told me I should join the regiment at Aldershot in a few days, when the colonel would inspect me and pass me into it. During the short time I remained at Manchester I made myself useful doing odd jobs, until orders came for the dismounted party to rail down to Aldershot, which we reached late one evening. The following morning I attended at orderly-room, and went before our commanding officer, Colonel T——. He was a fine, well-furnished, military-looking man, with a florid complexion, and an iron grey moustache. His principal feature was a great eagle nose, from which he got the name "Old Beaky" in the regiment. His manner was kind, and his advice short and to the point:—"Keep yourself smart and clean," he said, "and always be obedient. Support the credit of your corps to the utmost of your ability. And, above all, avoid drink, which is the pitfall of all soldiers."

I was now taken charge of by an old grizzly troop-sergeant-major, who wore four medals, and looked a fierce warrior, with his big moustache and little side whiskers. "Old Splodgers"—for this was the nickname given him on account of his big flat feet—possessed one or two eccentricities of manner which were a little trying to a nervous recruit. He never began to speak without giving a loud, hard, abrupt cough, and his favourite designation for everyone was, "you toad." As soon as we got outside the orderly-room he began at me: "H'm, you toad; come along and see your troop." With that he took me over to the stables, and calling out an old soldier, said: "H'm, Harris, you toad, look after this toad."

It was the practice in those days when, owing to long service, the percentage of recruits in a regiment was very small, to hand over each new one to an old soldier, who was known as an "old swaddy," and held responsible for the recruit's behaviour in barracks. Harris took charge of me, and at once proceeded to introduce me to the horses, and putting a brush and curry-comb into my hand, told me "to have a go at old Balaclava," pointing out a big bay trooper, with a terrible rough coat, which stood in one of the stalls. This animal had been through the Crimean war, and bore the marks of active service in the shape of a deep sabre scar on his forehead, and half of his left ear missing.

Pulling off my coat, I hung it on the bail, or bar between the stalls, and started to groom old Balaclava. But no sooner had I touched him with the brush, than he made a sort of half-rear in the stall, and threw his sound ear back in a way that induced me to chance the character of the trooper in the next stall by scuttling under the bail and against its feet, which made it nearly jump into its neighbour's premises. There was a roar of laughter from all the men, and it was some time before I plucked up courage to face old Balaclava again, who now stood looking as meek as a towel-horse. However, before I had time to have another go at him, the sergeant-major entered the stables, and called out "Tention" at the top of his voice; whereupon every man, except myself, ceased work in a jiffy, and stood bolt upright. I merely looked to see what was happening, and then gave two or three preparatory rubs of my brush against the curry-comb, wondering why Harris kept making all sorts of dumb motions at me with his eyes, and manoeuvring his fingers as though he were working off the deaf and dumb alphabet against time.

It was the captain, who had come in for inspection, and as soon as his eyes fell on me, he asked: "What have you got here?"

Splodgers, in a very stern way, came up to me and whispered, "H'm; why don't you stand to attention, you toad?" and began pulling me out of the stall, and shoving my hands down at my sides, explaining to the captain, with a salute: "A new 'emit, sir; just joined."

They walked round the stables, the captain commenting on each horse as he passed it, and when they had finished I was sent for, Splodgers whispering in my ear in a gruff voice, "Speak up, you toad; he's deaf"

The captain began asking me several questions to which I replied in a modified shout; whereupon he demanded whom was I bawling at? I learnt afterwards he was very touchy about his partial deafness, and I was glad when he turned away from me, and, the order for dismiss from stables being given, all the men went to the barrack rooms upstairs.

In the room I was taken to there were three tables down the centre, and fold-up bedsteads on either side, with shelves and pegs for kit and accoutrements above them. Soon there came a shout of "Look out for scaldings!" and a man ran up with a large dish of meat and a round tin of potatoes. Lumping them down on the table, he cried: "Come on; bring your *churries!*" whereupon some of the soldiers produced knives and began to cut up the meat into lots according to the number in the mess. Then each soldier took the portion that suited his fancy; but at least half-a-dozen men, after a look at the dish, lit their pipes and went off to the canteen.

Harris gave me a knife and fork and told me to wire in, and that if I felt peckish there was plenty extra to-day; but the meat and potatoes were both bad, and I made my dinner off bread. The meal did not take long, and directly it was over, most of the men began shaking down their beds and getting into them for an "easy," with their pipes alight. I helped the mess-man to clear away, and then stretched myself in a spare bed, thinking I had better do as the others did. Several of them offered me tobacco, but I said I did not smoke, whereupon they remarked, truly enough, that I would soon take to it.

After a bit the men who had gone to the canteen began to return, a few not quite so steady as they might be, and by three o'clock all the room was asleep except myself. I kept awake listening to the strange medley of noises made by the snoring of the men, and the rattling of chains, stamping of hoofs, and occasional neighing of the horses underneath.

There were fifteen men in my mess, fourteen of whom wore three or four medals. They were good-hearted fellows in the main, though a little short-tempered; and all bore signs of their long residence in India, where the regiment had been for nineteen years without coming home. They used many queer Hindustan names and terms, which it took me some time to get the hang of. For instance, they never spoke of knives, or salt, or bread, but always "Give me a *churrie!*" "Pass the *neemuck!*" or "Sling over some *rootee!*"

The next day I had to parade for foot drill, and was put in a squad with the other recruits, some of whom had already got their uniforms. From the tales I had heard about drill sergeants I dreaded them more than anything else, believing they took a delight in bullying, but I found the non-commissioned officer in charge of us patient, although strict, and the exercises not only easy but interesting.

The conditions under which men were enlisted in 1863 were for a one pound bounty and a free kit, the latter being supposed to include every necessary article. When I had been three or four days at Aldershot, Harris told me one evening to go up to the troop-sergeant-major and get my kit, and bring it back to him and he would show me how to put it by.

Making my way to Splodgers' quarters, I found him in his shirt-sleeves and slippers, dictating something to another man who was writing. Splodgers himself could neither read nor write, and consequently employed a soldier to do his troop accounts. Some time afterwards, when I was his clerk and knew him better, he read me a manuscript kept by himself in signs and hieroglyphics, which none but he could decipher. It was his diary during fifteen years' service in India. I often had an opportunity of examining it, and tried to make out the characters but beyond a few numerals like the English, the rest was Greek to me, being a series of crosses, and upright marks, and long and short dashes, which conveyed nothing to my mind, except vaguely suggesting the army signal code.

As soon as I entered the room the sergeant-major placed some papers in front of me to sign, one of which he pointed out as the receipt for the one pound bounty, and at the same time he slapped five shillings and ninepence down on the table, with the following statement of account:—

"H'm. Bounty, one pound. Deductions: one whip, so much; one cap for walking out, so much; one dandy brush, so much; one sponge, so much; one burnisher, so much. Total, fourteen three. Balance due, five nine. There you are, you toad; and see you don't make a fool of yourself."

I signed the papers and picked up the money, wondering what construction the authorities put on the words "Free kit." Then Splodgers took me to the store room, and gave me a variety of articles of dress, and my civilian clothes were put into store, and I never saw them again.

My uniform consisted of a pair of blue cloth overalls with two yellow stripes down the sides, a tunic of blue cloth with six cross rows of yellow braid in front, and two straight ones down the back, a stable jacket, which fitted as tight as a glove, and a second pair of overalls, called leathers. My arms and accoutrements were a muzzle-loading carbine, a sword, a pair of spurs, pouch and belt, and last, but to my thinking best of all, a bearskin busby, with a yellow bag and lines of yellow cord hanging over one side, and a white plume in front.

Sunday was the first day on which I wore my uniform. I crawled into it with as much care as if the different articles had been made of glass, and when everything was buttoned up and fixed proper, and I surveyed myself in sections in the piece of broken looking-glass which did duty for the toilet and shaving of everyone in the room, I heaved a sigh of satisfaction, and flattered myself I was a soldier at last.

CHAPTER 3

Regimental Life

I soon had many opportunities of forming an opinion of the regiment in which so many of my days were to be passed, It was at this time filled with seasoned and veteran soldiers, many of whom had been seventeen and eighteen years in India. Nothing delighted me more than to get one of these old soldiers "on a line" telling tales of *Kálapoosh*. They were very diffident about their own deeds; but when describing what their comrades had done, their tongues were loosened, and some of the stories beat anything I ever heard or read of.

The 14th Hussars contained as fine a body of fighting men and as smart a set of soldiers as any in the British army, their only fault being a liking for *pongelo,* for, truth to tell, they were hard drinkers. It must also be admitted that they were not as clever with the pen as with the sword, and in the matter of "the three R's" could not be compared with the young soldiers of the present day, who are scholars by Act of Parliament. But it is an ill wind that blows nobody any good, and my education now stood me in good stead; for of the fifteen men in my room, not one could write, and only one could read, and my ability to do both soon proved to my advantage.

It began in this way. One day an old soldier beckoned me aside, and asked me in a mysterious way to have a wet with him at the canteen. I thanked him, but declined; whereupon he produced a letter, and shoving it into my hand, asked me to read it to him. This I did, much to his delight, and after thanking me, he offered me sixpence (as I had declined a drink), which of course I refused.

"Well, I won't forget it, anyhow," he said; "and if you'll only write an answer back for me, I will boss your arms up when you come off drill, and if anyone rides rough over you, just you let me know, and I'll see to it."

This started the ball rolling, and in a short time I was reader and secretary to the whole room. There were some queer letters indited by me at times, for I always had a bit of fun in me, and it would come out when I had to write to two different girls from the same man, who had left a brace of sweethearts behind him at Manchester. Sometimes I slipped in a bit more than was dictated, and then, to the men's joy, the answers came back with unexpected remittances of postage-stamps which my persuasive pen had brought. There was this curious thing about it, that—although these old soldiers freely trusted me with their secrets—when it came to posting the letter, every man would put his own into the box himself.

There was one funny fellow, in particular, who often availed himself of my penmanship—a cockney of the name of Fruiterer, but always called *Rootee,* on account of his fondness for bread. He was a very "caius" (artful) chap, and had some well-to-do friends in London, from whom he often received money, which went as fast as it came, in grub—for Rootee was an exception to the general rule, and liked eating better than drinking. When I began to write his letters for him I came in for a full share of his feasts, i and he was always inventing new excuses to pile up the agony, and urging me to pitch his folks some extra thrilling yarn about his hardships, and especially his hunger. One day, when funds were very low, and he was desperately hard up for something to say, he asked me:

"'Cruity, scratch your head, and tell us something to sling at 'em."

I suggested, offhand, the first thing that occurred to me.

"Write home and swear you've lost a wheelbarrow while on stable-guard, and if you don't pay for it, Splodgers will have you sent to cells."

"That's the hammer!" he shouted, jumping up and slapping his knee. "That will knock the dollars out of 'em!"

The letter was written, and posted, and a sovereign came back within twenty-four hours—seventeen and sixpence being the price of the barrow, and the odd half-crown to buy an extra good one to appease Splodgers. The result of this shower of gold was, that old Rootee forgot his prudence, and "chanced his arm"—as the saying goes, when a man risks losing his stripes—by a visit to the canteen, which brought him about nightfall to the guard-room, and the next afternoon I had the sorrow of seeing him perspiring under pack drill. When I whispered in a friendly way he might find it easier to wheel his kit on a barrow, he glared at me, and didn't take the advice in the spirit in which it was offered.

Apart from becoming a bit of a favourite in the room, from writing the men's letters for them, I gained by it myself, for I soon earned a character for keeping my arms and accoutrements clean. I hope I accepted the commendation this brought me with befitting modesty, for, truth to tell, the men whose letters I wrote deserved it all.

I must not forget to mention one letter which I wrote on my own account, very shortly after I joined, and that was to Bill Thompson, telling him what a fine regiment I was in, and giving him to understand that soldiering was far better than sailoring, and I often wished he was with me. A few days after this I was sent for to orderly-room, and, to my surprise, learnt that Colonel T—had heard from my parents. The colonel told me I ought to have written to them, and that I must do so at once. My great fear was lest my father should claim me out of the Service—which he could have done, for I was under eighteen—and it relieved me to find he had made no mention of this. It ended in my getting a pass from Saturday till Sunday night, and going home to see the old people. I really think they were prouder of me than I was of myself, my mother expressing her joy and admiration at sight of me; though, afterwards, when she began to talk of my going to the wars, her tears came fast and freely. Of course, I saw Bill Thompson, and the last thing he said to me when we parted was:

"The spurs and tight breeches have done it, Ted, and I shall be with you before the week is out."

And sure enough he was; in the same station, but not in the same regiment, for he blundered, and took the bob for the 8th, instead of the 14th, Hussars.

One of the chief characteristics of our men was their fondness for the horses, and the care they took of them. The troopers, too, were real good ones, three and four years old, Irish bred, handsome-looking, and with plenty of blood, and, as the breeders put it, "fit to lep for a man's life." The few exceptions were a dozen or so old chargers, that had been transferred to the regiment after being sent home from the Crimea—such as old Balaclava—and these were used as a rule for training recruits at the riding-school. One of them was made over to me—a large bay, with four white stockings, who went by the name of Old Will. If he could have spoken he might have boasted that the head-collar was not invented out of which he could not wriggle. He was always slipping out of his; and he had a very bad reason for it—no less than thieving from his comrades. The nose-bags, which contained each horse's feed of corn, were always filled and slung overnight from hooks fastened to the ceiling, and dangled about three or four feet above the horses' quarters. Many a night would Old Will work his head loose, and go round robbing. Rearing up, and resting his forefeet on the back of the horse whose corn he was stealing, he tugged at the bag with his teeth till he got it down. Frequently he had two or three, and then he would be found in the morning, blown out like a wind-bag, and packed away in the same stall as Balaclava. This was another curious thing, for Balaclava hated every other horse, and lashed at them when they came near him, and while I was in the regiment injured two animals so severely that they had to be shot. But he never had an unkind word to say to Old Will, and whether in the stable or at the water-trough, they were the best of chums, which made us think they must have been comrades together in the Crimea.

Old Will was not such a wicked one as Balaclava, but he was

bad enough, and for the first week I was frightened of him; for whenever I went to groom or saddle him he would rear up and strike at me with his forefeet; and even when I fed him—and a decent sense of gratitude should have kept him civil—he had hardly seized a mouthful of corn before he would turn round and try to nip me by the shoulder, and once did so in a way which made me sore for a month. But I became used to him and his ways after a time, and, when my training days were over, I was quite sorry to transfer him.

One of the roughest experiences a cavalry recruit has in a life which is not all roses, is the riding-school. After I had been in the regiment a week, I was ordered to parade on foot, leading my horse, with a piece of felt, called a *numbdah,* strapped on his back instead of a saddle. We were marched off in file to the riding-school—a large building lighted from the top, and the floor covered to a good depth with tan, of which many a recruit knew the taste. After being-formed up into a circle, the rough-rider gave us instructions how to mount, but as we had no stirrups to help us, our frantic struggles to climb up were most laughable, and there was not one of the dozen 'cruities there who would not have given a day's pay for a ladder. However, after a bit, most of the lads succeeded in seating themselves; but I was so winded, and Old Will so restive and artful, edging away from me every time I tried to jump up, that I was clean beaten.

At last the rough-rider said that he would give me a leg up. Expecting Old Will to edge off again, as he had been doing, I made a tremendous semicircular spring round, directly I got the lift, flattering myself I'd be too clever for him. But it was he who was too clever for me, for he stood stock still this time, and I went clean over his back on to the tan, which raised a roar of laughter all round at my expense.

"When the ride is dismissed," said the rough-rider very solemnly to me, "just you bring a shovel and fill up that hole you've made in the floor." I felt savage enough at it all, but gulped down my temper, and next try I succeeded.

We now received a few instructions, the principal of which

were "Sit up," and "Look to your front." Then the order came, in a loud tone that made me jump again: "Walk! March!" Old Will, without any hint from me, started off, and finding his head loose, began trying to nip sections out of his leader's tail, for it was as much as I could do to balance myself on his back, without trying to guide or control him; and when, suddenly, the order came "Halt!" I was shot on to his neck, for he had stopped dead of his own accord.

The rough-rider now observed we managed the walking so well that he would try us at a trot. All we had to do, he said, was to "Sit still; keep your horse's head up; look through his ears, and you will never come off." This sounded simple enough, but it comprises the whole art of riding. We started off at a slow walk, our instructor standing in the middle, with a long whip in his hand which he presently cracked in a way that made Old Will wake up and start from under me so briskly that I found myself nearer his tail than looked well. I had just time to scramble back on to the *numbdah* when the rough-rider drawled out "Tro-ot," and off went the horses of their own accord. Before we had been once round the school I found myself leading file, instead of in my proper place about the middle of the ride; for Old Will did just what he liked, passing all the horses in front of him in succession, with, half a kick at one and a sly snap at another, whilst I jolted on his back like a bag of potatoes, until I tumbled off on to the ground, and for half a minute didn't know the hoofs from the tan. The ride was halted, and I was hoisted into my place again, and the order given to sit at ease.

And now the riding master and rough-riding sergeant entered, and the latter called out loud, "Tention!" in a voice which I soon came to know well, for during the next six months he was the man I most dreaded meeting when on horseback. For what with his circus whip and what with his patter, he kept me with the meanest opinion of myself it was possible for a man to have.

After a week's practice on *numbdahs* we were promoted to riding on stripped saddles, that is, saddles without any stirrups or fittings, which was a great deal harder and more insecure than riding bare-backed, for there seemed to be nothing to grip, the leather being polished slippery by constant cleaning. This tempted us to try and stick on by drawing our knees up, but it brought the constant cry from the instructor—"Keep your heels down!" which it took us a long time to learn how to do, not to mention the intolerable pain we sometimes suffered. I don't hold with stripped saddle riding, believing it destroys a man's confidence, and in many instances injures a good soldier for life by rupturing him; bare-backed exercise is in every way preferable.

After a couple of months' practice I was allowed to go out in the Long Valley with the other recruits, in charge of the riding master, and as I had now gained confidence, and was able to manage Old Will pretty firmly, I often made him go faster than he liked. But in return he took it out of me in the stable, for his was the hardest coat to get dry I ever laid a hand across, and he seemed to take a pleasure in dirtying his four white legs directly I had got them clean. This reminds me of an amusing story of which he was the hero, after I had done with him, and when he was in temporary charge of an old soldier named Paddy McCarthy.

A general horse parade had been ordered for one Saturday morning, and as cleanliness was the chief objects of these parades, and McCarthy knew Old Will's peculiar trick of dirtying his white legs after they had been cleaned, by rubbing one up and down against the other, he determined to be even with him. So after getting them as white as snow, he stayed behind in the stables, when the other men had gone to breakfast, and producing two pairs of worn-out white cotton stockings discarded by his wife, drew one over each of old Will's legs, with the remark—"Arrah, ye blatherin' brute, Oi've done yez this toime!"

Satisfied with his precautions Paddy bundled off to his breakfast, chuckling over his own cleverness Presently the turn out sounded for parade, and In a few minutes all the men had their horses ready except McCarthy, who, when the orderly-sergeant called the roll, was reported absent to the troop-sergeant-major.

The order was now given to mount, and just as we had settled down in our saddles, the voice of McCarthy was heard, crying "Stand sthill, ye murtherin' baste!" followed by some sounds which seemed as if Old Will was playing a waltz on the manger. The troop-sergeant-major, riding up to the stable door, called out to know when McCarthy was coming out.

"By jaybers, Sergeant-Major, not this side of Christmas," answered Paddy from within; "for this haythen horse won't let me shlip the shtocking off av Mm."

Just then the captain appeared, and rode round inspecting the troop, and the sergeant-major reported all present except McCarthy.

"And where's McCarthy?" asked the captain.

"He says he can't come before Christmas, sir," answered the sergeant with a smile.

The captain looked puzzled, and then told the orderly-sergeant to dismount, and see what was the matter. He entered the stable, but was out again under twenty seconds, his hand crammed to his mouth to try and keep down his laughter. Before he had time to pull himself together and explain, out bucked Old Will, his head-collar broken, and a wrinkled-up cotton stocking on each of his four legs, and after him Paddy with a pitchfork in his hand, and the completest assortment of curses in his mouth that was ever the property of one person. Old Will made straight for the parade ground, his head and tail cocked up at right angles to his body, throwing out his legs as proud as a peacock, and every now and then turning round and snorting defiance at McCarthy, who, after running a few paces, stuck his pitchfork in the ground, dropped his hands to his sides, and said he was ready to go to clink, but he'd be d—d if he'd parade that blooming horse again, not if it cost him his pension. Old Will galloped about a bit, and then came back and joined his troop.

About this time I was nearly getting into a nasty' scrape. During the general inspection of a regiment on parade it was the custom to tell off recruits as orderlies, to look after the barrack rooms and prevent stragglers entering them. On the occasion I am speaking of, there had been a "free-and-easy" overnight in our barrack room, and as usual a good deal of horseplay, during which most of the men's basins were broken, which caused great inconvenience at breakfast. When the troop was getting ready for parade, old Rootee Fruiterer came to me and whispered: "Look here, 'cruity, there's a chance for you to do a smart thing. While we are on parade, nip into the other rooms and collar sufficient basins to make good our damages. It's only fair, for they all had a hand in breaking ours last night."

This seemed to me just, and not much harm in it, so directly the troop had gone to parade, I prowled round and took a basin here and a basin there, until I had made up our complement. When tea-time came the other rooms missed their basins, and an old soldier from one of them came into ours to make enquiries. He asked me if I knew anything about them as I had been left in charge. I made no secret of what I had done, treating it as a joke, when to my surprise he ordered me to fall in between an escort of two men, and before I knew exactly what was happening, I found myself in the guard-room, where I remained all night, as much astonished as frightened.

The next morning I was taken before the colonel at orderly-room, and charged with the crime of "stealing basins." Theft, and especially theft from a comrade, is looked upon in the army as the very worst of all offences, and when I heard the charge I was fairly staggered. Colonel T—listened to the whole circumstances, and then pointed out what a serious effect the record of such a crime in my defaulter's book would have on my future career, and immediately altered it to "removing basins without leave." After rebuking the old soldier who had charged me, for his harsh treatment of a young recruit, he turned to me and said that he was of opinion I had acted thoughtlessly and without any criminal intent, and considered I had been sufficiently punished by a night in the guard-room. In dismissing me he hoped it would be a lesson to me for the future. And so it was, for the "crime," as altered by Colonel T—, remained in my defaulter's book till I left the army, to teach me that what may be considered only a practical joke in civil life, bears a very different complexion when a man is under the Queen's regulations.

The 14th Hussars remained at Aldershot till January, 1866, when it was rumoured that we were going to be sent to Canada on account of the Fenian invasion. But after an inspection, it was found we had lost too many of our old hands, and that the proportion of recruits was unduly large; and so, much to our chagrin, we were sent to Hounslow. and the 18th Hussars ordered to Canada in our stead.

Chapter 4

Hounslow

We left Aldershot on a bitterly cold and frosty morning in February, 1866, to march to Hounslow, and after detaching three troops to Hampton Court Palace and Kensington barracks, reached our destination between three and four o'clock in the afternoon.

Our new quarters were very comfortable, and in one point especially preferable to Aldershot, for there were no garrison provosts here, so that we enjoyed a corresponding amount of freedom. The garrison provosts, or military police, often make use of their power in a very arbitrary way, for let a man have a glove off, or a button undone, or hesitate in showing his pass, and he was immediately run in and punished, there being no appeal except a court-martial. The stringent and offensive manner in which the provosts at Aldershot performed their duties, made them hated and feared by all ranks.

The country round about Hounslow was pretty, affording pleasant walks in all directions. This suited me and my chum, Joey Harper, an old soldier, and a sober, steady man, who used to send most of his pay to his widowed mother, to whom I wrote his letters.

During one of my Sunday walks with Harper we found ourselves one evening close to a country church, about three miles from Hounslow, where it was the custom to bury any soldier who died at our barracks. Service was over, and several people strolling about the churchyard, examining the tombstones, which encouraged us to go in and do likewise. Presently we came to an inscription calculated to arrest a soldier's attention. There were only two initials "A.H," with the number of a cavalry regiment, and then the date, and these three words underneath: *Flogged to Death.*

I do not reckon to be particularly squeamish, but I must admit this had a great effect on me. I had heard of soldiers dying from sickness, or being killed in battle, or rotting away in an unhealthy climate, but *flogged to death* I had never heard of before. I looked round at Joey, and asked him what he thought of it, but he did not answer, only turned and walked away rather abruptly. A little later I questioned him as to what a flogging was like, but he dismissed the subject with a very few words, as if it were one he did not like to dwell upon. I had the curiosity to make enquiries about "A.H.," and found he had been punished for taking his horse out of stables contrary to orders, and insolence to a non-commissioned officer. It seemed a pretty small crime for which to flog a man to death.

There were several advantages in being at Hounslow. It was near London, and friends could run down to see us, and we got occasional leave to go up to town and enjoy ourselves. As our old hands left us, which they did very fast now, their places were mostly filled by cockney recruits, and this brought a lot of London folk to visit us, and have a look round the stables and barracks—a sight of which civilians never seem to tire.

Amongst those who entered the regiment at the same time as myself was one who acquired a character for being very light-fingered, and was known as the "Lifter." Within a few months he was twice up in front of the colonel for offences which were really theft, but which, as he was a young soldier, were so altered as to give him another chance.

It happened one Sunday morning that a visitor, in the course of strolling round the barrack-rooms, expressed a desire to obtain an army razor, not for its value, which was only five-pence, but because he had taken a fancy to the article. The Lifter happened to hear this, and offered to get one for a quart of beer; and this being promised him, watched his opportunity and stole one from the kit of a recruit.

This somehow came to the ears of his corporal, who ordered

him to the guard-room, and Colonel T——, much against his will, was obliged to send the prisoner up for court-martial. In due time the Lifter was tried, found guilty, and sentenced to fifty lashes, and to be dismissed the service with ignominy. When the sentence was confirmed preparations were made for carrying it into effect, and one day the whole regiment turned out for foot-parade in full dress, with arms, the officers in front of their troops, the same as for a general's inspection.

The Lifter was marched on to parade under charge of a guard, and with him all the other prisoners in confinement at the time, that they might experience the benefit of his example. When he reached the centre of the front of the regiment he was halted, and the adjutant, stepping up to the colonel and saluting him, received some papers, which he began to read. They detailed the finding of the court-martial, and the sentence awarded. As the Lifter's name and number were read out, he snatched off his cap and threw it on the ground in a devil-may-care way, and then took three paces forward in a jaunty, off-hand manner, and grinned out of insolent bravado.

The reading over, the regiment received the order, "Fours right," whilst the band moved up a little, allowing the guard with the prisoner to place themselves between it and the regiment; after which the word was given to quick march, and we proceeded to the riding-school to the strains of a merry tune.

Filing in, we packed ourselves four and five deep against either side. At the further end opposite the door stood a triangle, the farrier-major and two brawny farrier-sergeants, with their jackets off, their sleeves rolled up, and each holding a dreaded cat-o'-nine-tails. Up to them the prisoner was marched by the guard, and the doors were then shut. The floor being covered with tar not a sound was heard, and the silence was almost deathly. With the shutting of the door we seemed to be cut off from the sunshine outside, and the gloomy dead walls of the riding-school added an indescribable terror to the scene. By the triangle stood the colonel, the adjutant, the doctor, and the chaplain. Colonel T—— now called the regiment to attention, and then, turning to the farrier-major, gave the order in a husky voice—"Proceed."

At a sign from their superior the two farrier-sergeants seized the Lifter and began tying him up to the triangle. His jauntiness was all gone now, and he screamed at the top of his voice for mercy. At this a feeling of nervous disgust or sickening apprehension overcame many of the men, who were sorely worked on by the suspense of the scene. The farrier-sergeants hastened to perform their task, and in a minute the prisoner was triced up, and his shirt stripped from his back, which was exposed to view.

At this moment the chaplain stepped up to the colonel, and after saluting him, begged mercy for the poor devil, who was screaming and wriggling in anticipation. But Colonel T——, in a stern voice, pointing to the doctor, said, "The prisoner is now in his hands." Then looking at the farrier-major, he raised his hand as a sign to begin, and turned his head away.

"*One,*" cried the farrier-major in a loud, clear voice, for he was hardened to these scenes. Round swung the lash and fell with a sickening thud on the quivering flesh, whilst the Lifter writhed with the most ghastly contortions I have ever seen. Although my stomach turned at it, and I felt as sick as a dog, my eyes were fascinated by the spectacle. Slowly and methodically the farrier-major continued to count, the strokes falling as regularly, until twenty-five was reached, by which time the man's screams had dwindled into a low, prolonged moaning.

The doctor now stepped up and felt his pulse; and then signed for the punishment to proceed.

The second farrier-sergeant now relieved his comrade, and took up his position on the left, whilst the farrier-major resumed his count. At the fortieth lash the prisoner suddenly gave a convulsive jerk, and then hung limp. The doctor raised his hands, the counting ceased, and the falling blow was diverted. And a sigh of relief went up from officers and men alike, when the doctor stepped up to Colonel T—— and said—

"Sir; he can bear no more."

The insensible form was then untriced and made over to

the hospital orderlies, who were ready at hand with restoratives. When the Lifter had recovered consciousness, his shirt was pulled over his shoulders, and, escorted by the guard, he was assisted to the hospital. Directly he had crawled out of the building, the band struck up a lively march, to the tune of which the regiment filed out of the riding-school, and was dismissed.

The Lifter's military career, as far as the 14th Hussars was concerned, came to an end about a fortnight later, when, after being discharged as cured from the hospital, the other part of his, sentence was carried into effect. The regiment paraded as before, and the prisoner stood three paces in the front of it, whilst the sentence was read out. Then the regimental sergeant-major stepped up to him, and with a penknife stripped off every vestige of braid, lace, and buttons from his uniform, and the knob from his hat. Looking every inch a vagabond he was placed in front of the band, and marched to the front gate to the tune of the Rogue's March. As my troop came round the bend I was astonished to see him skipping and jumping about, I suppose at the prospect of his freedom. On reaching the gate a band boy walked up to him and gave him a kick behind, and then shoved him outside, and the gates were closed.

Then the Lifter thought he would have his turn. He first spat contemptuously in the direction of the regiment, and then putting his extended fingers to his nose, shouted out, "A soldier's farewell to you." But he had reckoned on his liberty before he got it, for at this moment two policemen suddenly appeared, and amidst the suppressed laughter of the regiment, seized him. We heard afterwards that he had been wanted for some time, and only got out of the clink to walk into the jug.

A far different scene from the one I have described took place on the second and last occasion on which I ever saw a man flogged. A soldier from the 14th who had deserted some years previously was recognised and brought in. A court-martial sentenced him to be flogged and dismissed the service, but the general commanding, out of a feeling of clemency which the prisoner was the last to appreciate, remitted the latter part of the sentence and only confirmed the flogging. We paraded as before and precisely the same scene followed, up to the tying-up of the prisoner to the triangle. But this man was made of different metal to the Lifter. He never uttered a word except to say to the farrier-sergeant, "Now then; come on, and be sharp about it," and received the whole fifty lashes without a word, though his back was black and blue, and we could see a regular check where the stripes crossed one another. When the punishment was over and he was untriced, he walked up to the colonel, saluted him with a grim smile on his face, and then spat a bullet out of his mouth, and declining any assistance, put on his shirt by himself.

"You're a brave man," said the old colonel impulsively, "and if you do your duty, by God I'll stand your friend."

The prisoner simply smiled and requested permission to join his troop; but this was not permitted, and despite his protestations that he was all right, he was ordered to hospital. The day he came out he deserted again and we never saw any more of him.

Within a couple of months of reaching Hounslow I was dismissed all drill, and on the morning that Colonel T—— conveyed this intimation to myself and several other recruits, a feeling of joyful elation came over me at being: a "full-blown soldier" at last. It brought with it many little privileges, such as afternoon in barracks with the other old hands, instead of on the parade ground, not to mention the proud satisfaction of mounting sentry at the front gate in full uniform. I was no longer a 'cruity, at the beck and call of everyone in the troop, but on an equal footing with them, and able to put up my dukes if they tried to come the old soldier over me.

This was the year in which the Hyde Park Riots occurred, when the populace demonstrated for the right of holding public meetings in the Park. One evening in July an order suddenly arrived for us to march to London, and within a quarter of an hour we were on the road. On reaching town we were accommodated in the Royal Stables at Buckingham Palace, our horses being picketed in the spacious riding school and ourselves in some of the coach-houses ordinarily used for the state carriages.

Whilst here we were much interested in looking at the celebrated teams of cream-coloured and black horses. The former were used for state ceremonies and weddings, and the latter for Royal funerals. They were all entire horses, and so nervous and subject to excitement, that, on a summer thunderstorm coming on, every door and window was at once closed and the gas lit all over the stables, so as to deaden the sound of the thunder, and minimise the effects of the lightning flashes.

On the second day I happened to be stable guard over the horses of my troop, and was standing in the riding school when a military-looking gentleman, dressed in civilian clothes, entered on horseback, and commenced asking me questions in a bluff but not un-genial manner. First of all he wanted to know who I was, and I told him stable guard over the horses; then what regiment was it, and I answered the 14th Hussars. Passing his eyes up and down the lines he remarked, "You have a fine lot of horses." Just as he was speaking an adjutant chanced to come in. Directly his eyes fell on the gentleman he almost broke his back in coming to attention, and at the same time roared out to me in a stentorian voice, "'Tention," which made me spring back from the force of habit, almost as smartly as he had done.

The gentleman on horseback now turned to him and asked him some question or other, and then I saw the adjutant relieve himself of the very finest kind of military salute and begin his reply with "Your Royal Highness," which brought sparks into my eyes and no mistake. It was H.R.H. the Duke of Cambridge I had been conversing with! The adjutant accompanied him round the riding school and then escorted him to the door, where he saw him out with a salute that couldn't be got into a picture. He then turned to me, and after asking me what I had said, remarked that I might consider myself a proud private soldier, for I had enjoyed the honour of an interview with the C.-in-C. of the British army.

Although the London mob knocked down the park railings, and defied the Government orders, the authorities, in the existing temper of the people, did not care to let loose on them the tremendous military force which they had collected, and the consequence was that our march to London merely resulted in a three days' visit there.

Life at Hounslow, with a few ups and downs, was, on the whole, very pleasant. I had got into the swing of duty by this time, and no longer found it irksome, and when I wanted a holiday I could generally get leave by putting in a pass. Occasionally, the routine of life was broken by a commanding-officers' field-day on the heath made famous by highwaymen; or, better still, by a grand field-day at Wormwood Scrubs, when we were sometimes brigaded with the two cavalry regiments of the Guards at that time quartered in London. These were termed "ladies' days," from the number of the fair sex who used to grace the scene. The operations always included the cutting and pursuing practice at the gallop, and as we passed the saluting point to the tune of *Bonnie Dundee,* we never failed in getting a roar of applause from the spectators, and a special waving of handkerchiefs from the ladies.

In November, we were ordered to take part in the Lord Mayor's procession. The majority of the men were told off as the advance and rear escort, but about forty—including myself—were sent up with that number of horses for the use of some extra mounted police. I had at this time a rather skittish young Irish trooper, which was not considered suitable for constabulary work, so I was ordered to take up Old Will instead. We marched under the command of the riding master, who was an Irishman by birth, but considered to have a Turkish appearance, and nicknamed Omer Pasha. On reaching the Guildhall, we dismounted, and unsaddling our horses, made them over to the police. Old Will fell to the lot of a stout and particularly pompous peeler, who looked him up and down with a troubled and anxious air. "Is he quiet?" he asked me in a whisper, slipping a shilling into my hand. "He's a wooden sheep"—said I—"on wheels." With that I got his saddle on Old Will's back, and told him to climb up.

Gathering the reins loosely in his left hand, the policeman mounted, but before he could get home in his seat, Old Will—

who evidently thought he had a 'cruity on his back—was off like a flash of lightning, and there was a merry five minutes of riding-school play in the courtyard of the Guildhall, as he dodged in and out of the other horses as if the rough-rider's whip were trailing behind him. As for the bobby, he convulsively dug in his heels and clutched hold of the pommel of his saddle with his right hand, trying to get a purchase on the reins with his left, which was jerking about somewhere on a line with the back of his head.

"Keep your spurs out of him, you bottle-blue marine!" shouted out Omer Pasha.

"Put the skid on the wheel!" I cried, as he passed me for the second time.

He did neither, for just then the saddle turned round, and he was deposited on the flags amidst the jeers of the bystanders. Of course, Old Will came to a dead halt, and stood waiting with a patient look in his face, just as he was accustomed to do at riding school when a recruit dismounted without leave.

When the police had moved off on our horses, we fell out and went to Kensington barracks by train. Here we had to wait six hours, with nothing to do, except partake of the hospitality—chiefly rum—of the many friends who had come to meet us. When we started on our return to the Guildhall Ave were all prouder of ourselves than plain water makes people, and Omer Pasha had a rare job to get us safely there. We had a long time to wait, during which the crowd seemed to consider it a duty to hand us drops of something short in an indiscriminate manner. The police came dropping in one by one, and it was not until close upon eleven that all the horses we had lent them were mustered, and we started for Hounslow. The night was fine, but bitterly cold, and never shall I forget the jinks we had on the road, or old Omer Pasha's face when he tried to trot us, but found we tumbled off. There was nothing to do but to walk us all the way home, and we did not reach barracks until four o'clock in the morning. Before dismissing us, Omer Pasha drew us up upon the parade ground and rated us properly for a quarter of an hour, whilst we sat shivering and very sorry in the cold.

About this time a great change took place in the constitution of the regiment, both as regard to officers and men. When I first joined it was full of colonels —in fact, there were so many that I found it the safest plan to address almost every officer by that title. They had all received brevet rank for their services in the Mutiny, and the majority of commanders of troops, though captains in the regiment, were field-officers in the army. During our stay at Hounslow, many of them were promoted to other appointments or retired, and their places taken by younger men, several of whom belonged to wealthy families and had plenty of money at their command, which they spent freely. Most of the old soldiers, too, had taken their pensions and gone, and the ranks were now filled with recruits, chiefly from London. I cannot say the change was a favourable one. There was the same amount of rough horse-play in the barracks, but not the same amount of good temper in the language used or in the practical jokes played. Selfishness began to creep in and take the place of the good fellowship that had existed between men who had passed the best part of their lives together, and often fought side by side on the field of battle. There had been a certain indulgence allowed to the old hands, and trivial offences were often overlooked by the non-commissioned officers when off parade and duty. The old soldiers, who had proved their merit on many a hard-fought field, understood and appreciated this, and regulated their conduct accordingly, never taking advantage of the leniency. But it was different with the new-comers, who availed themselves of this indulgent treatment off parade to exhibit slack behaviour on duty. The consequence was that stricter discipline all round was soon enforced, and the non-commissioned officers were ordered to be more particular in the performance of their duties. This caused crime to increase. In the army the term "crime" embraces all sorts of offences, serious and trivial; and the conduct of the regiment is gauged by the number of recorded crimes, and a man five minutes late for parade swells the total in the same way as a man absent from duty. This increase of crime was a great sorrow to our old colonel, who began to fear the regiment was losing its good name, as did also the old officers, who did everything in their power to avert it. For instance, our major, who was a colonel in the army, and a most kind-hearted officer, used to say, when a man was brought before him for the second or third time: "Pooh, pooh, my man! I cannot always be punishing you. Now if I tear your crime up, will you promise not to come here again?" Of course the artful dodger who was in trouble would say "Yes," and away he was allowed to go, laughing in his sleeve.

Many of the non-commissioned officers were really too young and inexperienced to be entrusted with the power they possessed, especially in what was practically a new regiment, for although when I joined it there were not twenty recruits in the ranks, when we marched out of Hounslow there were not fifty old soldiers left. The newcomers, too, were a difficult lot to deal with; they did not care whether they went to the guard-room or not; and it was a common thing to hear a prisoner say, as he was being taken to the cells, "What odds? It will be a rest. A clink ain't a grave!"

During our stay at Hounslow the 14th became very popular with the townsfolk, and what with amateur theatricals in the town hall and dances in the troop-rooms and barracks, varied with occasional trips to London, the winter passed quickly and pleasantly away. When, in the spring, the order came for us to proceed in detachments by march route to Edinburgh and Perth, there was a general feeling of regret at leaving the pleasant acquaintances we had made.

Chapter 5

A Long March

It was a lovely morning in April, in 1867, when my troop paraded for the march to Edinburgh. The regiment was to proceed in small parties, at intervals, for convenience of accommodation at the halting-places, and ours was the pioneer detachment. Colonel T—— drew us up and gave us a few parting injunctions, the principal being to keep up the credit of the corps and look carefully after our horses. Then he made the signal to stare, and with the band playing *The Girl I Left Behind Me*, we rode through the crowd of people who had turned out to bid us goodbye, and headed north.

The band soon left us and returned to barracks, and we marched along two and two, the captain and lieutenant at our head, Splodgers bringing up the rear, and everyone riding at ease—with pipes alight, laughing, joking, and talking—so that it was more pleasure than work. After covering a mile, and tightening girths, the order was given to trot, and we went along at a good pace; then pulled up to a walk and rode at ease again till "'tention!" and a second trot brought us to the middle of our day's march.

The captain now sang out for the sergeant-major, and a lane was opened by the troop "dividing the road," through which old Splodgers bustled up with the burden of importance on his shoulders. This being the first real march for many of us, we had our ears cocked and eyes purling to find out what was going to happen.

"It's about time for the White Jug, I think," said the captain, "see to it, Sergeant-Major."

Splodgers saluted and set off at a canter, and we followed at a walk, till a few minutes later we entered a village and discovered him standing in front of an old-fashioned country inn, with several men and girls round him, carrying jugs and mugs and cans of beer, and trays piled up with bread and cheese, generously provided, according to custom, by our officers. We did full justice to the refreshments, and after resting half an hour resumed our march. Soon a shout came down the troop: "Singers to the front!" and we formed up in three lines, the whole width of the road, whilst some rare songs with choruses were trolled out, in which our officers joined heartily. The horses seemed to enjoy it too, for they stepped out brisker and brisker as the singing went on; this lasted for an hour, when we were re-formed and broke into a good swinging trot which soon brought us to Watford, where we were to halt for the night.

Here we were met by the billeting party, consisting of a sergeant and private, who had been sent forward the previous day to arrange with the head constable of the place for our accommodation. Riding up to the principal hotel in the town, where our officers were to put up and which was our *rendezvous,* we were formed in line, and the sergeant proceeded to call out our names and stations something in this style: "Private Jones, Private Smith, two horses, The Red Cow"; handing them a billeting paper at the same time, whilst half a dozen of the onlookers volunteered to show the way.

Joey Harper and I found ourselves sent to The Swan with Two Necks, a small inn in a side street. As we rode into the yard, the landlord, a pleasant-looking countryman, met us with a cheery greeting and told us he had got everything ready. Leading the way to the stables he pointed out two stalls, heaped up to the horses' bellies with beautiful straw, the manner full of food, and two buckets of water standing ready. He then invited us to enter the house and see his missus, who had a drop of beer and a snack of bread and cheese ready for us, and wanted to know when we would like dinner. Joey thanked him, but said we were obliged to see our horses comfortable first, but could do with a drop of beer in the stables, which the good Christian at once drew for us.

"We've dropped into a good billet here," said Joey to me presently. "Mind how you go on, and don't spoil it."

"How spoil it?" I asked.

"Why, don't make a beastly fool of yourself, like a good many do when they've dropped on a soft thing, by getting drunk and making love to the landlord's women."

"No fear," I answered, as we took off our coats and set to work on our horses.

In about an hour we had them dry and groomed down, and the captain, lieutenant, and sergeant-major came their rounds. They inspected the horses' backs, noted the good accommodation and forage, and spoke a few kind words to the landlord, which greatly pleased him. Then Splodgers gave Joey and me our day's pay, which amounted to fourteen-pence each, and told us to parade at the *rendezvous* at nine o'clock the next morning.

Joey and I now went to dinner which we found the people had waited for us; and I am certain no one could have treated us better or made us feel more at home than the good publican and his wife. It seems they had a son, who was a soldier in the line, which may have accounted for their extra kindness to us. For they were but poorly remunerated for what they supplied, the government allowance being but ten-pence to pay for a hot dinner and a bed, and four-pence for two pints of small beer or one pint of ale. For each horse they received two shillings, and had to provide eight pounds of straw, ten pounds of corn, and twelve pounds of hay. Any extra meals we wanted we had to pay for ourselves; but we found that breakfast and tea were frequently given us free, and for every pint of beer we paid for we wore treated to a gallon, so that we did not come off badly.

I have described this first day's march and the billet at the end of it at some length, because with certain modifications and variations it serves for all that followed. During the thirty-six days we were on the road between London and Edinburgh, I found, with only one or two exceptions, that so long as we behaved well, folks did their utmost to make us comfortable.

The next morning we paraded in good time and marched off in the same manner as the day before; but the road being hilly we occasionally dismounted and led our horses, which eased both them and us. Our halt this night was at Dunstable, where there is a large straw-plaiting industry employing some thousands of young girls. As soon as the factories closed it was not a case of a soldier escorting his girl, but half-a-dozen girls to each soldier. In fact, it was a realisation of what Sergeant Gibbs had told me of the 14th Hussars having the pick of the lasses everywhere, and I am well within the truth when I state that at Dunstable the factory girls actually fought amongst themselves for the pick of the men The next morning there was sobbing and crying all round as we rode out of the town, escorted by a crowd of them, who vowed they would follow us to the end of our journey, until the first trot sounded, and soon made it a case of "the girl I left behind."

Nothing of note occurred until we reached Grantham, where a friend of Captain K—— resided. This gentleman rode out to meet us, and in the evening was very generous to the men, treating them to drinks, till he had quite a crowd round him. In our troop were two young cockneys who were suspected of being rather light-fingered, and it was noticed that they kept pretty close to this gentleman. In the morning we were paraded as usual, but were rather surprised to see Captain K——'s friend, and a strange gentleman in civilian clothes, accompany us when we marched off.

About two miles out of the town we were halted and told to divide the road, with our horses' heads inwards, and to remain sitting at attention till each man received further orders. The captain then posted the lieutenant at the head of the troop and the sergeant-major at the rear, with instructions to keep a sharp eye on the men, and see that no communication took place between them. Captain K—— and the two gentlemen now dismounted in the centre of the two lines, and a man was called out from the head of the column, ordered to dismount, strip his saddle, and expose to view every single thing he carried. The stranger, who turned out to be a detective, searched the kit, even going so far as to probe the saddle stuffing with a long needle, whilst the man was handled from head to foot, and finally asked if he knew anything about a gold watch which had been stolen from the captain's friend overnight.

In this way everyone was subjected to a thorough examination, not even the sergeant-major escaping, and the captain's own cart, which carried his kit on the line of march, was overhauled. All this took at least two hours, during which our feelings were far from pleasant, for, though it was a grief to us to be thus disgraced, our chief anxiety was for the detection of the thief, who had abused the gentleman's generosity. When everyone had been searched, Captain K—— turned to his friend and said: "I am sorry I cannot find your watch; but I have done my best. Whatever has become of it, you see it is not in my troop now." And with that we resumed our march.

Not long after this incident we entered Yorkshire and were, I think, nearly a fortnight in marching through it. It was in a town in this county, Northallerton, that I tumbled into the worst English billet I have ever had. My party was told off to the "Vine" public-house, and on reaching it, the landlord, a surly-looking fellow, asked us what we wanted. I handed him the billeting paper which showed he had to provide accommodation for four men and four horses. He called a helper, and told him to take us to the shed at the bottom of the yard—a tumble-down place not fit to herd pigs in. Of course we told him it would not suit us, upon which he swore it was "Good enough for soldiers!" and all we should get out of him. We then sent word to Captain K——, who came down with the head constable of the town, and after a deal of persuasion and threatening, forced the landlord to give us slightly better accommodation. But the man's back was fairly up by this time, and he kept strictly to the letter of the law, as laid down in the billeting warrant, and when we came into dinner we found just as much beef, pepper, salt, and beer, as was specified by regulation, and no bread or vegetables. Our remonstrances did no good; he said we were "only soldiers," and if we kicked up any row he would have the law down upon us. Of course we had to lump it as best we could, and we were not sorry that the "rats" got to his harness that night and nibbled holes in it, and the "cats" and "foxes" played havoc in his fowl-house.

At Newcastle-upon-Tyne we were called upon to assist in extinguishing a large fire that broke out the night we were there, in the public building the volunteers drilled in. We worked hard from ten o'clock till daybreak trying to subdue the flames, but only succeeded in preventing them from spreading. For our exertions we were publicly thanked, and some time after our arrival at Edinburgh the townspeople very kindly sent us each a complete new suit of walking-out clothes, a pair of gloves, a new whip, and three half-crowns to replace the damage done to our clothes.

Soon after leaving Newcastle we crossed the border, and the scenery rapidly changed, becoming grand and wild. The people also were different, their manners being colder, whilst the accommodation for ourselves and our horses was much poorer than it had been south of the Tweed. We were chiefly fed on mutton, of which we soon grew mortally tired. I remember at one place there was a very fat boiled neck of it placed on the table, with lumps of dough round it, supposed to represent dumplings, but as hard as bullets and quite cold. This being our fourth day of boiled mutton, our stomachs rebelled at the fare, and we sent for the old woman of the house, and asked her for something else.

"My gracious!" she replied. "It's a beautiful dinner, fit for the Queen herself!"

"May be, mother," replied our corporal, "but at least give us a bit of mustard to work it down."

"And a chunk of cheese to take the taste out of our mouths," added another man.

The demand for such luxuries as mustard and cheese appalled the old dame, and she threw up her hands in the air, shrieking out:—

"*What! What!* Mustard with mutting! And cheese for soldiers!" and bounced out of the room in terrible indignation.

We all began grumbling and growling now, and what should chime in just at this moment, as if mimicking us, but an old grandfather's clock that stood at the end of the room. It had to wind itself up before it could strike, and it began "Ghur-r-r-r" in sepulchral tones. This was altogether too much for us; we couldn't stand being mocked by a deaf and dumb wooden clock.

"Shoot me, but *you,* ain't the one to grumble!" called out the corporal. "Stop it, I tell yer. What! you won't? Take that then!"

With which he picked up one of the dumplings, and banged it right through the clock's face, and before you could say Jack Robinson, that martial article of furniture was being pelted with cold dough, until the grandfather who bought it wouldn't have known it from the pump in the yard.

We reached Edinburgh on the thirty-sixth day after leaving Hounslow, and proceeded to the barracks at Jock's lodge in the outskirts, receiving a hearty welcome from the 4th Hussars, whom we were relieving. Men and horses were in hard and good condition, and I think I may say that, with a few trifling exceptions, we had carried out our colonel's parting admonition to keep up the credit of the regiment and look after our horses.

We were soon followed by the other troops, one after another; but our numbers were smaller than at Hounslow, for we detached a squadron to Perth, and three troops to Hamilton, a place nine miles from Glasgow. The barracks at Edinburgh were in an old-fashioned pile of buildings, very comfortable in their way, and situated at the end of Queen's Park, and about a mile from the sea at Portobello, on the sands of which our field days took place.

About this time there was a great deal of anxiety created by the Fenian movement, and every military magazine was rigidly guarded, with double sentries at all posts. This made night duty excessively hard, and we fared little better in the day-time, having to provide constant escorts and guards for different Scotch notabilities attending the Quarter Sessions. The major in command of our wing was the youngest field officer in the service, and while he was temporarily at our head tried to rush discipline on the men with a strong hand, which made things very unpleasant all round.

Notwithstanding these drawbacks, the little time we were allowed out of barracks was spent in a most enjoyable manner. We got on right well with the Scotch girls, though I must add that, although fair and comely, their teeth were very bad, owing to their pernicious habit of eating sweets. "Where are ye going the noo, lad?" was their usual form of greeting when they met us. "Will ye no hae a sweetie?"

The Scotch are well known for their strict observance of the Sabbath day, and this we noticed, as well as the pronounced condemnation of drinking which they paraded. And yet I never saw in one day in any English town so many "fou' boddies" as I have seen on a single Sunday in Edinburgh. The Friends' Room in our canteen—a place set aside for soldiers to receive visitors in—was crowded by people who came to see us on Sunday, simply for the purpose of getting a wet, which they could not do elsewhere as all the public-houses were closed.

Soon after reaching Edinburgh, I obtained my first step of promotion. One morning Captain K—— called me out of stables, and after a few words of general commendation told me he was going to place my foot on the first rung of the ladder which might lead to a Field-Marshal or a court-martial; and that evening my name appeared in orders as lance-corporal. I was naturally pleased and proud, but it lost me my old chum, Joey Harper, who had no sooner heard of it than he said to me, "Now you're a Non-Com. I'll chuck you up, and have nothing more to do with you."

This may seem strange, but it will be better understood when it is explained that, although a corporal lived and messed with the men, it was considered a crime for him to be seen walking out with a private in the streets, and he was debarred from drinking with him in the canteen, a special room being set apart for corporals. The promotion only brought me extra duty, extra expense, and extra responsibility, without any extra pay, and certainly less sociability in the barrack-room. But it was compensated for by the hope that my turn would come at last to get my feet under the mahogany in the sergeants' mess, where in dignity and comfort I might forget all my troubles as a "lance-Jack," or "sergeant-major's greyhound."

Whilst stationed at Edinburgh, I was employed on one very pleasant duty. There was an old custom in Scotland that the reigning sovereign should once in a certain number of years visit the Border, and the Queen being about to do so this summer, an escort was ordered from the 14th Hussars for her Majesty's ceremonial progress. I was lucky enough to be chosen as one, and on a lovely summer morning we paraded in full review order, with shabraques, and under command of three officers, marched to Kelso, where the Queen was going to begin her journey.

We found two open carriages, each drawn by four horses, waiting at the station, and formed line in front of them with our drawn swords in our hands. The sun was shining brightly, and the sky one expanse of blue, whilst the green hills in the distance and the brightly-dressed populace in Highland costume in the foreground, made up a scene which was both picturesque and glowing.

Punctually to the appointed time the Queen's train steamed into the station, and the bands of the Volunteer regiments struck up the National Anthem. A few minutes later her Majesty appeared, looking remarkably well, and smiling and bowing all round. She exchanged many laughing remarks with one of the princesses who accompanied her, and the Duchess of Roxburghe in attendance; and about her person were the Dukes of Roxburghe and Buccleugh, and many distinguished Scotch peers and notabilities.

No sooner had the Queen stepped into her carriage and driven off, than the assembled multitudes broke out into deafening cheers, and we had the greatest difficulty in keeping our places, for our troop horses were some of the most spirited in the regiment, and kept plunging at the noise. Before long the crowd forced its way through the Volunteers who lined the roads, and surrounded her Majesty's carriage, unharnessed the horses, and began pulling it along at a great pace, the Queen standing up and laughing heartily, and at times clapping her hands as though she thoroughly enjoyed the scene.

We moved on in the rear, doing our best to perform our escort duties, but received orders from our officers to avoid interfering with the people. Nearing the centre of the town a halt was called, and an address of welcome road by the Corporation; and then a child about seven years old was held up to the carriage, and presented her Majesty with a bouquet; and I heard afterwards that she had been made a lady on the spot, in the same way, I suppose, as men are knighted.

The next day the Queen visited Melrose Abbey, and we were formed up fronting the entrance, in a rather confined strip between the royal carriages and a stand erected in our rear for spectators. When the Queen appeared she seated herself in the leading carriage, and whilst waiting for the suite to enter the others, my trooper, a clever mare, with an inquisitive turn of mind, poked her nose forward, and there being no room for me to back, managed to reach the floor of the royal carriage. Her Majesty immediately stretched out her hand and stroked Biddy's muzzle. I was half inclined to pull my horse's head up, but the Queen looked at me with such a pleasant smile that I thought I might be giving offence if I brought my horse to attention, and so Biddy enjoyed the highest honour that ever fell to a Hussar's horse, for it was not until the cortege moved on that her Majesty ceased stroking her, whilst I sat frozen to the saddle, cold and stiff as marble.

The proceedings of to-day were a repetition of what had taken place yesterday. During the journey to Abbotsford, where the Queen was to rest for the night, some of the remarks made by the Scotch countrywomen were very comical, and I remember one forcing her way close to the carriage and calling out, "Ay, woman, but you're lookin' bonnie the day," at which her Majesty smiled very kindly.

At last the gates of Abbotsford were reached, and passing through them the Queen found protection from the excited enthusiasm of her loyal Scots. The next day we escorted her Majesty to Jedburgh, and here our duty ended, and we returned to Edinburgh, carrying in our minds the remembrance of a Royal week, rich in incidents, such as none of us were ever likely to experience again.

CHAPTER 6

Scotland and Ireland

As a non-commissioned officer I found duty in Edinburgh exceedingly arduous, and what with the different guards and extra minor duties, I had little or no time I could call my own. The Fenian scare was at its height, and we had only "one night in bed," as the military phrase goes, or, in other words, were on duty every other night. On the top of. this came the extra vexation arising from the over-stringent discipline, which made the men discontented and difficult to deal with. So that although I was "on the road to a cocked hat," I found it none of the smoothest to travel; and when orders came for my troop to relieve another at Hamilton, I was quite glad to leave Edinburgh, notwithstanding its being a station most popular with the military.

Hamilton was the centre of a large mining district, and the barracks were built on the estate of the Duke of Hamilton, from whose woods and river just outside our walls I had many a good pigeon and trout for breakfast.

While here I received a letter from Bill Thompson, informing me that he also had won his stripes. His regiment was now at Manchester, and he gave me a graphic description of the execution of Larkin, Allen, and O'Brien, for the murder of Sergeant Brett, on which occasion the 8th Hussars had been detailed to keep order.

The young major, whom I have referred to, accompanied us to Hamilton. He was very fond of going about barracks after nightfall, trying to surprise the sentries and test their vigilance on duty. His chief military maxim—and he had a hat-full of them which he was always quoting—was blind obedience, which he said was the first duty of every soldier from the general down to the band boy, and he often pointed out that this doctrine applied to himself equally with the men. But like many in authority, he was not quite so particular in practice as in preaching, as the following anecdote will show.

Behind the mess at Hamilton was a wicket gate, of which every officer possessed a key, so that they could come into barracks without passing the main guard. This gate was in the centre of a long high wall, and the point where the two sentries who patrolled it met and challenged. One night two brothers were posted on this duty, and about twelve o'clock they heard a key turning in the lock, and saw a tall figure, clothed in civilian dress, quietly enter. Rushing forward they seized him, shouting out at the same time for the sergeant of the guard, who, when he came up with an escort, found the prisoner was none other than our major. He at once ordered the sentries to release him, but their reply was that their orders were to make a prisoner of any one breaking into barracks between watch-setting and *reveillé*.

"But can't you see it's the major?" cried the sergeant.

"Well, it may be the major," they replied, "but he is in civilian clothes, and we cannot distinguish him in the dark. And he's always told us the orders apply to him the same as to every one else."

This logic was irresistible, and it ended in the major giving his parole to his own sergeant before departing, when he no doubt cursed his fatal facility of quotation from the "Soldier's Pocket Book." Of course the sentries could not be punished, as they had simply carried out his own orders to the letter, though the "caius" chaps knew all along who it was they were apprehending, and were influenced by devilment more than zeal. They were called up before the major next morning, who complimented them on their watchfulness, but explained that their zeal should discriminate, and in fact cease, when it came to making a prisoner of their own officer.

A few nights after this, about two hours after "lights out" had gone, "Boot and saddle" rang out, and the alarm was sounded. In an instant all was hurry and bustle, and every one thought the Fenians had risen at last. It turned out afterwards that the Fenian sympathisers in Glasgow had determined to celebrate some Irish anniversary by an enormous procession through the streets on Sunday, which the Government intended to stop. As both sides were equally firm in their expressed intentions, some proper fun was expected. Off we started in the middle of the night at a smart trot, and in an hour and a quarter had reached the Cattle Market at Glasgow, and were admitted through the great iron gates, which were then closed and a strong guard stationed over them. Without unsaddling our horses we tied them up in the cattle pens, and then adjourned to the hotel inside the enclosure, where all the members of the Glasgow Corporation were assembled. They gave us a good welcome, and what was better still, a good supper, and we spent the next few hours stretched on the ground, with rugs and plaids to cover us.

During all this time we could hear the roar of tumult in the city, and towards morning the populace began to crowd round the gate of the market enclosure, swearing they would make haggis of the Hussars as soon as we showed ourselves. Before daylight we were formed up in a large open space fronting the gates, and at sunrise ball ammunition was served out with ostentatious parade, in full view of the mob who pressed against the gate, only twenty feet distant, threatening and abusing us. But this was the extent of their hostility, for not a stone was thrown. As the day wore on we heard by telegraph that the leaders of the people, overawed by the presence of the military, had abandoned their intention.

We were ordered to remain three or four days at Glasgow till quiet was completely restored, and during the time received everything we could want in the shape of meat and drink at the expense of the Corporation. Unfortunately, our young major had come over to take the command, and seeing how well we were provided, issued orders to the sergeant-majors not to serve out our pay. In these days it was the regulation to pay soldiers daily, and the men resented this infringement of their rights, and in rather an arrogant way demanded their money. The personal unpopularity of the major had a good deal to do with this, for he was a great stickler for regulations, and was now over-riding them. This was respectfully pointed out to him by the three troop-sergeant-majors, but he would not give way, and it came to this, that a serious outbreak threatened on the part of men actually there for the purpose of quelling disorder in others.

On hearing of the men's attitude the major, much against the advice of the non-commissioned officers, determined to go amongst them. They were assembled in a large dining-room in the hotel, drinking stout, and their tempers very uncertain, for they were shouting out in an opprobrious and unseemly manner. The major entered, and for a moment stood by the door looking sternly at the men, and then asked, in a sneering way: "Is there any one amongst you manly enough to tell me the cause of all this?"

There was a bit of a hush, and then, without a second's warning, and as if by instinct, a score of hands were lifted, and as many empty bottles crashed and splintered against the door, just as the major saved his head by withdrawing behind it. A moment after the three troop-sergeant-majors rushed into the room, and pointing out to the men the folly and certain consequence of their rash behaviour, exhorted them to remember the duty they were on. But they shouted in reply, "Make him give us our pay; we mean to have it."

The sergeants, finding expostulation was vain, said they would go back and see what could be done, and in a few minutes returned with the three days' pay due to the men. We learnt afterwards that these good fellows, knowing the temper of the men and the justice of their demands, advanced the money themselves, since the major would not.

Two or three hours passed, and then in walked the major

accompanied by an armed guard, and pointing to a dozen men in succession, "Take him—and him—and him," he said, until he had completed his list, and our ringleaders were handcuffed and marched off.

Next morning we set out, on our return, to Hamilton, and the prisoners were marched along through the open streets, chained to the horses of the mounted men, through crowds of the very people we had been sent to keep in order. Of course, it was considered they were Fenian sympathisers, and they were cheered to the echo; and in this state of disgrace the detachment marched back to Hamilton. The prisoners were tried by court-martial, and some got two years' imprisonment; but long before their terms were worked out their sentences were remitted, and the major sent in his papers and resigned the Service.

We remained at Hamilton till May, 1868, when we received orders for Ireland, and, marching to Glasgow, embarked on board a steamer, and reached Dublin the same evening. Within an hour of mooring alongside the quay we were all ashore, saddled, mounted, and ready for a long march of twenty-five Irish miles to Newbridge. This was the station where the regiment had been re-mounted after its return from India, and I had heard a good deal about it from the old hands. The barracks occupied an enormous extent of ground—in fact, the whole side of the principal street of the town, and were surrounded by a high stone wall, loop-holed for defence, and with a strong tower at each corner. Two sides of the barracks were flanked by the river Liffey, on the third side was the main street of Newbridge, and on the fourth an open space of waste land, colonised by a number of unfortunate women, who were tolerated by the authorities, and lived in thatched straw huts known as "wrens' nests."

The side of the main street fronting our barracks was chiefly occupied by public-houses, and low kinds of music and singing-halls, for the special recreation of the military. There was one hotel, frequented entirely by non-commissioned officers, its chief attraction being a billiard table. And a wonderful one it was, the bed being made of wood and the balls of stone.

There were no billiard tables in sergeants' messes in those days, so that this one was considered a discovery. But whilst many of our Non.-Coms. enjoyed themselves with the cue, I found a far pleasanter source of amusement in fishing in the Liffey. The sport is one of which I am passionately fond, and it delighted me to find the river full of trout, and nothing to interfere with my catching them, except themselves.

Two miles south of Newbridge was the famous Curragh of Kildare—a beautiful and broad expanse of the loveliest turf that horses' hoofs ever pressed. No matter whether it rained in torrents over night, the next morning regiments of cavalry and batteries of artillery might manoeuvre or gallop over it without a leaving a mark, the turf being short and elastic from the nibbling of thousands of sheep. Along the centre of the extensive stretch of down, and running from east to west, was a line of infantry huts, and in the summer a large contingent of cavalry was encamped under canvas at a place called Donelly's Hollow.

We had many fine field days on the Curragh, and one of them I shall never forget. There were five regiments of cavalry engaged, double that number of infantry, and about forty field-guns. At the further end of the Curragh, towards Rathbride, ran an isolated ridge, occupied by a skeleton enemy, and the plan of attack included the forcing of this position by the infantry, which was carried out in gallant style, whilst the cavalry, in two bodies, hovered on either flank, the left being composed of Lancers, and the right of Hussars and Dragoons.

Beyond the ridge the country fell into the level again, across which the beaten foe would have to retreat, and to make a nice finish to the day's operations it was arranged that a couple of squadrons from each body of cavalry should charge in pursuit. In order to accomplish this, they had to skirt the ends of the ridge, and then incline to right and left, until they met in the centre of the plain beyond, when they were to form in one line and charge.

My troop was amongst those selected for the right cavalry division, and as the signal to go was given away we dashed, slashing and cutting the pursuing practice in fine style; and after rounding the end of the ridge made for the point of juncture in the plain beyond. But now ensued an altogether unexpected development, for, as the two small bodies of cavalry approached each other, either through the excitement of the men and their horses, or through the impetus of their gallop, instead of wheeling so as to come into line they followed a diagonal direction, until they rode "bash" into one another, almost front to front at the point of contact. The Lancers lowered the points of their lances to avoid spitting our men, and some catching in the ground jerked the riders out of their saddles, whilst all of us came into violent collision. For a moment it seemed like a regular battle-field, many of the horses being bowled over, and others, with empty saddles, dashing madly about. As far as I myself was concerned, the feeling I had when I saw a smash inevitable was, "Look out for Phil Garlic" (a well-known military "mind yourself" expression), and warding off a thrust from a gallant Lancer, he received the benefit of a whack from my sword, and the next moment I came full tilt against one of his comrades, and we both rolled on the turf.

This untoward business occurred through the men being allowed to go too fast, and getting out of hand, and was the fault of the officers. Such a finale to a field day in time of peace has, I fancy, been rarely seen. The general and all the infantry, who had crested the ridge, were looking at us, as well as thousands of spectators, and the former came galloping down with his staff, and when he arrived within shouting distance of our officers, it was about the only time in my life that I felt no ambition to be a captain. On taking note of the casualties it was found that about half-a-dozen of our men were injured by lance-thrusts, and about the same number of Lancers from sword digs, whilst several of the horses had their shoulders put out from the effects of concussion. I am glad to be able to add that no ill-blood resulted from this nasty incident, which was just the sort of thing to start an inter-regimental feud; but the gallant Lancers and ourselves would not permit it to disturb our good-fellowship, and we remained the best of friends.

At the end of the drill season we proceeded to Dublin, and

were quartered in the Royal Barracks. I found the people of this city quite different from what I had expected. Amongst the lower classes a soldier in uniform appeared to be a mark for all the scurrilous abuse the Irish tongue could command, but with the lower middle classes a well-conducted man, who steered clear of discussing politics, could always be sure of very pleasant company, and there were several places of entertainment in the city where he might rely upon a good evening's amusement. One thing here was very different to the system in England and Scotland. Visitors to barracks wore not allowed unrestrained ingress and egress, but obliged to give their names and all particulars about themselves to the guard at the front gate before being admitted; a man was then told off to escort them to the particular soldier they wished to see, and back to the gate again when they left; the barracks, on account of the Fenian troubles, being treated almost in the light of a fortress on a hostile frontier.

About December came a sudden order directing us to proceed in full marching order to the railway station, where a train was waiting to convey us to the south of Ireland for election duty. Packing our horses into cattle-trucks, we steamed off for Cork, which we reached late in the evening. Our destination was Ballincollig, a place about seven miles off, on the banks of the river Lea. We at once commenced our journey, although it had grown quite dark before we started. We had not marched far before we found ourselves confronted by a roaring torrent, the river, owing to the late heavy floods, having broken its banks and overflowed into the road, which was two or three feet deep in water. There was nothing for it but to push on, and so, half swimming in some places, and half wading, we splashed and floundered along till we reached Ballincollig.

Although for some time uninhabited, this place had formerly been a cavalry station of some importance. But neglect and disuse had reduced the barracks to a woeful condition, for in the stables the weeds, chiefly from the dropping of the oats had sprung up to the height of about a foot, in which our horses were soon burying their noses. No gas being laid on, we were obliged to unsaddle and put our animals up by the dim light of a few miserable tallow candles, and when at last we had made them comfortable and were able to repair to our own quarters, we found a similar state of things upstairs. For the beds being stuffed with oaten straw, and the place as damp as a cavern, the seeds were actually sprouting up through the seams of the ticking. The rooms appeared as if they had not been entered for years. They had been in charge of some men of the Artillery Coast Brigade, who seemed to consider that their whole duty consisted in seeing that the buildings did not run away. Some of the artillery men were now told off in conjunction with ourselves to furnish a guard. My own post was in the main guard, and I was much edified by an argument between two of these Celtic bombardiers, who had fallen out as to whose turn it was to bake bread in the guardroom oven! In the morning a report was made to me by another gallant gunner in these words: "Och, sure Corpril, Oi've been on guard the furrust toime for tin years, and some thayfe has shtole me rug from undher me!"

There was a story about the cavalry regiment previously quartered at Ballincollig which, whether true or not, is certainly quaint. It had been so long in the place that it was popularly reported Government had forgotten its existence, while the men had taken up all sorts of civil pursuits, chiefly in the farming line. At last a general officer came down to inspect them unexpectedly, and on entering the front gate made himself known to the sentry, and seeing no men about, asked where the regiment was.

"They are all out harvesting, sir."

"Harvesting!" snarled the general, "I'll harvest them. Call the trumpeter."

"The trumpeter's away, your honour: but there's his son yonder, and he can give a blow."

He beckoned to the lad to come up, and bring his father's bugle, and when he arrived the general thundered out, "Sound the parade."

"The parade, sir, what's that?" asked the boy. "I never heard my father sound any parade."

"What the deuce does he sound?" asked the general; "I want to get the regiment together."

"Oh, if that's all you want, sir," answered the lad, brightening up, "I can soon manage it. It's 'Reapers In' you ought to have asked for."

It was in this queer, outlandish place that we found ourselves on this cold, dark, wet December night. Early the next morning we were split into small parties of twenty men, each commanded by an officer, and the one I was attached to was sent to Bandon to support the civil power during the election which was just beginning. After a rough, long march, through slush and mud, in many places fording streams (for the floods were out all over the country), we reached our destination and took up our quarters in some old dilapidated cavalry barracks perched up on the high banks of a river which ran through the town and divided it into two parts. Bandon was full of a riotous, screeching Irish mob, collected there for the morrow, which was nomination day, and all through that night, wet and tired though we were, we were kept under arms, and our horses ready saddled for any emergency. In the same barracks with us was a detachment of infantry, whilst a body of Irish constabulary was quartered in a large factory adjoining. It was anticipated that the election would be a most desperately contested one, conducted on the bitterest lines. The Conservative member who had represented the town for many years, was Colonel Bernard, a member of the family of the Earl of Bandon, whose estate and fine old castle stood on the opposite bank of the river. His opponent, a barrister named Shaw, was looked upon as the people's candidate. Bandon itself was not a very large town, but it was the centre of an extensive district, and the polling station was situated in the market-place, where five streets converged into one centre, and created peculiar opportunities for disorder.

But the Bandon Election is deserving of a chapter to itself, and so the reader must turn the page if he wishes to know how the Irish settled their political differences of opinion on this occasion.

CHAPTER 7

An Irish Election

When morning broke a hurried breakfast was served out to us, and then we were paraded with the infantry in the Barrack Square, where the commanding officer addressed a few words to us, the pith of them being that we were to keep our temper under the trying circumstances we should shortly find ourselves in. All this time the mob outside the gates were roaring and shouting out the name of Shaw, and working themselves into a perfect pitch of frenzy, which reached a climax when the gates were opened and the infantry endeavoured to pass out. They wore met with a shower of stones, and many of the poor fellows wore carried to the rear, bleeding from ugly wounds in their heads and faces, whilst soldiers and mob were soon fairly jammed in the gateway until it looked as if the latter would force themselves in, instead of the former marching out.

Our captain now gave the word to draw swords, and when the moment came, use them with vigour, but only with the flat sides. Presently the word was given for the infantry to stand aside, and then with a bound we were in the thick of it, laying about us right and left and keeping well together, for in this sort of a scrimmage a trooper once isolated is done for. We soon drove the rioters back, though they continued to face us, calling us all the bad names in Ireland, and paying little or no heed to the exhortations of several priests in their midst, who did their utmost to keep them in check, shouting out: "Whativor ye do, boys, don't touch the drag-hoons! Remember Dungarvan!" And well they might recall that name, for only a short time before a troop of Lancers, employed on duty similar to ours, were so badly mauled that they could stand it no longer, and turning on their opponents spitted them right and left, killing several and maiming many more. This gained for them the name—which is shouted after the Regiment to this day whenever they are seen in Ireland—of "Dungarvan Butchers."

As soon as we had driven the mob back, we formed outside the gate under a shower of stones, and made a lane for the infantry; and having once seen them into the street it was comparatively easy work to make a road to the court-house, or town hall, which was in the centre of the market-place.

Our next duty was to clear a way for the sheriff and protect him while he was receiving the nominations. This we accomplished with varying success; and between the cheers and curses of the multitude, and showers of stones, and flourishing of shillelahs, the two candidates wore nominated and a poll fixed for the following day week.

We now marched to Dunmanway, where a similar performance was gone through the next day, and we were then allowed to rest till Thursday, when we returned to Bandon for the election.

Early in the morning of the polling day the troops and constabulary marched into the marketplace and took up their several stations. The town was, if anything, crammed with a greater and more disorderly mob than on nomination day, and from a few words I overheard between the officers and the town authorities, I gathered that unusually rough work was expected, the contending parties being equally balanced, and both imbued with an undying spirit of victory or—break the other chap's head.

There were two polling stations, and the chief duty of the cavalry lay in keeping the road open for the electors to come up and record their votes. As it drew towards midday the voters began to come in thickly, and fighting started in real earnest. The constabulary had to bear the brunt of it, their work being to line the roads up which the electors came, and as the political opinions of every voter appeared to be public property, one half of the mob tried to kill him, and the other half to pass him through. The constabulary were consequently placed between two fires, and got pelted and clubbed impartially by both parties. Sticks and stones were as common as oaths and curses, and it made our blood boil to see the constant rushes of the mob against these plucky fellows, who lost their helmets, and had their clothes torn off their backs, till many of them stood in rags at their posts, with the blood streaming from their heads and faces.

Now and again, when matters grew desperate, the infantry came to the rescue, and clubbing their rifles laid stoutly about them; and I am open to say that the thuds of the butts falling on the heads and shoulders of the mob was pleasant music to us, who all this time were sitting with drawn swords, eager to be in the fray, but not allowed to make a move.

I will say this for the priests, of whom there were several present, that they used their best endeavours to keep the people from attacking the soldiery, constantly repeating the warning cry, "Remember Dungarvan." Behind the infuriated Irishmen groups of women, bare-headed and bare-footed, kept coming up in relays with their aprons full of stones, which they shot down by the side of the men, who kept up a perfect fusilade at everybody and everything. The mayor, who sat on horseback just in front of us, threatened every minute to read the Riot Act, but in reply the stones came hurtling along in his direction, just to remind him he was flesh and blood and law and order, to be pelted the same as everyone else.

After this sort of work had been going on for a considerable time, there suddenly came a tremendous roar from one part of the town, and a mounted constabulary man dashed up with the information that the mob had broken into one of the committee rooms and was wrecking it. The mayor gave our captain orders to follow him with his troop; and away we went, the crowd prudently opening before us as they recognised we meant mischief. We were too late to save the building, for the rioters had already entered it and demolished all the furniture and woodwork. But we went at them right and left, as they came triumphantly pouring out, and assisted by some of the infantry, managed to clear the wrecked house. We then formed up in a line in front of it, and there remained on guard, detaching a man every now and then as orderly to carry messages backwards and forwards between us and the rest of the troops.

Presently one of these orderlies—a man named Johnny Duckling—was struck by a stone as he neared us on his return, and fell from his horse, and for a moment we thought he was badly wounded if not killed. The troop waited for no order this time, but with one impulse dashed up to where he lay, the mob surging forward at the same moment to try and club him. We were too quick for them or they would, perhaps, have killed him. Some infantry and constabulary coming up, we handed Duckling and his horse over to them, and then proceeded in a serious way to take it out of his assailants. In spite of the remonstrances of our officers, who did their utmost to restrain us, we made up in ten minutes for all the insult, abuse, and injury we had been forced to passively suffer during the morning. It was not until our arms were tired with smiting that we returned to our station, whilst the mob, like beaten dogs, slunk back and glared at us under their eyelids from a very respectful distance.

The polling time was now about closing, and there was; a lull in the struggle until the results were declared. Both candidates were in the town, but Shaw, being the people's man, his supporters were far more numerous than Colonel Bernard's, and the question was, how to get the latter safely home. To cover his return to the castle our troop was divided into two escorts, and one followed an empty inside car, which was driven away with some parade and at a rapid rate to deceive the populace. A rush was made at it by the mob, some to attack and some to defend, whilst our men closed round and pretended to be in a state of great anxiety. This was the opportunity for Colonel Bernard, who at once stepped into the second car, and having a comparatively clear road in front of him, set off as hard as the horses could go. The first car had of course taken the castle road, but when it reached the river bridge instead of crossing it, as it should have done, the driver dashed down a road leading to the left. The mob only followed it for a short distance for they soon recognised they were on the wrong scent, and turning back reached the bridge at the same time that we did. Directly they saw the car we were escorting, they shouted out, "Here he is!" and surged forward to try and cut us off. But we were too quick for them, and managed to get our charge safely home.

Thus ended the first of the many elections I was engaged in during the old days before the ballot-box enabled men to save their skins and their consciences by swearing one thing and voting another. I may mention that Mr. Shaw was returned by four votes, so that the fight was as close as it was furious.

On our return from the castle, where we were most hospitably treated, we perceived that a change had stolen over the town. After a general victory there are never any enemies, for those that are beaten withdraw, or confess themselves partisans of the victors. It was something in this way now. The streets were nearly deserted, and the populace were all in the public-houses drinking from the bowl of fellowship. The few who came out to see us clatter down the street were no longer insulting in their remarks, and several of them cried out, "Well, bhoys, it's some fun you've had to-day, and it's been a glorious one for Ould Oirland." Others held out glasses to us, inviting us to get our horses done and come and show them "if we could dhrink as well as we could foight." In place of the bloodthirsty feeling that had previously been prevalent, everyone seemed to be claiming his neighbour as a friend. But the constabulary who followed us received an altogether different reception, for their appearance acted on the populace as a red rag on a bull, and many a curse of Cromwell was shouted after them as they passed to their quarters.

The next morning we were off by daylight to Dunmanway, where a similar scene was enacted. The Sunday following we marched to Skibbereen, and here the officer in command of the troops pursued different tactics to secure peace and order. The town could only be entered by one of two roads, being surrounded by bog and river. Guards were placed over both, who permitted no one to pass into the place until he had first deposited his blackthorn. This was a masterly move, for most Irishmen regard their shillelah with the same reverence as a soldier feels for his rifle, or a Hussar for his sword. Man after man came up, but when the terms of admittance were explained, they glared savagely at the Sassenach tyrants, and then, with a flourish of their national weapon, turned right about face and returned, baffled, but not demeaned. None but those who possessed a vote would consent to surrender the token of independence they prized so highly, and as the best part of the rough element consisted of non-voters, who merely wished to be present for the fun of a faction light, and the excitement of cracking a fellow-patriot's skull, this excellent precaution excluded large numbers of the lowest class from the town.

Such was the sort of work we were employed in for nearly three weeks in County Cork. Nomination day in one place, polling day in another, turn and turn about, until the elections were over and Mr. Gladstone was elevated to power to continue the policy of coercion and cultivate the leek he was to swallow a few years later.

When the election duty was over, instead of returning to Ballincollig, our various scattered detachments received orders to converge on Cork, where we all met at a given date, and from whence half the regiment proceeded to Dundalk, and the other half, which it was my lot to accompany, by march route to Dublin.

Our first day's ride was a very long one, as many a cavalry soldier knows, for we had to cover twenty-eight Irish miles before we reached our halting-place at Fermoy, where we found little enough comfort to compensate us. Marching in England and Ireland are two very different things. In the most distressful country there is no hot meal provided for the soldier when he reaches his billet at the end of a day's march, a slight additional payment, called marching money, being granted him in lieu thereof. Out of this he has to provide everything for himself, for he receives nothing from the person he is billeted on, except the use of cooking utensils and fire. Then the billets themselves are very poor places as a rule, rarely, if ever, being in an inn, and a man may have to put up at a crockery-shop one day, a baker's the next, a draper's the third, and a butcher's the fourth, and so on. The accommodation is of the most comfortless description, and I often felt as though we were in a foreign country and amongst people alien to us in everything. Constantly, in an Irish billet, I have lain in bed and counted the stars through a great hole in the roof, and although the landlord protested that "Glory be to God, *his* conscience was clear enough to enable him to sleep with the stars shining down upon him," I never quite looked at it in that light. If it happened to be a Friday, deuce of a sniff of honest meat could be got for love or money. Then again the people were prejudiced, if not against us personally, against our uniforms. Sometimes, if we schemed to get at the soft side of them, they would try to make us comfortable, but they had not the means to do much, for the country was poverty-stricken. Many a time as we sat down at a separate table to a fairly good dinner of our own foraging, the family—whom, if appearances went for anything, we should describe in England as well-to-do tradesmen—gathered round a square table, bordered with a rim of wood, and messed off a great heap of potatoes boiled in their jackets, seasoned with a little salt, and washed down with butter-milk, and we'd hear them sniffing at our meat as though the smell of it was a treat.

Our horses fared as badly as ourselves, seldom enjoying a decent stall. It was a common thing during the rainy weather to have to bail the water out of the stables (which were always sunk slightly below the level of the ground) so as to make them inhabitable. Our arms, too, were a constant source of anxiety to us, and before we broke off to our billets we always marched in a body to the local police barracks, and deposited our carbines there for safe custody, calling for them the next morning.

In most of the stables the horses kept company with pigs, ducks, and fowls—an arrangement that was not without its advantages when we had to forage for ourselves; and though sometimes we got an old crow that wasn't worth a shilling, I fear the owner had to give us credit. I don't seek to defend this, and I admit H troop deserved their name of the Forty Thieves; but if they broke the Eighth Commandment, it was because without doing so they would at times never have broken their fast.

What with the discomfort of bad billets and long marches in snow, sleet, and cold, we soon seemed to have all the spirits washed out of us. Even the time-honoured institution of "The White Jug" was forgotten by our officers, whilst "The Girl I left Behind Me" never existed on the line of march, for if Biddy or Kathleen were once seen talking to a Saxon soldier she was "for it" the next time she went to confession. Glad we were to reach Dublin and take up our old quarters in the Royal barracks, just in time for Christmas-day. Our officers, as if to make up for the discomforts we had recently gone through, vied with each other in providing a handsome spread for the men, and there was a sort of general holiday for a week.

We remained six months at Dublin, and the only thing of general interest that occurred during this time was the public entry of the new Lord Lieutenant. We furnished the escort, and I had a good opportunity of noting his reception, and could only wish it had not been at the expense of so much mud to our troop, for what missed him hit us.

There was an incident that happened at Dublin of which I must not omit mention. This was the discovery of an old veteran of our regiment, who had sounded the charge for the 14th Light Dragoons (as they were then) at the battle of Talavera in the Peninsular War. One day this old chap, who was about eighty years of age, came toddling into barracks. He was an undersized man with a boarded face, wrinkled and scored, and a white moustache. He was dressed in the uniform and three-cornered hat of the pensioners at the "Old Man's House"—as the official residence of the Commander-in-Chief in Ireland is called. Soldier-like, some of our men asked him up to the canteen, and when his tongue was loosened, and he told them his name was Heffernan, and he had been trumpeter in the regiment in the Peninsular War, it is no exaggeration to say that he might have swum in beer if he had been so disposed. As it was he took more than was good for him, and had to be sent home in a cab, and was punished by a month's confinement to quarters. When his term was up he was invited to our sergeants' mess, and there accorded a grand reception. They cheered him, and chaired him, and at last set him upon the table with a trumpet in one hand and a glass in the other. First of all he quavered out a song called *The Ragged Brigade*, which graphically described the condition and personal appearance of the Fourteenth at the end of the Peninsular War, Then he sounded the charge with his trumpet as he had done at the battle of Talavera more than sixty years before. I never saw men so strangely stirred as these notes blared out; they were silent for a moment, as if they were waiting for the faint echoes to come back from Long Ago, and then they rose and burst out into ringing cheers. The old man on the table was to us a precious link with the past, even though he looked but as a ghost of departed glory, Our officers invited the old hero to their mess, and took upon themselves to see that he ended his days in every comfort, furnishing his rooms and giving him plenty of money. But he only lived to enjoy their bounty for a year.

The drill season began at the end of June, and we were again ordered to the Curragh. Here we were under canvas, in the old-fashioned bell tents, and to our discomfort it rained nearly the whole time. It happened that the authorities were contemplating the formation of a new camp for cavalry, and Colonel G—— was in charge of the survey. He applied to our commanding officer for an orderly to attend him, and, although a corporal, I was selected for the post. The reason was because my horse, a very handsome young bay, just dismissed from the riding school, wanted a little better stabling than the ordinary troop horses had, and on this account I was told off for duty with Colonel G——, who had a good stable attached to his quarters. Many a swinging gallop I enjoyed behind him during his daily visits to the site of the proposed new camp, and for nearly three months was in close attendance on him, holding his horse whilst he was engaged surveying, and oftentimes sharing his field lunch with him. Some years later when I attended the funeral service at Canterbury Cathedral to commemorate his death at Khartoum, my thoughts wandered back to the pleasant rides I enjoyed with him in 1870, on the velvet turf of the Curragh of Kildare.

October brought us orders to march to Longford from whence my troop and two others were detached to Athlone, or, as it is called in the army, from its situation exactly in the centre of Ireland—the Knob of Hell. The town is situated on both banks of the beautiful river Shannon, and connected by a splendid drawbridge. The barracks were built on the Roscommon side of the river, near the ruins of an old castle made famous by a siege in the days of Cromwell. The garrison consisted of a mixed body of troops of all arms, and amongst them a newly raised battery of field artillery, made up of volunteers and horses transferred from other batteries. The men were as wild a lot as I have ever seen, and one day, on being ordered out for one of their very frequent marching-order parades, some devilment of discontent seized them, and instead of turning out spick and span in the usual manner, they painted their horses with blue and yellow to represent zebras, mounted them bare-backed, having previously armed themselves with mops and long scrubbers, and then proceeded to the snow-covered parade ground and indulged the rest of the garrison with an imitation of a mounted war-dance. Nor would they return to their stables till the fit wore off them. With the exception of one or two of the ringleaders, who were rather severely punished, the rest of the men were let off easy, and after this explosion, settled down soberly and steadily to work; and the battery soon achieved a reputation for smartness, second to none in the service.

The Fenian movement still continued to be a source of anxiety to the authorities, and Lord Strathnairn, the commander-in-chief in Ireland, who inspected us about this time, was very much addicted to sounding the alarm and exercising the troops in all sorts of dodges, so as to teach them to take the field in a quick and efficient manner. Soon after Christmas a change was considered necessary, and our G troop was ordered from head-quarters at Longford to Athlone. We had given it the usual incoming welcome, and most of us were in the town introducing the newcomers to our friends and acquaintances, when we were suddenly surprised by hearing the "Boot and saddle!" and "Turn out!" We all hurried back to barracks wondering what was up, the general opinion being it was one of Lord Strathnairn's false alarms. But on entering the barracks the sergeant-majors ordered every man to seize the first horse he could get, and ride down to the railway station. Such a confused scene in a cavalry stable I have rarely seen, for everything had to be done in the dark, it being past ten o'clock, and the place only lighted by two or three wretched lanterns. Within a quarter of an hour we were all drawn up at the station, where we found the infantry filing into a train, and heard the battery of artillery come rumbling up. But when it came for us to entrain, there was a considerable delay for want of trucks and we had to wait several hours. We then steamed off to Tuam in county Galway, where we arrived on a Sunday morning, much to the astonishment of the townsfolk, when the bells were ringing for mass, and forming a junction with the other troops, marched through Tuam into the open country that led to the wilds of Connemara.

Everything appeared in its usual aspect, till we saw some smoke rising in the distance, and as we neared the place found it was issuing from a large rickyard. The cavalry now pushed on to reconnoitre, and came up to the farm, which had been burnt down, and the cattle houghed and maimed. It was a cruel thing to see the poor dumb brutes standing there bleeding, and their owners wringing their hands and calling down the curses of heaven on the wretches who had ruined them.

We beat the country up for some days, but without any results, although it was certain that the Fenians had been in arms in the locality, for Tuam harboured many of their leaders, and bodies had been seen quite recently drilling at different points on the wild treeless hill-sides. At the end of a week the artillery and greater part of the infantry returned to Athlone, and most of our detachment accompanied them. But fourteen of us, myself included, under command of an officer, were left behind as a sort of personal bodyguard to the Bishop of Tuam, who was a brother of the Earl of Bandon, and we took up our quarters in the house of an Orangeman, named Fenten, who owned a baker's and publican's business close to the Bishop's palace.

Chapter 8

An Irish Informer

We remained some time in Tuam, where we were very comfortable. The officer in command was an easy-tempered young gentleman, and our sergeant, old Joe Parry, a very popular Non.-Com.; and we had easy times of it. I was told off as cook and caterer, and had to exercise all my wits and ingenuity to satisfy the mess. Our favourite dish was a young kid which could be purchased for ninepence or a shilling, and when baked in an oven heated with turf and served with plenty of vegetables (supplied from the Bishop's garden), made an excellent dish. Fowls were cheap, a good one being sold for sixpence, and a "nest" of eighteen to twenty-four eggs cost only four-pence; other things were on the same cheap scale, so we lived like fighting cocks on our fourteen-pence a day.

The Dean of Tuam constituted himself our chaplain and visited us twice a week. He invariably began his ministrations by ordering a pint of beer all round, and after we had drunk it, would say: "Now, men, your pots are empty, let us pray." And when devotions were over he ordered us another pint of beer all round before going away.

Not un-frequently we were invited up to the Bishop's palace, and his lady often showed us a collection of curios which interested us much, as they contained a number of uniforms and arms worn by her ancestors previous to and at the battle of Waterloo. These visits always concluded with wine and cake, handed us by footmen in livery—an attention which nearly took our breath away the first time.

Although things were so comfortable for us, they were not quite as pleasant for our landlord Mr. Fenten. Every day brought him an anonymous threatening letter, usually with a picture of a coffin for a crest, and himself lying in it with a dagger through his vitals. These caused Fenten considerable alarm although he was as bold and determined a man as ever stepped; but the bravest of the brave cannot but be uneasy when confronted with dangers he cannot see, meet, or guard against.

The state of nervous apprehension into which Fenten fell, and my own imprudence nearly cost me my life one night. My bedroom was situated at the top of the house, which stood in a large courtyard, with a pair of tall wooden gates leading to the road. After seeing our arms safe of an evening Sergeant Parry troubled nothing more about us, and, having formed acquaintance with a very pleasant family in the town whose house was always open to me, I often chanced my arm, and stayed out an hour or so beyond locking-up time. When I returned to quarters I used to climb over the gate and get in at the kitchen door, which there was a knack of opening from outside.

Coming home rather late one night, I scrambled over the gate and slipped into the kitchen right enough, and proceeded to creep upstairs in my socks. I suppose I made some noise which aroused Fenten, for after I had passed two nights and turned to mount the third, I saw something indistinct standing on the landing above, and simultaneously heard the click of a gun being cocked.

Instantaneously it passed through my mind that I had often heard Fenten declare he would, without compunction, shoot any Fenian at sight, who entered his house after dark, and was fully prepared for them in the event of their attempting to carry out their threats against his life. Quicker than lightning I ducked my head, and as I did so a loud report rang out, followed by the crashing sound of broken glass, as a charge of buckshot went through the window at my back.

"It's me, Mr. Fenten," I shouted out, fearing he would let fly the second barrel.

Hearing my voice he dropped his gun, and rushing downstairs to me with open arms, cried out: "My God! corporal—have I shot you?" and when he found I was uninjured threw his arms round me and burst out sobbing like a child.

Of course the report roused the whole house, and in less than a minute every man in it was round us. Fenten, recovering himself, explained, with a ready resource, that he had fetched me out of bed, thinking he heard someone moving in the house, and had fired at what looked to him like a man escaping down stairs; and this invention saved me from getting into serious trouble.

Whilst stationed at Tuam, which I may here mention was an active Fenian centre, we often noticed a smart well-dressed man who lived nearly opposite to where we were billeted, and it was the general remark amongst us that we had seldom seen a finer specimen of humanity. He was about six feet tall, as upright as a dart, and of a military appearance, with, perhaps, just a little bit of swagger; but he was one of those whom it suited. He had a handsome face, with pleasant eyes that seemed to invite a civil remark, and assure a civil answer, and he sported a large moustache. One night I was rather late in returning to quarters, and I daresay found the cold air did not mix well with potheen, for I experienced some difficulty in climbing over the gate, which seemed to me considerably higher than usual Seeing this, who should come up but our fine-looking man, and in a pleasant tone of voice, asked me, "Comrade, can I be of assistance to you?" I thanked him, and we got talking, and he offered me a cigar, and asked me to come over to his quarters across the road and have a glass with him. But it was already very late, so I told him I would look him up some other evening, and with that he gave me a leg up, and I found my way into the house.

A night or two after this I was going out for a stroll and ran up against him. He repeated his invitation, and this time I accepted it. He took me to a large, fairly well-furnished room, which had something the appearance of an office, for a couple of desks and an *escritoire* stood near the window, and the walls were lined with pigeon-holes for papers.

Noticing my curious gaze, Deasey—for so I will call him—observed, "Oh, there is more business done here than your people think," and then drawing chairs to the fire, produced a large bottle of spirits, and a couple of glasses with the remark: "Help yourself, and you'll find a drop of stuff there that you don't get a sniff of every day. It's never paid a penny to the Sassenach, whereby it's pure and wholesome drinking for a patriot."

I stopped an hour and found him a most pleasant and entertaining companion. He appeared to have a good deal of the American in him, for most of his yarns were about the Civil War in the States, in which he had taken an active part. But what astonished me more than his stories, was his intimate and accurate knowledge of the movements and numbers of the various troops in Ireland, and the able way in which he discussed the personal qualities and military abilities of the officers commanding regiments and brigades. He seemed to know something about everyone, and a great deal about most. His conversation possessed a sort of fascination for me, and this first meeting led to several others, and I passed many evenings in his company, until we became very friendly.

Although I was not without my suspicions, he never made any attempt to draw me out or obtain information from me, and so I associated with him quite freely—especially as he did the better part of the talking. One evening, when he had taken more of the potheen than usual, he startled me by remarking, "Now you are a non-commissioned officer in your Queen's army; but I suppose you will hardly believe me when I tell you I am a commissioned officer."

"In the United States Army, I suppose?" said I.

"Well, no—not exactly; but in what you call the Fenian Army—that is, the Army of Ireland."

I was taken aback at this bold confession, but tried to turn it off by saying, "Well, whatever army you are in, you do it credit."

He smiled, a bit pleased at this, and then taking out a roll of papers from a drawer at his elbow, observed, "Here is my commission and one or two others," holding them up in his hands and partly unrolling them for me to see; "And this," he went on, pointing to a particular one, "belonged to a scoundrel who is dead now. If you like to hear his story, and have time to listen, I will tell you how we serve informers in our nation."

I told him I should be very glad to sit and listen; and this is his story, given, as far as I can remember it, in Deasey's own words.

No doubt you have noticed in the Protestant Cathedral here at Tuam, the bent and grey-headed old verger. Well, that man had a son, Michael Kavenagh, a smart and intelligent young fellow with half and half leanings towards the Cause, who offered to join us if we gave him a commission. His request was granted, and one night we swore him in at the Cathedral altar, not to desecrate the building, but just to bring home to him the solemn nature of our oath of fidelity to the Brotherhood. For a time he seemed heart and soul with us, but by degrees a change came over him, and he fell away—without our knowing it, however; and one morning he was missed and no one knew where he had gone.

Not long after this there came a rumour that someone had turned traitor, and was going to swear an information at Tuam court-house. You have doubtless seen the inside of it, and know how it is arranged. There is the body of the court, with places for magistrate, lawyers, prisoners, and jury, and then a barrier, with space behind for the public. Up above a gallery runs three sides round the court, and, sitting in it, you can look down on everything below.

The Government apprehended great danger and commotion from the divulging of this informer, and took proportionate precautions. In all sorts of quiet ways extra constabulary were drafted into the town, and when the court-house doors were thrown open it was found that the public were excluded from the gallery, which was filled with police.

The body of the court was soon packed to overflowing with men whose hearts were in the Cause. Some had assisted in Michael Kavenagh's swearing-in at the Cathedral, and all were on the tip-toe of expectation to discover who the informer was. Had they suspected it was Kavenagh there were many who would have put a good few Connemara miles between themselves and Tuam court-house on that fatal day.

The hour struck, and the magistrate entered from the back of the court and took his seat, and all the doors were closed, and silence ordered. Then he rose, and, in a very impressive manner, spoke as follows:—

I am here to-day to administer justice, and do my duty as resident magistrate of this district. God forbid that I should have to give an order which would cause blood to be shed. But you know me, most of you, and that I shall not shrink from doing my duty. And I therefore solemnly warn you that if but a hand is raised, during the course of the day's proceedings, against the man who will be brought before me, I shall uphold the law, and your blood be upon your own heads.

Then he looked up significantly to the officer in command of the constabulary in the gallery, and resumed his seat.

"With ball ammunition—load!" rang out the word of command from above, followed by the rattling of firearms.

Then came the order:—

"Present!"

With a simultaneous movement the muzzles of fifty rifles were depressed over the gallery railing, and brought to bear upon the crowd in the well of the court.

A silence still as death followed. The doors had been bolted, and our men saw they were trapped like vermin in a hole.

The magistrate signed for the informer to be brought in. A curtain drew aside, and Michael Kavenagh stepped up to the elevated seat prepared for him. As the crowd recognised him a yell of execration burst from their throats, and a dozen revolvers leapt out, and were pointed towards the table at which he sat. ,

"Stop!" cried the magistrate, lifting up his hand with an imperious gesture. "For God's sake stop and reflect! Down with those revolvers, for the first shot fired will be the signal for many of you to be hurried into eternity."

Slowly and sullenly the weapons were lowered, for, darker

than the magistrate's warning, deadlier than his proclamation, were the black muzzles of the rifles that lined the gallery, and the eloquent click of the triggers as they were being cocked. The curses of hell burst from hoarse throats, and gleaming eyes glared fiercely upwards, filled with hatred and fear.

Michael Kavenagh laid his information, describing how he was sworn in against his will as a lieutenant in the Fenian army. With this and a dozen other lies he perjured his dastard soul. Then he was asked if he recognised in court any of the men who had been present at the Cathedral when he was sworn in; and he answered "I do," and pointed out several whom he named.

The magistrate made a sign to the officer in charge of the constabulary, and a score of policemen were sent down, and under cover of their comrades' rifles, apprehended the men whom Kavenagh had betrayed. Then the informer rose, and hurriedly left the court, whilst scorching curses and threats were hurled after him as he went.

Deasey paused in his tale, and drew a long breath. Then he poured out a very strong draught of potheen, and drained it before he continued:

We looked for him, watched for him, lurked for him, and laid traps for him, but Michael Kavenagh had vanished. At last we heard that he had been sent to London, and some of our agents followed him there. But before they arrived he had been shipped off to America. Our advices went out to our friends across the water, and we almost felt sure of our revenge, when suddenly he doubled back, and returned to England again, and at last we lost touch of him altogether.

He had gone to Australia, with English gold in his pockets, and an order for land, on which he might settle down safely. And he might have escaped us, but for a woman. His sweetheart lived at Tuam, and the girl loved him, and consented to join him; and when, one day, she suddenly left the town, we knew we had the clue. We waited, waited, waited. We did not know where she had gone, but her parents still remained in the old home, and we felt sure letters would come to them. But a year passed before we found out what we wanted. We had friends in the post office, and every letter addressed to the girl's parents was opened and read, and then resealed and delivered. One of these contained Michael Kavenagh's assumed name and address, and the same week one of our men was outward bound for Australia.

Kavenagh had settled down on a farm a little way up country, and was prospering. He was a father, too, for his wife had just borne him a son. He had grown a long beard, which completely disguised him; and time and immunity from danger had brought ease to his mind. He began to think he was safe and forgotten. But the Brotherhood never forgets.

One evening there came a travelling pedlar, to his farm—one of those itinerant merchants who are common in the colony. His wares were good and cheap, and he soon got into conversation with Mrs. Kavenagh; and when her husband returned from work the pedlar asked if he might remain for the night, as he was tired. Kavenagh willingly gave him welcome, and after he had been provided with a hearty meal, asked him, in the cool of the evening, if he would like to have a stroll round the run.

They started out, Kavenagh kissing his wife and infant son before he left. Presently they came to a secluded spot.

"I have something to show you," said the pedlar; and, drawing out a revolver in his right hand, and a photograph in his left: "Michael Kavenagh," he asked, "do you know this?"

It was a photograph of Kavenagh himself, taken at Tuam when he was a younger man.

As the doomed traitor looked up his whole past life uprose before him, and he knew his hour had come. His face grew ashy pale, and the sweat poured from it like water. Clasping his hands, he begged for mercy, for the sake of his wife and child.

"You showed no mercy, Michael Kavenagh," said the pedlar. "You sold your brother men for English gold. Mercy is not for you here or hereafter."

"My wife! my child!" the wretched suppliant gasped.

"I give you five minutes to pray for them, and make your peace with God. Do not waste a moment of it!"

Kavenagh heeded not the advice, but continued to beg, and implore, and shriek for a reprieve. The pedlar never spoke again, but kept his revolver covering his victim, and when his time was up sent a bullet through his brain.

Deasey's face had grown strangely hard as he sat there, with the firelight flickering upon it, bringing into relief deep, stern lines I had never seen before. As he neared the end of his story his speech grew slower and slower, and the last few words were spoken in a whisper. Then he rose to his feet.

"Death to informers," he hissed between his teeth; and the next moment, lifting his eyes to heaven, he called out in a loud, clear voice, as if to justify the crime—

"And God save Ireland."

"I do not like your stories, Deasey," I said; "I want no more of them."

"Ay, ay," he said, shaking his head solemnly, "but it is the story of men whose hearts are beating with every throb for Ireland— who are waiting for the day to dawn when we shall stand erect in the field, under our country's flag, not crouch in the bogs and treeless wilds of Connemara. We fear not the issue, but these informers so destroy us, that sometimes I think Freedom's morn will never break. It is the curse of our land that it breeds traitors, such reptiles as this Kavenagh. You are a soldier, loyal to your Queen; I respect you for it. But say now, how would you treat a comrade who betrayed your country to the enemy?"

I did not reply, for all he told me seemed so in opposition to my ideas of right and loyalty. "Goodbye, Captain Deasey," I said to him, "we must never meet again."

He shook my hand, and smiled a strange smile. "Perhaps we may," he said, as he saw me to the door. But that was the last time I ever saw him.

During the three months we were at Tuam we gained the good opinion of the inhabitants, and made many pleasant acquaintances. We seldom, if ever, entered a public-house, having plenty of entertainment elsewhere. As for potheen, there was a glut of it, for I believe more "mountain dew" was distilled in the wild hills within a short distance of Tuam than in any other part of Ireland. And talking of the national beverage reminds me of the following anecdote which gave us all many a good laugh.

About a mile out of Tuam stood a shanty in which lived a widow woman, of the name of Maloney, and her two sons. She owned a potato patch about two miles off, and kept an old donkey to carry in turf and "taties." This donkey was well known in Tuam, and indeed the Government excise supervisor had long kept an eye on it, suspecting that on occasions it carried contraband goods, though unable to prove it.

One morning there was a terrible hullaballoo at the widow's shanty, and going up to the crowd collected in front of it, what should I see stretched out on the bare ground but poor old Neddy, blown out to an enormous size, and to all appearances in the throes of death. The widow crouched over him, wringing her hands and crying, "Och, wurra, wurra, the baste's dyin', the best frind a widdy ever had."

The crowd was both sympathetic and interested, for it is seldom that a chance occurs of seeing a donkey die. Some hazarded one opinion, and some another, until the doctor, who had been sent for, arrived. He had long physicked man and beast in the neighbourhood, but the complaint from which Neddy was suffering completely baffled him. It was a sight to make a stoic laugh to see him standing over the animal, scratching his bald head, trying to find a Latin name for the malady. At last he gave it up and acknowledged, "For the life av me, Misthress Maloney, I cannot tell what ails the baste."

Just then the excise supervisor happened to ride by, and reining up his horse asked what was the matter.

"Wurra, wurra, me donkey's dyin'," wailed the widow.

Hearing this he dismounted and walked up to where poor Neddy lay like a log, while Mrs. Maloney adjured him by all the Saints in the Calendar to suggest some remedy out of his extra knowledge and earn her blessing. The supervisor stood for a moment, wrapped in deep thought, and scrutinising the animal intently. Then he stooped down, and lifting up the donkey's head applied his nose to its nostrils. A sniff sufficed him, for he at once dropped the head, which fell thwack to the ground, like a lump of lead, and straightening himself up, said in a severe official voice:

"Misthress Maloney, the donkey's *dhrunk!*"

With that he searched round the shanty, and came across a large tub sunk in the ground as if to catch rain water, but which was half full of pure potheen. It then came out that the night before, the widow's sons, having finished their last journey in the dark, left Neddy to his own devices. He, roaming about in search of water, came across the tub, and the lid being insecurely fastened, pushed it aside and drunk his fill till he got what I suppose may be called "the staggers." The widow's sons were at once apprehended and taken to prison, and later on received a very heavy punishment.

About Easter, orders came for us to join our troop at Athlone, and a couple of days' march brought us there, and about the same time I was promoted to full corporal, which increased my pay without increasing my responsibility or expenses. A full corporal in those days was considered the best paid man of his rank in the regiment, for with his step he had no extra gold lace to mount, and as he continued to mess with the men, he had no sergeant mess expenses to shell out; and as he groomed his own horse, no "batman" or soldier-servant to pay. All his extra money was clear gain, and from often wanting a bob, he now frequently had an extra one to spare.

It never rains but it pours, and very soon after I was promoted full corporal, an old sergeant, named Sappy, who had charge of the young horses, left the Service, and I was selected to succeed him. This was an unexpected rise and greatly improved my prospects, for Colonel T—— was passionately fond of his young horses and took particular interest in them. These remounts—as they were called—were always kept by themselves and under the charge of a non-commissioned officer, who was responsible for their welfare to the colonel and veterinary surgeon, and who enjoyed several privileges, such as relief from petty parades and all day guards. The number of remounts varied with the season of the year, but on an average there were about thirty of them. When I went to headquarters at Longford, to take over the appointment, I must say my elation of spirits was a good deal tempered by doubts as to my ability to fill it, for the duties were of a very difficult and responsible nature. My only qualifications were a great fondness for horses and in my having been a "young horseman" from the time I finished with Old Will. I suppose I had caught the colonel's eye, having trained two or three young animals which happened to turn out well. Anyway, he selected me for the post, which was considered one that led to quick promotion if a man could give satisfaction, as it brought him daily under the colonel's personal observation.

CHAPTER 9

I Get My Sergeant's Stripes

My next promotion came to me far sooner than I could reasonably have looked for it, for within a very short time Colonel T—— made me a lance-sergeant. In the ordinary course I would not have been due this step under two years, but it was given me in order that I might have more authority over the men in the young horse stables. Of course it made a vast difference in my life, for I passed from the benches and bare deal tables of the barrack-room to the luxury of the sergeants' mess. After six years of barrack life the change was a very marked one; the food was much superior, and there were mess waiters to attend to our requirements. I acquired a share in a room with two other sergeants; never again did I groom a horse, for I had a batman now to look after mine and furbish up my traps, and there were the club-like conveniences of the mess to make the evenings pass pleasantly.

On the other hand, a lance-sergeant's rank carried no extra pay with it, and was the hardest position of all to keep up, for there were extra clothes to provide, and as a sergeant never wore fatigue dress, his uniform had more wear and tear to stand. The subscription to the mess came to a shilling a day, and this, after paying my batman, left a very small balance for my other expenses. And so, although I had finer clothes on my back, my pockets were often empty. Still there was corn in Egypt somehow or other. My chum was caterer to the mess for a month, and of course, during that time I wanted for nothing so far as liquid refreshment and other little extras were concerned. The nest-egg he put by tided him over for a month or two, and then it came his turn at the canteen, which was as good as a ten-pound note in his pocket; and as really good comradeship existed in the sergeants' den in those days, it was always a case of share and share alike.

Where a lance-sergeant benefited most was in the matter of society, for he could always get the choice of an upper servant in one of the tip-top families, or a tradesman's daughter; being now in a position to give invitations to the frequent dances given by the mess. In return for this the young ladies would look after the sergeants out of barracks, and lacked no liberality in returning our hospitality. Civilians can hardly understand the vast social difference that exists between the sergeant and the private soldier. The former is always expected to act as a gentleman, and treated as such, whereas the latter is often looked down upon as if he belonged to a lower caste altogether, although both originally came from the same class; nor is it always the really best man of the two who wears the stripe.

Early in July we were ordered from Longford to Cahir, and soon after our arrival there the Franco-Prussian war broke out, and there was a general hope in the army that somehow or other England would be drawn into the contest. I shall never forget the vociferous shouts of joy that went up from our men when one evening at stable parade an order was read notifying that we had been placed in the first army corps, and that the regiment was to be augmented at once. All was now bustle and activity, each troop being increased, and new recruits coming in fast. Of course this added to my work a good deal, for in addition to the extra horses brought in to meet the augmentation, a great many old ones were weeded out and replaced by young ones, which had to be trained in double quick time.

When the war craze had died away I had a trip over to England, of which I must make mention. A deserter from another regiment, who had fraudulently enlisted in ours, gave himself up. It was the custom at this time to have a witness when a recruit's kit was served out to him, to attest his signature, and I was frequently called upon by the sergeant-major of my troop for this purpose, and had done so for the deserter I am writing about. I was consequently told off for the double duty of escorting him back, and giving evidence at the court-martial, and took him to Waterford, where we embarked on the steamship *Cymba* for Milford Haven.

This steamer was a cattle-boat and carried but few passengers, and on this occasion her cargo consisted of fat pigs for the London market. The night was a dark and stormy one, with a high sea running, and the captain hesitated some time before putting out; and when we did make a start, the weather we encountered was terrible. By the time we had reached mid-channel the sea was running mountains high, and the *Cymba* rolling in the trough of it like a buoy adrift. The squealing of the pigs as they were shuffled and shaken up in the hold, combined with the howling of the gale, and the breaking of the waves, created such a pandemonium as I never wish to be in again. All that night we lay at the mercy of the storm, unable to make any headway, and when the morning broke all the captain could do was to keep the *Cymba's* head before the gale. That day and the following night we continued to be tossed about in the raging seas, and on the third morning the engineer reported that the coal was exhausted.

It now became a matter of critical urgency to keep up the fires, and without a moment's hesitation the order was given to use the pigs as fuel. Two men went below, and a rope being thrown to them they made it fast to a fat porker, and up he came. A knife was then stuck into his throat, and he was pitched into the furnace, where he frizzled and flared up in a way I would never have believed possible, had I not seen it with my own eyes. And now another element was added to the storm, for in addition to the shrieking of the wind and the roaring of the sea, the whole ocean was pervaded with a beautiful aroma of roasted pork, and never do I sit down to a bit of it for dinner to this day, but that scene comes before me.

At the end of the fourth day the storm abated, but instead of being anywhere near Milford Haven, we found ourselves steaming into Greenock, on the coast of Scotland. By this time I had had enough of the *Cymba,* so getting a railway warrant, I trained my prisoner down to Aldershot, and after the court-martial, returned to Cahir.

Nothing of any particular interest happened here, and early in 1871 we returned to our former station at Ballincollig. Here a great change had taken place since our last visit, the barracks and stables having been renovated and made habitable. Although the town was a hotbed of Fenianism there was a large gunpowder mill situated close to the barracks, and the employees were notoriously Fenian sympathisers, if not actual Fenians themselves. The necessity of taking special care of our arms was now impressed on the non-commissioned officers, and orders were given to all barrack-room orderlies never to allow the men's quarters to remain unguarded.

In spite of these warnings and the precautions taken, we suffered a serious loss one night during the progress of a theatrical performance, which everyone was attending. Seven carbines were stolen from a room at the top of a three-storey block. As soon as the theft was discovered, a thorough search was made, and the colonel and officers offered a reward for their recovery, but they were never discovered.

The seven owners of the carbines, and everyone who could in any way be connected with their loss, were made prisoners and kept in the guard-room for three weeks; and a court of enquiry was held, but without eliciting anything, and in the end the men were permitted to return to duty. Almost immediately afterwards volunteers were called for to make up a draft going out to the 18th Hussars at Bangalore, in India, and the men who had been confined over the stolen carbines, so resented the suspicion of their loyalty, that they one and all volunteered and left the regiment, to the great grief of our colonel.

For some time past sundry changes had been taking place

in the educational department of the Army, which resulted in attendance at regimental schools being made compulsory. All recruits had, in addition to their drill, to spend an hour daily over their mental improvement, and it was made a serious crime to be absent from school and punished accordingly. This innovation affected the old trained soldiers as well as the recruits, for everyone in the regiment was required to obtain a third-class certificate, without which no man was promoted to lance-corporal

On the top of this came another general order, which cut the non-commissioned officers very hard, for whatever their professional ability, promotion to full sergeant was absolutely prohibited to those who did not hold a second-class certificate. To gain this, an examination in reading, writing from dictation, composition, and arithmetic, had to be passed, but even this limited amount of learning stumped many of the smartest non-commissioned officers, and it was queer to see elderly men spending every spare moment of their time in working to improve their education. Not a few swore they had enlisted for soldiering, not scholaring, and resigned themselves to fate; but what was ruin to many was good fortune to me, for I passed the examination, and a vacancy occurring just in the nick of time, was promoted to full sergeant long before my turn.

Another innovation, or rather a radical change, was also introduced in the conditions of service. A man was now enlisted for eight years with the colours and four with the reserve, and could obtain his first good-conduct stripe in two years instead of three. Nor were the officers unaffected by the march of improvement, for purchase was entirely abolished, promotion went by seniority, and competitive examinations became the order of the day for all ranks.

When the drill season came round, the 14th went to the Curragh again; but I missed this, as I was ordered to Dublin with the young horses, and remained there till October. Being now a full sergeant I found society in the Irish capital very pleasant. There were many regiments quartered there, of all arms of the Service, and during the winter hardly an evening passed without a dance at one or other of the sergeants' messes. These were well patronised by the young ladies of the middle classes, and after attending half-a-dozen of them, I enjoyed quite an extensive acquaintanceship with more pretty girls than I had ever seen before in one city. For go where you will, the round world over, you will not find a more lovely face or a more graceful figure than is the heritage of the grey-eyed girls of Ireland.

Every now and then a sergeants' ball was given to which the officers and their ladies were invited. These were grand affairs, and generally commemorated some battle in which the regiment giving it had taken a part. Ours always took place on the 22nd of November, the anniversary of the battle of Ramnuggur; the 17th Lancers gave a "Balaclava" ball; and the 16th Lancers perpetuated the memory of Aliwal. In addition to these festivities, there were pleasant picnics, when the weather grew warmer, to the Vale of Avoca, not forgetting a visit to the strawberry gardens in that direction. In fact, take it for all in all, there is no pleasanter station for a sergeant of a smart cavalry corps than "dear, dhirty Dublin."

And for me it was especially pleasant, for here and now I became acquainted with the young lady who afterwards became my wife. And so what with enjoyable hours out of barracks, and congenial employment within them with my young horses, I never had a happier experience during any part of my soldiering.

We remained at Dublin till the end of our service in Ireland, which lasted six years altogether. In June, 1874, we received orders to proceed to Aldershot in the usual detachments, but as I had a number of young horses in training, I was sent on independently with thirty old soldiers on steady, trained horses leading the remounts — the whole under command of the riding-master.

On our arrival we found the regiment, which had preceded us, quartered in the "Dust Hole," a term applied to the North Camp at Aldershot. The dry winds and sands of this place were a great change after the mist and damp of the Curragh. Close to us were the tents of the 2nd Life Guards, between whom and the 14th an old friendship existed, and very soon after our arrival their corporals' mess (there is no rank of sergeant in the Guards) sent our non-commissioned officers an invitation to a "free and easy," to be given in our honour.

The mess tent of the Life Guards was a very large one, and everything was done to decorate it and ensure us a hearty welcome. When we assembled there after evening stables, a jollier lot it would be hard to find. The chair was occupied by the regimental-corporal-major of the Guards, with our regimental-sergeant-major on his right hand, and hosts and guests intermingled down the table.

After we had settled down, a few raps from the chairman brought silence, and bidding all charge their glasses, he gave the first toast of "The Queen," which was honoured by all standing. Seats being resumed, a song was called for, and our regimental-sergeant-major opened the evening with *There's a land that bears a well-known name*, and after it, agreeable to the usual custom, gave a toast, and wound up by calling on one of the Guards to follow.

In this way songs and toasts alternated, until at last it came to the turn of our old farrier-sergeant Johnny Walker. He only knew one song, and could rarely be persuaded to sing it, but if he once started he would never stop until he had warbled out the whole thirty verses. The refrain, given in a most comical manner, with his eyes shut and his features screwed up out of recognition, ran:

"Oh, call him back again,
It will ease the Frenchman's pain,
'Ride on to death or glory,' cried Napoleon!"

The song itself gave a detailed historical account of Bonaparte's doings, omitting nothing from his rise to his fall, and Johnny Walker had precious little breath to spare when he got his hero to St. Helena. He had still his toast to propose, and this was it:

"When war is on and danger nigh,
'God and the soldier!' 's all the cry;
When war is over and all things righted,
God's forgot and the soldier slighted."

Roars of applause greeted him as he resumed his seat, his whole face wreathed with smiles and beaming with contentment. For this white-haired old sergeant was a favourite with everyone, being the last of our old Indian warriors, and the only one left in the regiment who had ridden at the charge of Ramnuggur under Colonel H—— in 1848.

The chairman now called for order, and when silence was established, rose and said:

"Gentlemen of the 2nd Life Guards.—It is now my pleasing duty to propose, with full military honours, the toast of the evening: 'The regimental-sergeant-major and non-commissioned officers of the 14th King's Hussars.' Charge your glasses and drink the health of our gallant guests." Then in a stentorian voice he gave the order: "Prepare to mount!"

Immediately every Life Guardsman rose, glass in hand, and placed his left foot on his chair. "Mount!" rang out the word of command. Simultaneously each individual sprang up and brought his right leg on the table, and in this position drank our health with musical honours.

When the ceremony was concluded, singing was resumed, and one of our youngest sergeants—a noted lady-killer in his way—gave us, *Her bright smile haunts me still,* a trifle through his nose, and for his toast proposed the following, which is not unknown in the Hussar regiments of the Army:

"Here's to the Hussar, and the Hussar's charms,
And the pretty girl he holds in his arms.
May he be rammed, damned, jammed,
And cast into the north corner of Hell,
The door locked, the key lost,
Not a blacksmith to be found
Within a mile of the ground
To let the man out who speaks ill of the Hussar!"

And he then resumed his seat, and eased his fatigued nose in a beaker of grog.

A few more songs and toasts went round before our regimental-sergeant-major rose and called on us to return the compliment paid us by the Guards; which we did with similar ceremony—for mounting the table, glasses in hand, was a custom long in vogue in the 14th. After this the loving-cup was produced. This piece of plate had been brought over from our mess for the occasion, having been presented to us years before by the 2nd Life Guards in token of amity and friendship. It was filled and passed round, until it had completed the circle of the table. And in this connection I may mention that for years a custom existed in the 14th—and no doubt still exists—of sending the loving-cup round the mess-table every New Year's Eve, when the health of the 2nd Life Guards was drunk; and no matter in what part of the world we were quartered, a telegram, wishing them a Happy New Year, was always forwarded, oftentimes flashing the message over thousands of miles of land and sea.

Aldershot in the drill season is a place where the active part of a soldier's duties is thoroughly rehearsed. There were generally about three cavalry regiments encamped there during the drill season, and as many more in the permanent barracks in the South Camp, and often additional regiments were under canvas at a place called Cove Common. Of infantry there was a very large force, and a full complement of Artillery, Engineers, and Commissariat, making a very respectable total, sometimes augmented by large bodies of militia. The field-days were on a very grand scale, and used to draw thousands of spectators to follow the operations of mimic war.

We learnt more of soldiering here than we had done at any other station, being at it all day, and every day, which left us no leisure at our disposal till the evening, when we found ample compensation in the numerous entertainments going on. There was a good theatre attached to the cavalry canteen in the South Camp, admission to which was free to all ranks, the expenses being defrayed from the profits of the canteen.

In another theatre there were splendid plays performed by the officers and their ladies, sometimes assisted by a star from London; but a charge was made here, the proceeds being handed over to some benevolent institution.

When the drill season came to an end, the 14th moved into permanent barracks at the South Camp, and remained there for the winter, relieving our old friends, the Scots Greys—usually known as the "Old Jocks"—who entertained us right royally before they departed. A fresh batch of young horses arrived just about this time, which kept my hands pretty full of work till the spring, when the 8th Hussars marched into camp; and it was a great delight to me to meet my old chum, Bill Thompson, again, who had also been promoted to sergeant.

And now there came one of those breakings of old ties and associations, which bring sorrow to soldiers in the same way as they do to civilians. In May, 1875, we lost our old commanding officer, Colonel T——, on his promotion to major-general. We knew a good friend was leaving us; and I shall never forget his farewell parade. More than thirty years had he been in the regiment, having entered it as a young cornet in the forties, and for the last ten years commanded it. He was a living link between us and the old generation which had made the regiment's name famous on many a battlefield.

After the usual inspection and march-past on foot, Colonel T—— formed us up into a hollow square, and taking up his post in the centre, addressed us for the last time. He told us that this was the last parade of us which he would hold. In looking round him, he said, his eyes only fell on two men who had been in the regiment as long as himself; but although the old veterans had dropped away, and younger men had filled their places, it pleased him to feel that they were inspired by the same spirit and discipline that had made the name of the 14th Hussars respected wherever it had served. He exhorted us to use our utmost endeavours to keep up that good name, and, above all (the ruling passion was strong) "Look after your horses, men!"

We were to remember how very often from the merest trifles sprang the most grievous disasters. And this he explained by an illustration, which I have always remembered:

"For the want of a nail a shoe was lost; for the want of a shoe a horse was lost; for the want of a horse a man was lost; for the want of a man a regiment was lost; and for the want of a regiment a battle was lost."

This was a piece of deductive reasoning which the youngest soldier present understood and remembered.

Then the colonel touched a more serious note, and the fine old man's voice faltered, and behind the great eagle nose, which stood so imperiously out, the eyes were dim and sorrowful. He thanked us —every single man there, from the officer who was to succeed him down to the last-joined recruit—for the hearty support he had received during his tenure of command. Then, raising his broad, stalwart form to its full height, and attempting, with a soldierly effort, to overcome his gathering emotion, he finished up:

"Officers, non-commissioned officers, and men of the 14th Hussars: I am forced to take my farewell of you, and God knows it almost breaks my heart to say good-bye."

Wheeling hurriedly round to hide his face, he walked away, amidst a tremendous burst of cheering. Once, and once only, he turned, and taking off his busby, waved it in the air. Alas! it was the last time we ever saw him, for he died a few months later at Cheltenham.

Chapter 10
Kálapoosh

The command of the 14th Hussars devolved upon Colonel C——, who was a more reserved gentleman than Colonel T—— and not quite such a *beau sabreur* of the old school. But he had seen service, the best part of his career having been spent in the regiment. I think, if anything, he thought more of his non-commissioned officers than Colonel T—— did, and being a man of means, was very liberal to us, treating us, amongst other things, to the Derby, and the Cup day at Ascot.

The autumn manoeuvres this year were held at Chobham Ridges. I thought Ireland was a pretty rainy place, but it was nothing to this, where it poured night and day like an Indian monsoon, which made living under canvas very unpleasant. But it was even harder on the horses, who were never dry, and up to their knees in mud and mire. Once or twice, out of sheer desperation, I believe, they broke loose and stampeded all over the place, to the amusement and excitement of the men, who enjoyed the hunt after them. A notable figure in these hunts was the young Prince Imperial of France, who was attached to one of the regiments in camp, and who had as good a seat on horseback as any young officer I ever saw. We did not do much but soak and swear at Chobham, and were very glad to return to dry quarters at Aldershot when the manoeuvres were over.

By this time my last batch of young horses, being fit for the ranks, had joined the troops, and as we were very soon to embark for India no fresh remounts were sent to us, and I had little or nothing to do. It happened that a man in our regiment gave himself up as a deserter from another in Ireland, and I was told off to take him to Dublin. I have mentioned my engagement to a young lady in that city, and I thought my trip there might be turned to the best advantage by getting married; so, plucking up courage, I applied for leave to do so, through the captain of my troop, and received it.

At Dublin I unexpectedly found myself in clover. The prisoner belonged to the 3rd Dragoons, and it appeared that in India, some years previously, the 14th had twice entertained them when on the march, without their being able to return the hospitality. Now that they had got a sergeant of the 14th in their moss, their old regimental-sergeant-major said that I must make up my mind to receive as proxy for my regiment, all the arrears of hospitality due, and on this score I was treated like a duke all the time I was in Dublin. Whilst waiting to give my evidence at the court-martial I made all arrangements for my marriage, which took place directly it was over. When my leave was up, my wife and I agreed that as there was only a very short time before the regiment embarked for India, it was no good starting house-keeping at home, and so I reluctantly consented to leave her behind in Dublin with her friends till we were about to embark, and returned to the regiment alone.

During my leave the 14th had shifted quarters to Colchester, where I rejoined them. After reporting myself at orderly-room, I went to the sergeants' mess, where I received the usual amount of chaff on my marriage. Presently the regimental-sergeant-major came in, and remarked that a sergeant had suddenly fallen sick, and he wanted a substitute for the main guard. He then happened to catch sight of me, and coming forward, offered me his congratulations, and was so civil, that I thought I would volunteer to help him out of his difficulty, although I had never yet done a sergeant's guard, my work with the young horses exempting me from it. He accepted my offer with thanks, and asked me to go and get ready at once for guard mounting. "But," he added, "mind and be extra careful, for there's a rough lot in the clinic, and one man especially who has made a couple of attempts to escape, and you know what that means." He referred to two prisoners who had escaped a short while before, for which the sergeant-in-charge had been tried by court-martial, reduced to the ranks, and sentenced to a term of imprisonment.

I joined the guard and took over the keys and prisoners, who were all, saving one, confined in what was called the dry room. The exception was the man who had made the two attempts to escape, and was in consequence locked up in a solitary cell at the back of the guard-room, out of hearing of the sentry.

On going to the place to take over charge, the sergeant I was relieving warned me to be careful of him, as he was a notorious clink-breaker. I looked at him through the spyhole in the door; he was a surly-looking customer, of the lowest type found amongst the cockney recruits, and a stranger to me.

The cell seemed strong enough, but I noticed there was only one lock on the door, and if it could by any means be forced there was nothing to hinder the inmate from getting off. I cannot explain why, but I did not feel satisfied about Wylie, and would much rather have had him in the dry room with the others, than in the detached building out of sight and hearing. So on my return to the guard-room I took counsel with my corporal, who was an old soldier, and then sent an application to the adjutant, requesting sanction to transfer the prisoner to the dry room. In a quarter of an hour an answer came back, written on the back of my application, which stated that the adjutant had ordered the prisoner to be placed in the solitary cell, and he must remain there. After showing this to the corporal I was about to crumple it up and toss it in the fire, when he checked me, saying, "I shouldn't destroy it"; so I slipped it in my pocket.

I did not fail to take an occasional look at Wylie, throughout the night, but on each occasion he was to all appearances sound asleep. In the morning, shortly before the relief was due, I ordered the corporal to take the solitary prisoner out of his cell to perform his ablutions. He went out of the guardroom, but was back under half a minute, crying out—

"Sergeant, he's gone!"

"Who's gone?" I asked.

"Why, that blackguard, Wylie."

"Wylie gone?" I repeated; "you're dreaming, corporal; you've been to the wrong cell. I saw him less than an hour ago, safe and sound."

But it was no dream; for when I went there I found the lock had been picked by a long nail, which Wylie had secreted, and that the bird was flown.

There was nothing left but to send a report to the regimental-sergeant-major, who at once came down and greeted me with the words:

"I told you to be careful, sergeant, and now you have let this happen. I have no alternative but to place you under arrest."

I handed him my arms and the keys of the guardroom without a word, and a sergeant being called I was marched off, a prisoner, to my quarters. As I passed the barracks I was greeted with jeers from the men of a troop whose rooms overlooked my way. This I felt very severely, although their behaviour was not personal against myself, but the expression of the popular sentiment, "No breaking, no making," which meant that if non-commissioned officers were never broken, there would be no promotion.

I cannot describe how acutely I felt my position, as I sat in the solitude of my room, realising nothing clearly except that a prisoner under my charge had escaped, and I must suffer for it. Only a few hours before how bright my prospects had seemed! Promotion had been very rapid, I was just married, and everything looked prosperous and happy. And now it was all changed, for, on the first blush of it I thought my fate was bound to be the same as that of the sergeant to whom the regimental-sergeant-major had so pointedly referred when he warned me to be extra careful. I felt conscious that the very caution he had given me would go against me. I need not state how often my thoughts wandered to my wife, and how I worried myself by speculating how she would receive the news that I was reduced to the ranks and in prison, for such I had made up my mind would be my fate.

The next day I was taken before Colonel C——, who called upon me to state anything I might have to put forward.

I gave him a detailed account of my actions from the time I mounted guard till I was relieved, and mentioned that I had expressed my doubts as to the security of the cell, and applied to the adjutant for leave to transfer the prisoner to the dry room.

"And what was his answer?" asked the colonel.

"I have it here, sir" I replied, producing my letter with the reply written on its back. The colonel took it from my hand and read it, and then handed it to the adjutant who was standing by, asking, "Is this correct, sir? "

The adjutant, of course, replied in the affirmative, and evinced his anxiety to clear me, repeating that Wylie had been confined in the solitary cell by his express orders, and that he had written the answer to me in the full belief that he was acting for the best.

The colonel now turned to me, evidently well pleased at what he had heard, for he spoke quite cheerfully:

"You have done a very sensible thing, Sergeant, not only in representing your doubts to the adjutant but in keeping his reply. I will order a court of enquiry into the matter, and whatever the result may be, I am pleased to think you have done your duty."

The next day the court assembled, and after examining the cells and the guard-room, acquitted me of any neglect of duty, and I was released from arrest.

Active preparations were now going on for the approaching departure of the regiment to India, and doctor's examination and vaccination were the order of the day. Our arms and accoutrements were subjected to searching tests and inspection by trained armourers on behalf of the Indian Government, to whom they were about to be transferred. Of course we left our horses behind us, to be taken over by the 18th Hussars, whom we were going to relieve. At last the day of embarkation was close at hand, and all was ready for H. R. H. the Commander-in-Chief, who inspects every regiment prior to its departure for foreign service. Our inspection passed off with credit, and we received a few words of commendation from the Duke for our past good conduct, and so ended our last parade, as a body, in England.

Just previous to this my wife had joined me, and was lodging with a friend in the town of Colchester. When the fatigue party, with the women and children, were started off, I was sent as non-commissioned officer in charge, and on the 3rd January, 1876, we marched out of barracks and through the snow to the railway station, headed by our band and attended by a large crowd of civilians. Our special train ran through London, and we reached Portsmouth in the afternoon, drawing up on the jetty close to where the troop-ship *Euphrates* was moored, and we were soon all aboard. The next day, about noon, the regiment arrived, and the men were at once embarked and told off in messes of twelve to the places they were to occupy during the voyage. We were fortunate in being accommodated on the main troop-deck, and not on the dark one below, which was occupied by a regiment of infantry and a battery of artillery. The total number on board amounted to nearly 2,000 souls, there being 1,300 men, 100 officers, 170 women and children, and the ships' company.

It may occur to a civilian that this enormous number of people could only be accommodated with the greatest difficulty and inconvenience in so confined a space, but such was not the case. The most wonderful arrangement and discipline prevailed, and there was room for everybody; and no one seemed to be in his neighbour's way. The tables were so fixed that they could be taken down at night and hammocks slung for the men. There were three meals a day, breakfast at eight, dinner at twelve, and tea at four o'clock, and considerable variety in the food. For instance, one day we had pea soup and boiled pork; the next, salt beef and plum pudding, which was the favourite dinner, and much preferred to the tinned beef and mutton, and preserved vegetables, which were served out in turn. Fresh bread was baked on board twice a week, when every man received a ration, but on other days biscuits only were served out. A pint of beer was allowed for dinner, and this was all the liquor the men got, for none was allowed to be sold. There was, however, a canteen on board, kept by the master-at-arms, where we could buy eatables if we felt hungry.

The women and children fared very well, for they were allowed bread every day; they messed with their husbands at some tables set apart for them at the end of the deck nearest their quarters, and drew the same rations as the men. But in addition to the ordinary fare many little extras were provided for them in the shape of condensed milk, sago, arrowroot, and preserves, by the authorities on board—a liberality which they never experienced in England. Every night at eight o'clock the doors of the women's quarters were closed, and sentries posted over them to prevent all ingress or egress. It was rather hard on the sergeants' wives, for although they enjoyed better quarters and treatment on shore, here on board there was no difference between them and the wives of the privates. This they felt very much, especially when they were subjected to annoyance from the wives of men whom their husbands might have had occasion to report in the way of duty. This was very easily done and there was no redress.

The discipline on board ship was of a most stringent character both amongst the men and women. Perhaps the thing most felt was the restriction on smoking, for the men were only allowed to puff a cloud from ten to eleven in the morning, and six to eight in the evening. At these times the troops were all huddled up in one place forward of the main mast, but the married men were allowed to join their wives on a portion of the upper deck, amidships, set apart for them. There were, of course, always a great many men on duty, and these had to help the watch in such avocations as they could lay a hand to. The punishment usually meted out for petty crimes was stopping a man's beer for so many days, which was shown in his defaulter's book as equivalent to an equal number of days confined to barracks. As regards general duty, there was a parade in bare feet once a day, and the men were employed as much as possible in cleaning the ship, and furnishing the various sentries, of whom a great number were posted about. Everything was done, in reason, to make the troops as comfortable as possible. In lieu of the tight clothing we wore on shore, a complete sea kit was served out to us, consisting of serge clothing, a wicker and canvas helmet, sea soap for washing our clothes in salt water, and a pound of tobacco known as "navy sixes" and very good smoking it was. Of course we had to pay for the kit ourselves.

It was a bitterly cold day when the great white troopship steamed out of the harbour at Portsmouth, the band playing a lively air, and the crowd assembled on the quay giving us a hearty God-speed. Amongst them were many poor girls, some with children in their arms, who had come down to see the last of the husbands who had married them without leave, and were now obliged, by the rules of the Service, to leave them behind. And there were sights that made the eyes sore, in some of those pale tear-washed faces that hid themselves behind the little child, so that its father might see it for the last time.

We met with pretty rough weather down the Channel and through the Bay of Biscay, the *Euphrates* rolling as these mountain-high troopships can roll; and there was a great deal of seasickness amongst all ranks, the women and children suffering worst. On the first Sunday we passed Cape St. Vincent, and the weather being now clear and bright, could distinguish the objects on shore quite plainly, and even hear the distant pealing of the church bells; and this with the blue sky overhead, and the calm sea around, was like a taste of Paradise after the Purgatory of the Bay.

Divine service on board was a solemn and impressive ceremony, and especially so on the first occasion. The chaplain, in his white surplice, stood beside a drum, draped with the Union Jack, which served him as a reading-desk. On one side of the quarter-deck the sailors were drawn up in their blue and white uniforms, and on the other, the different troops, in their full dress, but bare-headed. The ladies, women and children were seated on forms in the centre, the whole deck being densely packed. When the hymns were struck up, I do believe every single man joined in them, and the volume of sound must have floated far over the waters, perhaps to the shore itself. The troops stood throughout the ceremony, filing in and out of their places at the word of command, just the same as if on parade.

Before reaching Malta my wife fell in for a slice of luck. The lady of one of the officers on board being in a very poor state of health, required some one to attend upon her, and my captain's lady recommended my wife, so that she was berthed aft during the rest of the voyage, and no sergeant's wife had a more comfortable trip out than she did, and when we reached Bombay she received a very handsome present for her services

There were plenty of amusements on board. Dramatic entertainments took the lead, the performers being drawn from all ranks, and the stage improvised in the waist of the ship. Nigger concerts were another very popular form of amusement. On a couple of nights in the week, if the weather was calm, the band played on the quarter-deck, and after the saloon dinner a dance was got up, to which the sergeants and their wives were always invited. During the daytime card-playing was the chief pastime indulged in by the men, in which they were joined by the ship's company, who were soon initiated into "Twenty-five or I lost it!" In barracks cards are strictly prohibited, and nominally so on board ship, but the law was more honoured in the breach than in the observance. Of an evening, if nothing more exciting was going on, a sing-song would be extemporised, in which the sailors joined, and provided the musical accompaniment in the shape of fiddles and concertinas. In fact, between Jack and ourselves there was always the heartiest good-fellowship, although there was one restriction, very strictly enforced, which forbade us from visiting each other's quarters.

Not infrequently the days were varied by a fire alarm, so that the troops might be well posted in their stations in the event of a real fire breaking out. It was surprising, when the bell rang, to see with what alacrity every officer and man reached his allotted station, and within five minutes or less of the first clanging, the order "Silence!" (equivalent at sea to "'Tention!") was shouted and every one of the two thousand souls on board was standing at his appointed place. Only the throbbing of the restless screw could be heard, as the boatswain, from the bridge, standing by the officer in command, shouted out the various orders or piped his melancholy whistle. On these occasions the women and children were all bundled off to their quarters below, no distinction being made between officers' wives and the others, and it was no uncommon thing for one of the ladies, who might protest at being disturbed, to be lifted bodily off her feet by order of an officer and carried below to her cabin.

Fire-alarm practice was varied by another which, if my recollection serves me right, was called "Prepare to leave the ship," and was exercised to prepare us for a collision at sea or shipwreck. The trooper carried an immense number of boats and rafts, all ready victualled and with the necessary gear in them, and these could be launched under a minute. When the alarm was sounded the men took up their stations as before, the women and children again hurried below, and in an incredibly short space of time the officer in charge of each boat would shout out, "All ready to lower away, sir."

We passed through the Suez Canal with the usual number of groundings and haulings off, and entered the Red Sea. The heat now became intense, and awnings were rigged up forward, as well as aft, whilst about a third of the men were permitted to sleep upon deck at night, in turns, a privilege that was greatly appreciated.

When we were nearing the Straits of Babel Mandeb we met the merry old troopship *Malabar* (broken down as usual) homeward bound. The 18th Hussars, whom we were relieving, were on board, and many greetings were exchanged between the two ships, our band playing *Home, sweet home,* as a compliment to them, and they responding with a hearty cheer. But although the well-known air and the circumstances brought back to the minds of all of us thoughts of "England, home, and beauty," I do not think there were many who would have changed places. For before us was the life of adventure and excitement in a foreign land, which most of us had been looking forward to for so long, and of which we in the 14th had heard so many yarns from our old hands before they drifted out of the regiment.

On the evening of the thirtieth day after leaving Portsmouth we steamed into Bombay harbour, and took up our position for the night in line with the men-of-war anchored there. The next morning we landed in tenders, and entered a train ready waiting to carry us to our destination, which was Bangalore. Starting a short time before noon, we reached Poonah in the evening, and de-training, marched to the rest-camp, where we were soon sleeping our first sleep on the soil of Kálapoosh.

CHAPTER 11

Cantonment Life

The *reveillé* sounding at daybreak, awakened us to our first day's soldiering in India. Going out of my tent I found the sun rising above the horizon. But what a different sun to that which we catch glimpses of in England; it seemed like a great ball of fire, angry and fierce-looking. The morning was, however, pleasantly cool, and I was glad to see signs of breakfast being prepared by the native cook, within a few yards of where my tent was pitched, in the encampment known as the "married quarters."

Walking over to the main camp I learnt the orders for the day, and on my return found that my wife had improvised an excellent meal, consisting of a broiled fowl, for which she had given fifteen pence, with eggs, curry and rice, bread and coffee. She had also engaged a native girl as servant, who was to wait on us as long as we were in Poonah for a salary of four-pence a day. She was a jet black lass, with her well-oiled hair drawn smoothly off her forehead, and hanging in a big knot on her right shoulder, and her face was not unpleasant to look at. She wore a tight-fitting bodice, and a large cloth wrapped round and round her waist, forming a petticoat, beneath which her bare feet disclosed a massive silver ring on each great toe. She also had silver ornaments on her ankles, any amount of silver bracelets on her wrists, and a necklace of silver coins, which caused me to wonder how the mischief she raised all this jewellery on "fourpence a day, and feed and clothe herself."

The men were busy in camp, cleaning up their arms all day,

and being ordered to keep in their tents, the time passed wearily enough. The next afternoon a parade of the whole regiment was called, so that we might be inspected by the general commanding. Never in my experience did the 14th Hussars present such a ragged spectacle for a general's parade as on this occasion, for we were still in our board-a-ship serge suits, and our helmets battered with many a dent received between decks.

After the parade was over we had leave to roam about a bit, and several of us went to the cemetery to see a large obelisk erected to the memory of the officers, non-commissioned officers, and men of our regiment who had died or fallen in action during our last tour in India. There were many names on it which I had often heard mentioned during the early days of my soldiering, and as I stood there looking at the monument, and wondered in what forgotten spot, or ploughed-up field, or wild jungle, the bones of many of these brave fellows lay mouldering, the thought came to my mind that I hoped I should do my duty as well as they had.

About five o'clock the following evening we were formed up and marched to the railway-station, and packed rather closely into a special train. It was quite dark when we steamed off, but before long a brilliant moon rose and lit up the surrounding country. The speed we travelled at was very moderate, but it was much cooler than we had been led to anticipate, and the journey would have been comfortable enough if we had had room to stretch our legs, but with eight men crammed into a compartment only meant to squeeze in ten, there was no chance of a sleep. Several of the more adventurous spirits climbed on to the roofs of the carriages, whore they enjoyed a lovely moonlight ride, without any tear of bridges or tunnels, there not being one for the train to pass under. At every station we stopped at, water-carriers ran up and down the platform, singing out "*páni, páni,*" and right glad were we to replenish our water-bottles several times during the night.

Just before daybreak we reached a rest-camp, for it is the custom in India for troops to travel by night and halt by day. Stumbling out of our carriages in the dark, we made our way to our temporary quarters, and found an excellent breakfast ready for us. Resting there the whole day, we started again in the evening, and in this way, travelling by night and halting by day, covered the long distance between Poonah and Bangalore, which place we reached on the 14th February, 1876.

Here the general commanding the station and his staff met us, and headed by our band, and others from the European and native regiments, marched three miles into barracks. It was a very different experience from entering an English garrison town. There were, certainly, plenty of black eyes, and, may-be, pretty faces, but they were all hidden behind the brown mask of the dusky Eves of India. But if the native beauty of Bangalore was a little off-coloured, so were the 14th Hussars, for we were still in our board-a-ship slops. And, as illustrating this, I may mention that a few months afterwards, whilst shopping one day in the Thieving Bazaar, I chanced to drop upon a lady's diary exposed for sale amongst a lot of old books, and, prompted by curiosity, turned to the page for the 14th February and found the entry: "The 14th Hussars arrived at Bangalore to-day. Didn't think much of them!" Of course the book went round the regiment after that, and "Didn't think much of them" came to be a rare take-down expression with us.

On reaching barracks and breaking off, I was directed to the part of the cantonment in which my quarters were situated. They were in a long row of stone houses with verandahs, and at the door of one was a tall European girl, who asked me my name. Upon my telling her she bade me enter, for they had been looking out for me a long time. Inside I found a neatly-furnished room, with a good meal ready on the table; whilst beaming in another doorway was a fat, jolly-looking, old Indian woman-servant, who answered to the name of Kitty. Then I learnt to my surprise that two or three men of the 18th Hussars, before they left, had handed over the furniture in this house for me. On enquiring their names, I recognised the men of the 14th who had left our regiment at Ballincollig, after the row about the seven stolen carbines, and volunteered for the 18th. I had kept up a sort of correspondence with them and this was the result of it. The European girl was the daughter of Conductor Jackson, who was in charge of the provost prison in Bangalore, and who appeared very soon and gave me a hearty welcome.

I soon made myself comfortable in my little home, and although life in all its bearings was very different from soldiering in England, I did not regret the change. My house consisted of a sitting-room, two bed-rooms, and a bath-room, with a kitchen and cook's house in a detached building in the rear. There was also a bit of a garden, and as gardening was always a hobby of mine, I determined I would soon have it under crop.

The advantages of married life in India soon became apparent. Whereas in England a soldier's rations had to suffice for his family as well as himself, here food was allowed for the former, and, in addition each married woman drew sixteen shillings and a child five shillings a month, whether the husband was a non-commissioned officer or only a private. My own pay was four pounds a month, and there were very few of those vexatious deductions which whittle down the soldier's shilling in England. For what was called "messing," I paid a penny a day, and this supplied me with vegetables, rice, tea, coffee, sugar, and condiments. Two pounds of meat and two of bread were provided daily for my wife and myself free. My other expenses were sixpence a month for the library, and a shilling a month for the sergeants' mess. After the first heavy outlay in providing Indian clothing, which we had to pay for ourselves, the upkeep of our uniforms was nothing like so heavy as at home. Last of all, we kept servants to do our work for us, Kitty for my wife, and a "boy" for myself; and Government provided a native *syce* or groom to look after my horse.

The privates were as well off in their way as the non-commissioned officers. The only deductions from their pay were a penny a day for messing, sixpence a month for cooking, the same for cleaning materials and hair cutting, and eighteen-pence a month for washing, which, owing to the white kit, was a heavy item. There was one restriction, however, which was felt very sorely by many of the men, and that was the limitation in the quantity of liquor they were allowed to buy. No one could get more than three pints a day, and two drams of arrack. The former cost fourpence-halfpenny a quart, and the latter three-halfpence a dram. They were issued only at certain hours, and the canteen was never open till eleven o'clock, long before which many men had raised a thirst. The arrack was not a very palatable beverage, having a sickly taste, but the men tumbled to it in time and liked it mixed with hot coffee at night. It was a pure spirit, and not unwholesome, and if the men had only stuck to it instead of flying, to the vile country liquor, appropriately named "Billy Stink," from its disgusting smell, they would have kept healthier, and disease and crime been less prevalent. "Billy Stink" could be bought surreptitiously from the natives at ninepence a bottle, and I have no hesitation in saying that a quart of it was sufficient to drive six men, not used to it, raving mad whilst under its influence.

The liquor traffic at the canteen was conducted by rule and routine. Every man who went up for a pint or a dram had to call out his name and troop, whereupon the corporal on duty referred to a board in front of him where, on a line with each man's name, were three holes and a small peg. As the first pint was served the peg was stuck in the first hole, and at the second and third number two and three holes were pegged. After this, if a man attempted to come the "double," he was met with the answer "Pegged up!" and not a drop could he got out of the canteen-sergeant for love or money. The only way open to him of obtaining more than the sanctioned allowance, was by buying a comrade's share, but for this, even if he could discover a man willing to sell, he generally had to give double price. Professed abstainers and men in hospital were "noted" at the canteen, and no liquor could be drawn in their names. Of course, a temperance man could "come down the pole," simply by telling the canteen-sergeant he had had enough of it; and this often occurred, for many men would abstain for a month on trial and then give it up. In my humble opinion, all these elaborate precautions restricting the supply of good wholesome liquor were wrong, and caused more drunkenness than they prevented, for they drove men to "Billy Stink" to stay their craving. No red tape regulations could keep such men from boozing, and if get drunk they must, it was far better they should do so on pure spirit than on bazaar poison.

Attached to the canteen was a coffee-shop, kept by a native contractor. Here tea and coffee were obtainable at all hours, as well as stews and savoury country dishes for supper, and European groceries and tinned provisions of all sorts. As the scale of prices charged was fixed by a regimental committee, it was very reasonable.

Whilst on the subject of refreshments I must not forget to mention a native liquor called toddy, a quart of which could be bought for a halfpenny. It was obtained from the sap of the date-palm, and when fresh, tasted like a mixture of milk and honey, being free from any intoxicating qualities. But directly fermentation set in, which it did when the toddy was exposed to the sun or kept too long, it turned it into nasty stuff like sour butter-milk, and caused diarrhoea and dysentery, so that its sale was soon stopped after our arrival at Bangalore.

And now a few words about the horses. They were a mixture of nearly all the breeds found in India: Persians, Kandaharis, Turkomans, Northern Indians, and country-breds, with a few Cape horses and perhaps half-a-dozen entires, three parts Arab bred. Of mares there were not a score in the regiment, whereas in England we often had more mares than horses. Seventy-five per cent, of our troopers were greys of one shade or another, and all were much smaller and lighter than those we had been accustomed to at home. The Arab-bred came nearer perfection in symmetry, beauty, and temper, than any horses I have ever seen, and they were soon snapped up as chargers by our officers.

The strength of our regiment in India was six troops, each containing seventy-six horses. A native groom was told off to every four horses, and agreeably to the customs of the country, the men each paid them a shilling a month in addition to their government pay. On Thursdays (which are always full holidays in India) and Sundays these syces had entire charge of the horses, even to exercising them, and very good bare-back riders they were. Though occasionally given to drinking, they did their work well. When we first went out, our men, I am sorry to say, took to knocking them about a good deal, and on the slightest provocation, but this was soon put a stop to, and anyone caught at it severely punished.

Of course this native help made stables far easier work than in England. After morning exercise or parade the men changed into fatigue dress and groomed their horses down, and were then done with them. In the evening there were stables again for an hour, and this was all they had to do in looking after their animals.

After our arrival at Bangalore we were allowed a short rest, and then came constant parades in the morning for riding-school—to get our riding-seats, and foot parade in the evening—for fitting on our new clothing, about which Colonel C—— was very particular, the white overalls being sent back to the tailor's shop time after time for alteration. After this duty and drill were a great deal less severe than at home. On exercise-days the *reveillé* would sound at about five in the morning, when the native cooks brought coffee and biscuits to each troop bungalow. Then the men got up, dressed, and proceeded independently to the stables, where they found their horses all ready saddled, and nothing for them to do but to mount. After an hour's exercise came stables, followed by breakfast and saddle-cleaning. After this the men were free till evening stables, and after that till watch-setting; the first post being sounded at half-past nine, and the last at ten o'clock. Just before the latter went the orderly-sergeant called the roll in the bungalows—a term constantly applied to barracks in India—and examined the pegs to see that every man's carbine and sword hung in its place. "Lights out" was sounded at a quarter-past ten, but this was a nominal call, for they were kept burning in the soldiers' quarters all through the night.

Exercise-days were varied by an occasional commanding-officer's or adjutant's field-day, ordered perhaps once or twice a week. But in the cold weather there were many divisional field-days and parades, which often kept us out from two or three hours before day-break till nine or ten o'clock in the morning.

With the exception of the fifty men or so who were on duty for the day, the others had too much time on their hands, and this, broadly speaking, is one of the curses of a soldier's life in India. For five days a week the men had, as a rule, nothing to do between ten in the morning and five in the evening, except eat, drink, sleep, and roam about, at their own free will, over the country. There was no roll-call and no restrictions were placed on their movements or their dress, unless they were going into cantonments, when they had to wear the regimental uniform. I think, as a rule, the men got too much to eat, and ate too heavily for the climate they lived in. Their breakfast at eight o'clock consisted of a great piece of meat, cut off, probably, from an animal killed that morning, fried by the native cooks with onions, or made into a curry. Dinner was at one o'clock, and was served by the four or five table-boys attached to each troop, who always enquired beforehand, "What master have for dinner?" the rations being cooked differently and separately for each man, according to his taste. Tea consisted of a basin of that beverage and anything the men liked to add to it from the coffee-shop; and at supper they could obtain what they wished, ready cooked, from the same place. The food was very plentiful and good, excepting the meat, which, unless stewed and mixed with vegetables, was tough and unpalatable.

It was the being waited on by so many servants, both in stables and barracks, that led to the weary hours of forced idleness that spoilt many a smart man. In giving the soldier native help in his work, the idea of Government was to avoid exposing him to the sun. To keep within the barracks during the day was the constant admonition dinned into his ears by those in authority over him. This soon had its influence on the men, and set them brooding over what they thought must be a deadly climate, when so much care was taken to confine them indoors. I do not deny that there is a great deal to be said against the climate, and in favour of the economy of sparing Europeans when native labour is so cheap; but in my opinion the theory was carried too far with us, and some got nervous, and actually predisposed to the alarming ills which it was the intention to ward off. For what with being fed up to the chin, and having nothing to do to digest it or work it off, I often fancied the men would have been far healthier and hardier with less of the nigger and more of the sun. The majority of them were of the labouring class, and had for many years regularly done a hard day's work. Suddenly they found their work being done for them, and the result was that soldiers who kept in good condition on English rations grew stale and soft-fleshed on Indian ones. There is an old proverb which says "Idleness is the root of all evil," and if this may be applied to the average British soldier in India, the long, long, weary day from ten to five—seven mortal hours with nothing to do but to keep out of the sun—has been to blame for many a crime committed, many a constitution wrecked, and many a man gone wrong.

But monotonous as cantonment life was for the men, it was often worse for the women in the regiment. There is no European in India whose lot is harder than that of the soldier's wife. However good and industrious a cook or housekeeper she may be, she must not put her hands to any of the legitimate duties of her sphere; for if she does, the natives look down upon her at once, and this is fatal to the proper self-respect she should have. And so it follows that she has not even so much to do as her husband, but is forced to sit and moon in the house from daylight till evening, wishing in vain for the domestic occupations of England. Can one wonder if some of these poor women, more especially those without children to brighten their homes, left for long lonely hours by themselves whilst their husbands are away drinking at the mess or the canteen, and with no one to give them a word of warning, listen sometimes like their mother Eve to the voice of the tempter and fall? When a case of this kind occurred and was brought to the notice of the colonel by the regimental provosts, the punishment was both severe and effective. The woman's disgrace was published in regimental orders, as follows:

> The wife of — having embarked on the troopship — for passage to England on the 3rd instant, is struck off the strength of the regiment from that date for misconduct.

The punishment fell heavily on the husband too, for not only was his home broken up, but he had to return to barrack-room life, and there amongst men who knew his domestic history, soldier on as a single man till his term of service expired.

The mention of native servants reminds me of how I came to engage the "boy," or personal servant, who looked after me during nearly the whole of the time I was in India. When we arrived at Bangalore the country was suffering from a water famine, and every week matters grew worse and worse. The natives and their cattle were dying all around us by scores, and deserting the villages and flocking into the station where Government was doing its best to feed them. The water in the station was very low, and even the European troops were put on a limited allowance. The sight of the living skeletons brought under our notice every day, as they staggered along the road, I shall never forget, for their bones literally protruded through their skins, and many dropped down in the ditches by the roadside, and died.

One morning I was in charge of the troop at exercise, and as we were riding along I saw stretched out under an old tree a woman who had died from starvation. A living child was still feebly clinging to her breast, and the skeleton of another, a little older, lay dead across her lap, and beside her stood a third, the phantom of a boy of about twelve years old, trying to scare away the crows that were hopping inquisitively round. The sight turned me sick, and I could not stand by and do nothing. So I ordered the *Muccuddum,* or foreman of syces, who was riding behind me, to dismount and take the twelve-year-old boy to the lines, and see him fed

"No, no, Master," he objected; "Master have nothing to do with black niggers. Their time come die: they die—leave them die."

This was all very fine coming from a fat, sleek *Muccuddum*, who had pickings out of all the syces' wages; but I told him I could not agree with him, and if he did not obey me at once I would have him chucked out of his snug billet by hook or by crook. Very reluctantly, and much to his disgust, he dismounted and seized the boy, and in spite of his screams and struggles, lifted him on to his horse and took him back to the lines, where he was fed for a day or two. When he had improved a bit, I brought him up to my quarters, and christened him Harry. Kitty, our old woman servant, took charge of him and initiated him into the duties of my "boy." I never regretted what I had done, for Harry grew up to be a faithful, hard-working, merry lad, and repaid me a hundredfold.

Chapter 12
Soldiers' Pets and Pastimes

We soon settled down to Indian life at Bangalore, and adapted ourselves to its conditions. As there were no young horses to look after, I was still on regimental duty, and so had plenty of time to make my new quarters snug and ship-shape. There was a nice bit of garden ground in front of my house, but as no rain had fallen for some months, and the heat was increasing daily, nothing could be done with it at present. For similar reasons the tanks and rivers were all dried up, so I could not pursue my favourite pastime of fishing. A book from the library helped me to pass an hour, and there was a billiard table in the sergeants' mess, but this always seemed to lead on to peg drinking, which I never cared for, and failing any other occupation I took up the study of Hindustani.

Government encouraged both officers and men to get a little of the *bát* down their throats by rewarding those who passed the lower standard with a donation of nine pounds, and twenty pounds for the higher, whilst a successful examination in the "highest proficiency" brought the lucky linguist over a hundred pounds. Candidly speaking, the first two were not hard, and with application and the help of a *Munshi,* or native tutor, I mastered the lower in a few months, and received my nine pounds, of which my black "coach" claimed a third. The twenty pounds for the higher I gained during my second year, and here I rested contented, for the highest standard required very close study, and a natural gift for languages. Still, there were some men in my regiment who passed it, and, strange to say, one of them was an habitual drunkard, whose defaulter's sheet was filled with the red tokens of crime. Not only did he master the language, but in time superseded the native *Munshis* as regimental teacher, and was much preferred by beginners. In this way he earned hundreds of rupees, which all went, as fast as they came, in drink. He had only three objects in life: to keep as far from a horse as possible, being a terribly nervous rider; to argue with a *Munshi* over the *bát;* and to get fuddled as frequently as he could. If he had expended the energy he had devoted to those objects on a worthier cause he would have been a successful man in life, but it was not in him, and he lived and died a "wrong 'un."

After the regiment had been a few months at Bangalore the non-commissioned officers began to think it was time to make the acquaintance of the society of the cantonment. So a sergeants' dance was arranged, and invitations sent out to the members of the European messes, with an intimation that we should be glad to see any of their civilian friends, especially those of the fairer sex. The night was eagerly looked forward to, and when at last it came there was no dearth of guests, especially ladies, and our M.C. was at his wits' end to find partners for them all. First of all came our own contingent, and a few of the ladies' maids in the service of the officers' wives. This division sported the rose of old England on their cheeks, and retained their English grace and healthfulness of figure and face, contrasting very favourably with the other European women present who had been in the country a long time, as their pale cheeks and listless manner showed. Then there were a few elderly dames, whose husbands enjoyed snug billets on the staff at Bangalore. Last of all was the Eurasian brigade, all more or less dusky, their complexions being finely shaded off from delicate primrose yellow to rich chocolate brown. The primrose dames did their best, with plenty of powder and good judgment, in choosing the colours of their dress to come as near English brunettes as possible. They were often comely and pleasant-looking, but their darker sisters, who sported bright and loud colours, and whose country origin no art could conceal, found few admirers. One and all, however, danced with spirit, and enjoyed themselves thoroughly, except one lady, who being annoyed at something, resisted all the blandishments of the partners our M.C. brought forward when it was too late, repulsing them with the somewhat comically-sounding reply: "Hum do teen dufait bolta hum don't dance!" [I have two or three times told you I don't dance.] These entertainments brought us into touch with the cantonment and civil population of the station, and led to many acquaintanceships, renewed at the band stand, which was the general *rendezvous* every evening.

Nearly all the senior sergeants kept a horse or pony of their own, called in the language of the country *tattoos,* or more briefly *tats.* As soon as we had established our private studs, mounted paper-chases were started, and jackal hunts; or failing a Jack in the flesh, we chased him in the spirit in the disguise of a lean, fleet pariah dog, who often led us a merry burst. Our hounds, or "bobbery pack," were made up of drafts from the various barracks, and ran straight and fast when they didn't stop to quarrel amongst themselves.

In all our sports and pastimes we received every encouragement and assistance from Colonel C———, whose kindness and liberality to his non-commissioned officers in England I have mentioned. Here in India he extended his generosity to the men, and though he has been dead many years, I'll be bound there is not a man in the 14th Hussars, who served under him, but remembers him to this day.

Many of the men took up some pursuit as a hobby, such as keeping pets, training birds to talk, catching cobras, collecting butterflies and the like. I think the birds at Bangalore were the first things to attract their attention, for they were so different to the English ones. There were three varieties that frequented the barracks: sparrows, crows and kites. First in everyone's affections came the sparrow, for he was in evidence everywhere. He was very much like his English brother, only cleaner, glossier and tamer. He would fly in at the open verandah, when the men were at meals, and without the least fear hop about on the tables and help himself to a bit of anything he fancied, often perching on the edge of a basin and tasting the milk or cold tea. The men encouraged them, and never attempted to drive them away, for all looked on the sparrow as one of the few links between us and old England, and whatever else was trapped or shot, the little brown bird never had a finger raised against him, for we loved him in India as we did Robin Redbreast at home.

Artful old Jack Crow was quite a different customer. His character was as black as his looks. Still the men never killed him in barracks, though the crows took care to give a wide berth to anyone carrying a gun outside them, for they knew the use of it as well as the armourer-sergeant. Jack Crow was a professional thief, a felon in feathers. It was the custom for the native "boys" to carry the soldiers' dinners across from the cook-house to the barracks in open baskets, and these the crows considered it their duty to requisition. If ever the boys' attention was diverted for a few seconds, down hopped a crow in a twinkling and whipped off a piece of hot steak or a chunk of pudding, and flew away with it to the roof of a neighbouring bungalow. And then it was a sight to see the native cook gesticulating and cursing the old crow, who between each mouthful would caw back at him in an insulting way. Our men delighted in devising traps to catch these crows, and cunning as the birds were, they could be enticed into a room and captured. And now they had to submit to a badge, or, as I think they regarded it, the decoration of captivity. A thin piece of wire was inserted between the two holes in their upper beak, and a button, or disc of metal, or little bell attached—each troop having its distinctive token—and the birds were then let loose, none the worse for the operation. In time nearly every crow in barracks wore one of those symbols of capture, and as they attached themselves to particular buildings, we could always tell which troop they belonged to by the badge they wore. Mighty proud Jack Crow grew of his Legion of Honour, especially of the bell, and it was a comical sight to see a row of these birds perched on the roofs, shaking their heads up and down, tinkling their bells, and seeming by their actions to say, "Me got medal, too, same like soldier sahib."

Kites, the third variety of barrack birds, spent most of their time soaring and circling high in the sky. But should any servants pass along with a piece of meat exposed in a basket on their heads, or even in a plate in their hands, often a kite would swoop down with incredible swiftness from a tremendous height, and sweeping it off with his claws, fly up again and devour it on the wing. It was great fun to see this trick played on a raw recruit who might be crossing from the coffee-shop with a savoury stew he was licking his lips over in anticipation, until there came a whistle of wings and a rustle of feathers, and off went the solid part of his feast, leaving him only the unsubstantial gravy. At meal-times these kites would descend and circle screeching round the bungalows; and the men, when they had finished their meals, would often toss the bones and fragments in the air, which the birds never failed to catch with their claws before the morsel reached the ground. These kites served a useful purpose as general scavengers, and the men were strictly prohibited from shooting them.

The tame or domestic birds, kept in cages, were chiefly parrots and minahs, the latter being a sort of starling. Many of these were brought round for sale, and could be purchased for a copper. Some of the men went in for teaching them to talk, and a common method of doing so was to lower a cage some distance down a well, and then lean over the edge and shout down the expressions the parrot or minah was required to learn. Many an orator was turned out in this way and sold for twenty or thirty rupees. Sometimes a man with a touch of caustic humour not un-combined with business acumen, would teach his bird the uncomplimentary nickname of his troop-sergeant-major, and, when it was proficient, hang its cage up in a commanding position, where to the delight of the men, but chagrin of the victim, it would give public utterance to the obnoxious designation. I remember one instance in which a sergeant was so derided, that to stop the annoyance he bought the parrot for a large sum of money and then wrung the poor bird's neck.

Of course, there were many four-footed pets kept in barracks by the men, no restrictions being placed on their doing so. Dogs were the most popular. They were generally chained up under the shade of the trees between the troop bungalows, and their principal delight was a bandicoot hunt. The bandicoot is a monster rat, a regular elephant among rodents, and has lots of fighting in him. Great numbers infested every building and stable, and provided rare sport for the terriers. There was always a good market for really game dogs amongst the wealthy natives and Europeans; so that dog breeding and training was a source of profit as well as pleasure. Next to dogs came monkeys, but their dirty and mischievous habits prevented them from becoming favourites, and they were not nearly as popular as the mungoose, a bright-eyed, merry-mannered little creature, something like a large grey ferret, which everyone seemed fond of. The mungoose was clean, easily tamed, and affectionate, and soon evinced a great attachment for his master, These animals were generally kept in the bungalows, fastened by a chain to the men's cots, who frequently carried them out for an evening stroll, and took them to the canteen, snuggled away in the insides of their coats, from which they peeped out, all wide awake, with their little ferrety eyes purling round. The mungoose is supposed to be invulnerable to the bite of the most venomous snake, but this is not the case, for I have witnessed many of their plucky combats with cobras, and though they generally killed the snakes, it would sometimes happen that the mungoose missed his spring, and got bitten by the reptile. He would continue his attack and generally killed the cobra, but he always died himself in a few minutes. The mungoose's method of attack is singular; having come upon a cobra in the open, he begins racing round and round him at a great speed, taking care however to keep out of striking distance. The cobra rears itself up, expands its hood, and with its eyes tries to follow the rapid circular movement of its enemy, turning its head quickly first to one side, then to another as its assailant disappears and reappears in the course of its circuit. This constant motion at length forces the snake to lower its head for a rest, when the mungoose seizes the opportunity, and springing forward fixes its teeth behind the cobra's head and, in spite of its contortions and writhing, holds on like grim death till it is dead. If the mungoose misses its spring the snake has its chance, but whether bitten or not, the mungoose always returns to the attack. These deadly combats are, I am persuaded, the result of a natural antipathy, for the mungoose never eats the snake. It was the great bravery these plucky little animals exhibited in attacking so deadly a foe that endeared them to every soldier's heart.

Most of the married people kept pigeons, ducks, rabbits, and fowls. Amongst the latter were some grand specimens of the Indian game or fighting cock, and many a sporting match used to be brought off in the dry ravines around Bangalore, their sandy sides and bottoms forming fine natural pits. The natives were very fond of cock-fighting, and the taste soon spread to the men of our regiment, and I must plead guilty to a weakness myself for what I have heard called a demoralising sport. Many of my neighbours kept a fancy bird or two, and each man had an opinion of his own, and bragged about what his cock could do, and at last, an opportunity offering, I determined to keep one as well.

Our riding-master, old Omer Pasha, had a rare bird which I had often admired. It stood nearly three feet high, and its leg was like a young ostrich's. It was very decently behaved as long as it was let alone, but if ever a cock crew within sound, he would stalk off and kill it as a matter of duty. Omer Pasha was mighty proud of him, and nearly every day had some fresh victory to recount, of which I generally got the benefit. "Bedad, sargint," he would say to me, "the cock's fit to foight a loion!" But one day he had another tale to tell, for old Crusoe—obviously its name—had fallen foul of one of Omer Pasha's favourite goats, and pierced it to the brain with one stroke of its powerful spur. I arrived just as the deed was done, and found Omer Pasha in a tearing-rage over the death of his goat.

"Away wid the bird, sargint," he cried to me, "before me timper gits the bether av me. The murtherin' baste has killed the swatest goat in Bangalore, and I never wish to see him any more at all!"

I was not long in securing Crusoe, and carried him over to my quarters under my arm, while he "cwarked" like a young elephant trumpeting. After a few days' confinement he got used to my place and I let him run loose. Then I began to experience trouble; for the other cocks in the neighbourhood began to try and come the old inhabitant over Crusoe, and he killed off enough to stock a poulterer's shop. The end came when he got the blood fever on him, and breaking into Conductor Jackson's yard, depopulated it. Jackson was a friend of mine, and so I curried Crusoe.

I have never seen such a place for butterflies as Bangalore. Many a time a flight of them, so thick that it almost resembled a snowstorm, would pass the barracks. In the woods round about, some large and handsome specimens were to be found, and many men made a hobby of catching and preserving them, selling the collections to officers or their ladies for large sums of money. They varied their outdoor hunts by collecting cocoons of the moon moth, as we called a large variety which had a transparent circle on each wing, and often measured seven or eight inches across. When these moths were issuing from the cocoon, they required the greatest watchfulness and patience on the part of the men, for if they were not killed directly they unfolded their white wings, a few flaps against the muslin cages rendered them useless as specimens. It was an amusing sight to see a great brawny man sitting up all night waiting for a moth to come into existence so as to kill it at the right moment, and displaying a patience and alertness that would have done credit to a sentinel in war-time.

The large dry ravines and hollows in Agram plain, in the vicinity of Bangalore, were the home of vast numbers of cobras, whose bite was certain death. Notwithstanding the risk, there were men who hunted them, and appeared to find a fascination in the sport. Armed with a six-foot length of bamboo, split to the first joint and a wedge inserted to keep it open, and carrying a small vessel of bread and milk, they would proceed to search the banks for a trail leading to a cobra's hole. The rice and milk was then deposited in front of it, and the man took up his station quietly on the top of the bank. Presently the cobra, attracted by the bait, would poke its head out, and down would come the cleft bamboo and pin its neck to the ground.

Then holding it firmly, the cobra-catcher would kill the reptile, either by striking it on the head with a stick or stone, or often by a kick with his boot. The prey was then brought to the barracks, and flayed in the same way as an eel, the skin being preserved and always selling for a rupee. The body after being parboiled was buried, when the ants soon picked the bones clean. These were threaded on wire in the correct order, and the skeleton formed a curiosity which always commanded a good price.

In connection with the cobra catching a very remarkable incident happened, which showed that the snake had its revenge in one instance. A man who spent most of his time in this pursuit was taken to hospital one day, complaining of a great pain in his right foot. It was examined, and the toe was found to be slightly scratched and very badly inflamed, whilst the symptoms were those of snake-bite. But the man strenuously denied that he had been bitten, although acknowledging he was a cobra hunter. Blood-poisoning set in, and he died. As is always the case, his kit was sold by auction in his troop, and a young fellow bought his boots.

In a few days he had to go to hospital suffering in a similar manner. The doctors questioned him closely, but he dreaded snakes too much to even approach them, and had no knowledge of even having seen one lately. His right toe, he explained, began to hurt him the very day he had first worn the boots purchased at the auction of his dead comrade's effects. He died in great agony, and the symptoms confirmed the doctors' suspicions that it was a case of snake-poisoning. The boots that both men had worn were now sent for, and it was discovered that the fang of a cobra, charged with poison, had pierced the toe of one of them before it had broken, and that the point protruded inside, and to this was due the death of the two men. This incident occurred under my own observation, or I should have hesitation in relating a story which almost sounds incredible.

Of course many men went in for *shikar*, but in the earlier months of our stay at Bangalore there was no sport to be obtained, the drought having exterminated or driven away all game for miles around. But after the much needed rain fell there was plenty of shooting to be obtained. Fishing was fairly good at a place called Godgoodi, which was full of canals teeming with coarse fish. I may here mention that no restrictions were placed on the men who engaged in these expeditions, for they might wander about where they liked and shoot at what they pleased, the owners of the fields being perfectly indifferent to trespassers so long as they and their cattle were not hit.

In addition to these hobbies and individual pastimes I have mentioned, there were of course many general and public ones, such as cricket, races, and the like. These were shared in by all the Europeans of the garrison, and many a good afternoon's sport used to come off on the *maidan* or playing-ground. In tent-pegging and lemon-slicing several of the native cavalry joined, and these competitions were not only very interesting to the spectators, and exciting to our men, but taught the latter a great deal and increased their dexterity with their weapons and their mastery over their horses. And I must confess that in these particular trials of skill the native mounted troopers, on their lithe, active country-breds, more than held their own, and I picked up many wrinkles from watching their practice; on the other hand, they could not compete with the Europeans in feats of strength or endurance.

After the monsoon burst and rain was plentiful, there was gardening for those who took an interest in it. Every soldier could obtain a plot of ground, and seeds and necessary tools, whilst prizes were offered for the best cultivated gardens to encourage the men to go in for the occupation. Moreover there was a good deal of money to be made by it, for vegetables and garden produce always found a good market.

 I think I have now shown that not only did those in authority do a great deal to assist the European soldier in India to find pleasant and profitable employment for his leisure hours, but that there were many ways open to men, according to their individual inclinations, of occupying or amusing themselves. There was really no excuse for a man to soak in order to kill time. Of course we had the usual percentage whom nothing could wean from the old curse, which seemed to be bred in their blood and in their bone. But there were others, better men and better soldiers, who appreciated what was being done for them, and acknowledged with gratitude their obligations to officers like Colonel C———, who made the men's welfare their study, and treated the private soldier as a rational being, by removing many of the old galling red-tape restrictions which often defeated their own ends. Colonel C———'s object was to draw the men from the canteen by holding out to them wholesome means of amusement and rational methods of occupation, and this done he left it to their common sense to choose between the two. From personal observation I can vouch that the result was a diminution of crime, a decrease of drunkenness, and fewer occupants of the hospital. And as one who has experienced both phases of soldiering, I unhesitatingly assert that a soldier's life in England cannot be compared to the one he leads in India, either for pleasure, for comfort, or for profit.

Chapter 13

Pallida Mors

We had not been long at Bangalore before the continuation of the hot weather and the want of water began to tell upon the health of the regiment, and there were many sufferers from intermittent fever and dysentery. The first-mentioned disease soon claimed a victim, a private in my troop, who died early one morning, and as burial follows death within a few hours in India, his funeral was fixed for the same evening.

My troop was ordered to parade in full dress without arms, excepting twelve of the men who carried carbines, and were called the firing party. A black horse, to represent the dead man's trooper, was robed in a costly black velvet pall, embroidered with a white skull and crossbones (this was peculiar to our regiment), with a plume of black ostrich feathers on its bridle. Across the saddle, supported by the collar chains, dangled the dead soldier's spurred boots, toes reversed. The horse was led by two men, cloaked in black, one on each side holding it by a new pocket-handkerchief passed through the rings of its bit. Those handkerchiefs, when the ceremony was over, were always kept by the men as a memento.

Preceded by the band, mute at present and with the drums draped in crape, we marched to the mortuary, where we found a gun-carriage drawn up, with six horses attached to it. The troop now broke off, and each man uncovered and filed into the mortuary, to take a last look at his dead comrade as he lay in his coffin. The lid was then screwed down, the troop formed a lane, faces inwards, the firing party presented arms, and the six pall-bearers, all chums of the deceased, carried the remains out, and placed them on the gun-carriage, covering the coffin with the Union Jack, and depositing the deceased's arms and helmet on the top.

Whilst this was going on, the firing party rested on their reversed carbines in an attitude of woe, and when everything was ready the cortege started forward at a slow march. Contrary to the usual marching order, the shortest and youngest privates led, the older and taller men followed, the non-commissioned officers came next, and the captain brought up the rear. Another curious thing was that the men stepped off by their right—instead of by their left—foot, as is customary. When we passed the guardroom the sentry turned the guard out, and for once and once only in his career, the poor dead private received a "present arms."[1]

After we had marched out of hearing of the hospital, the band played the *Dead March* in *Saul*, after which we struck into a quick step, but fell slow again as we neared the cemetery, which was quite two miles distant. Here the remains were met by the chaplain, in his surplice, who preceded them to the grave, reading the burial service as we followed slowly after with uncovered heads. The firing party now formed up in two lines, one on each side of the grave, and when the service was concluded, at a whispered word of command fired three volleys into the air, the band playing the solemn notes of a funeral dirge. After the last echoes had died away, amidst a few chords which sounded like the stirring notes of the *reveillé,* the men formed up and marched back to barracks at a quick pace and to a lively air.

The mention of the mortuary reminds me of a weird story connected with it, that gave me the greatest start I ever had in my life. This "dead-house," as our men called it, was situated about a hundred yards from the hospital, being the last building on that side of the cantonments. It was a very lonely spot, hidden from view by a belt of dark trees, and further isolated by a wide *nullah*, or dry ravine, in which many cobras lurked. Whenever a body

---

1. The "present arms" is *really* to "an armed party commanded by an officer."

lay in the mortuary it was the custom to post a sentry there, with orders to knock against the door now and again with the butt end of his carbine in order to scare away the rats, bandicoots, and other vermin which infested the place. The post, both from its solitude and the nature of the duty, was shunned by everyone, and particularly by young soldiers, whose imaginations were worked upon by ghastly stories told them by older hands of what they had seen and heard when on sentry there.

One evening, when mounting guard, I found a sentry had to be furnished for the mortuary, and I accordingly told off one for the post. After watch-setting I went the rounds, and then returned to the main guard and sat down for an "easy." About midnight I was suddenly startled by the cry of "Sergeant of the guard," and going out was told something was wrong up at the hospital, and the call had been passed for me. I made my way there as quickly as possible and found that the sentry stationed over the dead-house had deserted his post, and neither the threats of the corporal, nor the advice of his comrades, could induce him to return to it.

I asked the man, who was deadly pale and trembling with nervous excitement, what was up; but all I could get from him was that there was "something" in the dead-house, and it "called to him like a voice from the tombs." Ignoring his fears I pointed out to him the serious consequences of deserting his post, and the additional shame he would have to endure of being laughed at by the regiment. But he would not budge an inch. "I can stand their laughing," he observed, "but I can't stand *that*," jerking his thumb towards the direction of the dead-house. Then as I spoke sternly to him not to trifle over a serious matter, but return at once to his duty, or take the consequences, he took off his belt and throwing it on the floor, exclaimed, "There! put me in the clink, Sergeant. I'll do two years sooner than go to that post again."

There was nothing to do but to post another sentry, and I called for a volunteer. This put the men on their mettle, and a soldier of some years' standing responded, and accompanied by the corporal we set out for the dead-house. We walked along without speaking, for there was something uncanny and awe-inspiring in the task on which we were bent, and in the dark night and black shadows of the trees that surrounded the dreaded house where the dead man lay, and an involuntary shudder ran through me as I saw by the light of the waning moon, which was just rising, a large cobra glide across the path leading to the mortuary door. Around us reigned a silence still as death, broken once only by the weird howling of a pack of jackals on the plain beyond.

On reaching the dead-house we all halted, and I bent my head down to the keyhole to try and catch any sound within. But I heard nothing. I then made a circuit of the building, without finding anything to account for the sentry's scare. As I returned, the new man was popping a ball cartridge into his carbine. "Man, ghost, or devil," said he, in a grim voice, "they'll have the benefit of this if they come any of their hanky-panky tricks on me"; and with that he came to attention at his post.

I was just turning to go back, when my eye caught sight of a grated window, probably intended for ventilation, in the side of the dead-house, and about eight feet from the ground, and the thought occurred to me to have a look into the place as the moon was shining full on to it. So calling to the corporal, I asked him to give me a lift up, the grating being a little beyond my reach, and with his assistance I got hold of the bars, and pulled myself up.

As my eyes reached the level of the aperture a sight met them which paralysed me. For there, within a few inches of me, and with the moon shining full upon it, was the white, scared face of the dead man, and his eyes staring into mine with a lack-lustre look Then a low voice proceeded from his lips, and I heard him ask, "Chum, what's the time?"

I gave a yell and dropped to the ground, and the next moment was panicking away, followed by the corporal and sentry, after the latter, either by accident or in his excitement, had fired off his carbine. But they never caught me, and I was well ahead of them at the hospital guard-room, into which I dashed, to the consternation of the men, and throwing myself down upon a bench, panted to regain my breath.

In a few seconds the corporal and sentry had arrived, and everyone was crowding round us asking what was up. My first words were, "My God, no wonder that poor fellow deserted his post." Then turning to the corporal, I said, "Send for the key of the dead-house at once."

It was soon brought, and everyone left the guardroom to accompany the hospital sergeant to the mortuary. The door was opened, and then it was all explained, for there lay the poor inmate in his shroud, doubled up on the stone just under the ventilator at which he had appeared to me.

It seems the doctor had given him up that morning and told the orderlies he had only a few hours to live. After midday the poor fellow had gone off in a faint, and this had been mistaken for death, and as it was too late then to hold the usual *post-mortem*, the body was removed to the dead-house. There at midnight, he had come to his senses, with the result I have recorded.

The doctor was sent for and everything done to try and revive the poor fellow; but he was dead indeed now, and the next day filled the grave that had been dug for him whilst he was yet alive.

Within six months of our arrival at Bangalore, our good colonel, who had done so much for us, was suddenly taken ill and died within a few hours; and although a different cause was assigned, it was the general belief that he had been carried off by cholera. I could fill pages with the description of the sorrow and gloom—I might almost call it the dismay—caused in the regiment by Colonel C——'s death. Although he had only been in command for a comparatively short time he had endeared himself to all ranks. On the day of his death an order was issued that no trumpet was to sound, no band to play, and, except for guard-mounting, no duty to be done by the regiment for a week. The effect of this was such as a civilian can hardly credit. A sense of oppression overwhelmed everyone, and never have I passed such a long, dark week as that silent one at Bangalore, when never a trumpet sounded and the very life of the regiment seemed suspended.

Colonel C——'s funeral was conducted in exactly the same way as that of the trooper which I have described. Death levels all ranks in the army as he does in the outer world. It was of course more fully attended, for every man in the 14th Hussars was present, as well as a great number from other regiments, and all the officers from the garrison, and personal friends from the civil station. But for the rest, colonel and private both received the same military honours.

The command of the 14th Hussars now devolved upon Colonel A——, and under him a great change was wrought in the regiment. He was altogether a different type of officer to our two last colonels. His one aim was to bring us to the highest state of efficiency and discipline—ready to go anywhere, and do anything, at three minutes' notice. He was an enthusiast at soldiering, and his highest ambition was to be sent on active service. As a disciplinarian he was particularly severe, and especially so with his non-commissioned officers, rarely overlooking a fault, and never listening to an excuse, but, still, always scrupulously just—a little too just, we sometimes thought. I need not add that he made us all sit up to attention, and gave us plenty to do. His first reform was to order the dismissal of all the native servants employed in the barracks, except those sanctioned and paid for by Government. This was resented by the generality of the men, who had grown accustomed to the luxury of private domestics; and when it was followed by another order, encroaching on the sacred Thursday full holiday, by instituting a general horse-parade on the morning of that day, the murmuring was deep, if it was not loud.

Little by little Colonel A—— overhauled every detail of drill, paying especial attention to the musketry instruction, in which, up to this time, most cavalry regiments were rather backward. As we now possessed a good weapon in the Martini-Henry carbine, he was determined we should know how to use it. Alterations in the cavalry drill were also introduced, and most of the spare time the non-commissioned officers had was spent in making themselves thoroughly acquainted with the new system. Drills and parades became the order of the day, and the barrack-cots had less of their master's company than had previously been the case.

Of course, the horses came in for their share of being stirred up, and never during my soldiering did I experience such stiff field-clays as under Colonel A——. "On the move" was the constant trumpet-sound; and move, move, move it was. The horses, taken as a lot, were not young ones, many having been several years in the service, and soon the hard work on the iron-hard ground began to find out the weak spots in their legs, and many had to be cast. They were replaced by an entirely new breed of horses, which was beginning to be imported from New South Wales, and known as Walers.

For some time past it had become apparent that the supply of Indian-bred horses was not equal to the demand of the Cavalry Remount Department, and, hence, recourse was had to new countries for supply. With the advent of these Walers the young horse stables were re-started, and I returned to my old post in charge of them, and prepared to receive our first draft of fifty remounts.

Never shall I forget the day they arrived, each led by a native groom. The first thing that met my eye was a huge brand on the shoulders of every horse, in some cases eight and nine inches long, forming a most unsightly scar. The horses were from four to five years old each, rather heavier in build and bone than English ones, and lacking blood and breeding. The majority of them were mares, and they were of all colours except grey, which was rarely found.

The order was given to turn them into the stables, and I told off a man for each horse. With their native grooms these Walers were fairly quiet, for they had submitted to them on their first landing, after a long. passage in a sailing-ship, when their spirits were broken by fatigue, hunger, and confinement in the dark, close-packed hold, and they had not strength to rebel. But now, directly a European approached them they lashed out, and jibbed back, and were as frightened as antelopes, showing such signs of aversion to the white faces and military dress, that in many cases our men could not handle them to take off their halters, and were actually obliged to ask the natives, who had come with them, to do so.

It took months to get over this timidity, and in some horses it proved quite incurable, for no matter how kindly and gently treated, they never ceased to dread the approach of the rider. All were more or less addicted to buck-jumping, and it was a very long and tedious job to get the worst ones to take the saddle quietly, for the moment they felt the girths tighten they would bound like a ball some feet into the air, trying to make their heads and tails meet between their legs. But trained they had to be, though it caused many practised riders to experience a nasty fall, generally preluded by a somersault in the air.

Towards August signs of the monsoon, or rainy season, which had long been looked forward to, began to show themselves. Instead of the brilliant blue skies and staring sunshine, heavy clouds drifted overhead, and there was a succession of violent dust-storms. The dry, crisp heat gave way to a sultry, damp atmosphere, that was far more trying; and we sweltered at the least exertion. Punkahs were not provided at Bangalore, although they are found in nearly every plains station in India; and we felt the want of them. At last, one day, after a tremendous storm of wind, thunder, and lightning, we heard a pit-pat, pitter-patter of raindrops, and in five minutes down it came in torrents. Every European—man, woman, and child—immediately rushed out into the open air by instinct, and enjoyed the cool, impromptu bath. For seven months we had not seen a single drop of rain, we had lived in a bakehouse heat, we had walked over burning soil and breathed in impalpable dust, and now it was delicious to feel the spattering of the great raindrops, and the very pores of our skin seemed to open and drink in the refreshing moisture.

The rain continued steadily morning and evening for some weeks, and the weather soon grew cooler. But now fever became prevalent, and a great number of our men were down with it. Our parade-ground being turned into a quagmire naturally put a stop to drills, and we began to enjoy easy times again. As for the country, the change it underwent was magic. The grass sprang up so quickly we could almost see it growing, the trees clothed themselves in smart new gowns whilst we were looking at their toilette, and it really appeared as if we had been transported in the twinkling of an eye from the Desert of Sahara to an emerald isle. No Government could have proscribed the wearing of the green and the national colours of the Muhammadan, and the Irishmen had it all their own way.

Some weeks passed, and then the monsoon began to wear off, and we had a taste of that most dreaded of all scourges, cholera. What a sound that first whispered warning is, when, with bated breath, the news passes on from mouth to mouth! The first man that was struck down was a private in D troop; and I can well remember the effect when the word went round that it was cholera. A sudden and un-definable change took place in everyone immediately. Men who had long been teetotallers, and had not touched a drop of liquor for months, rushed to the canteen, clamouring for arrack, all their ideas of abstention being thrown to the winds, and their one aim being to pour as much spirit down their throats as the rupees they had saved while "up the pole" could buy for them. The canteen-sergeant reaped a rare harvest, for at times there was almost a fight amongst the men who should be served first. No one said much, but, plain as printed words, could be read the haunting question on each man's face: "Who is going to get it next?" Whilst their husbands were indulging in Dutch courage at the canteen or sergeants' mess, the poor women suffered in suspense, dreading the swift, sudden, unseen strokes with which this fell disease strikes its victims down.

The first fatal case was a married man, named Ikey Payne. He was one of our regimental bruisers, and had been the hero of a famous fight at Aldershot in 1864, his opponent being also in the 14th. And now, by a strange fatality, this very opponent was the second victim, and within a few hours of each other he and Ikey had been floored by the same fighter. Then the cholera stopped, and we thought it had left us, but about a fortnight later it came again.

Early one morning I was called to one of the troop bungalows at *reveillé* and there saw an awful sight. During the night, out of thirty-two men in one division of the building, fifteen were seized. The rest of the troop were only separated by a partition wall, reaching but half way to the ceiling, so as to permit of the air circulating, and yet not a single man on that side of the wall had been touched. Some unseen barrier rose between the two to stay the progress of the plague.

Of the fifteen men attacked, the majority were corpses before sunset; but outside the fatal building there were only two cases. It was almost as if a shell had fallen on a particular group of cots, and expended its malignant powers upon their occupants. And, stranger still, the natives told us that exactly the same thing had happened once before to another regiment stationed in these very barracks.

I need not dwell on the gloom that settled down on us after we returned from the funeral of these poor cholera victims, and for many a long day afterwards there was the ever-present dread of a return of the dire disease. My own anxiety at the time was very greatly increased by the state of my wife's health, for she was expecting her confinement; and it was a happy day for me when she got safely through her trouble, and presented me with a little daughter.

In February of the following year it was decided to send out a Commission to Australia to impress upon the breeders of Waler horses the necessity of adopting a better plan of rearing the young stock I was selected as one of the two non-commissioned officers who accompanied the Commission, and after a pleasant voyage we reached Brighton, in Victoria, where we were received by a deputation of breeders. The points urged on them were the advisability of importing good sires from England; the necessity of stabling and handling the young stock, instead of letting them run wild like mustangs; and, above all, the discontinuance of the barbarous practice of branding them with such enormous irons, which not only disfigured the horses, but seemed to give them a shock they never got over. The advice was readily adopted, and its fruits became apparent in two or three years. In 1874-5 the wretched skeletons of beasts that were bundled ashore at Madras, more dead than alive, were often sold at ten pounds a head. In 1879 the Government price was sixty pounds a horse, and there was a large and lucrative private demand, which must have put many thousands of pounds into the pockets of the breeders in the colony.

I was only a month in Australia, and rejoined my regiment in June. Soon after this a vacancy occurred for a rough-riding sergeant-major, and I was given the post. It was a good piece of promotion, and added a shilling a day to my pay, besides various windfalls incidental to the situation. For instance, there was always a tip when an officer's charger was dismissed riding-school; and, again, there were many young officers qualifying for the staff who were obliged to gain an equitation certificate, and these, when they got through my school, invariably remembered the schoolmaster. Besides this, a rough-riding sergeant-major was always sure of as much private work as he had time for, such as breaking-in and training horses for civilians or wealthy natives.

And so my new position, although it entailed many new duties and new responsibilities, was a good one. Day after day I began work at dawn, and rarely finished riding my last charger till ten o'clock. I was at it again by three, and continued busy as long as there was any daylight. But it paid me, and it agreed with me, for I got into hard condition, and found myself all the healthier and happier for the extra work.

CHAPTER 14

Court-Martialled

In the autumn of 1878 the usual Southern India Rifle meeting was held at Bangalore. It was a sort of Madras Presidency Wimbledon, and attended by all the best shots, civil and military. To increase the interest the authorities determined to wind up the meeting this year with a day devoted to inter-regimental sports, and offered several valuable prizes for competition.

The ranges were on some high ground just outside Bangalore, and on the sports day I think every single inhabitant of the station who was not on duty, or incapacitated by illness, was present. A good programme had been arranged, and there was a great deal of keenness evinced over the competitions. A large number of refreshment booths were erected on the ground for the convenience of the spectators, but the regulations were very strict against supplying liquor to soldiers, although, unfortunately, this did not prevent them from being treated by civilians.

We had a large four-horse brake belonging to the sergeants in the regiment, and this, with another borrowed for the occasion, conveyed the wives and children of the non-commissioned officers to the ground. My wife was unable to go, being very near her second confinement, and I wished to remain at home with her, but she persuaded me not to miss the opportunity of seeing such a good afternoon's sport, and much against my inclination, and, as it turned out, sadly to my detriment, I yielded to her solicitations and went.

The first few competitions passed off well enough, and the

shouting over the winners increased the spirits of the military spectators, for there were representatives of at least fifteen European regiments competing. As the excitement increased there was more and more liquor consumed, and this began to tell upon the soldiers, who were eagerly following the doings of their respective champions, and warmly cheering them when they won. I myself did not feel quite happy in my mind, for I could not help thinking of my wife all by herself at home, and wishing I had not come; and as I sat on my pony, and observed what was going on around me, the thought occurred to my mind that with a little more drink there would be a general row, for the regimental party feeling was beginning to rise very high over the results of the various competitions. Soon isolated drunken squabbles and fights began to take place between men of different regiments, and things looked nasty.

It now came to my turn to ride in one of the races, and although I won it, I was disqualified over some technicality which I would have avoided if the rules of the meeting had been printed, and this made me very angry. At last the final item on the programme was reached—the tug of war, by which time the general excitement had increased to fever-pitch, and as each beaten team retired, it was evident their backers were not satisfied. Suddenly a hot dispute broke out over a particular trial between an infantry and an artillery team, the men on the beaten side crying out against the decision of the judge, and before anyone could tell how it happened, off came the belts, and the whole body of soldiers on the ground was engaged in an Oriental reproduction of Donny-brook Fair. It was not a fight of regiment against regiment, but an indiscriminate lashing out all round, with no object that I could see except the pure and simple devilment of the thing.

This disastrous climax had been brought about in a great measure by the want of forethought on the part of those in authority in omitting to circulate printed rules and conditions under which the various competitions were to be conducted. Differences of opinion and points of argument constantly arose, owing to misunderstandings, followed by wrangling and quarrelling, until the whole culminated in a regular riot.

As soon as the turn of affairs became apparent, the ground was rapidly deserted by all the civilian spectators, whist those who had erected refreshment booths made ludicrous haste to pack up their goods and get off, fearing that the soldiers might begin looting. The scene was indescribable, fighting going on in every direction, and the officers calling on the non-commissioned officers to assist them in quelling the disturbance. But discipline and obedience had vanished, and seeing at last that they were powerless to restore it, the officers made their way to barracks to procure what further aid they could.

I was sitting on my pony all this time, and forgetting the eleventh commandment in the army, "Man, mind thyself," rode to where I saw a mob of our men mixed up with the European and native Infantry, and began using my best endeavours to part them. But it was of no avail, for threats and persuasion were alike thrown away, and the fight grew fiercer and fiercer as the men warmed to the work, and I found myself gradually drawn into the vortex and surrounded by a mob of infuriated and half-maddened soldiery.

And now the officers who had ridden off to the barracks, having collected what men they could, sent them up as pickets to quell the disturbance; and I perceived one of these pickets coming up to the place where I was, being able, from my position on horseback, to look over the heads of those around me. I immediately shouted out to the men to knock off and make tracks, warning them they would be very severely punished if taken prisoners in the act of rioting. Hearing this, and at the same time seeing the picket forcing its way through the crowd, most of them acted on my advice, and I was left almost alone, when, to my astonishment, the corporal shouted out: "Collar hold of that sergeant on the pony and run him in, for I heard him telling the men to slope as we came up!"

In spite of my protestations I was dragged from my saddle, and my captors were marching, me off to the guard-room, when I appealed to an officer, who had come upon the scene, to interfere. Although he could not and would not release me after being made prisoner by the picket of another regiment, he allowed me to go under escort of a sergeant of Infantry to my own quarters, and there I had to spend the night and next day as a prisoner.

On the second day, after Colonel A—— had "weighed off" a good few of the men implicated in the row, my turn came to go before him. On my crime being read, I found I was charged with being drunk and creating a disturbance. I was naturally much incensed at having been made a prisoner, and more so at finding such a serious crime preferred against me. The colonel was greatly angered at the conduct of the men, and as little disposed to be considerate as I was to be humble. When then he asked me, in a hard official voice, if I had anything to say to the charge, I indignantly denied being guilty, and instead of speaking in the tone and manner I should have adopted, answered hotly and unguardedly, declaring I had used my best endeavours to quell the disturbance, and considered it very hard that the result, instead of being to my credit, should have placed me in the position I found myself.

Had it been another occasion I think Colonel A—— might perhaps have conducted the inquiry himself, but, as I have before said, he felt acutely, what he considered, the disgrace brought on his regiment, which he fondly imagined he had drilled and trained into a superiority above all others. He made no allowance for the excited feelings of the men; their misconduct had touched his pride, and when a commanding officer is suffering in that way it is bad for those brought in front of him. After hearing the evidence of the Infantry picket, he struck off the latter part of the charge—"creating a disturbance"—as it was not proved; but the drunkenness being stuck to by the corporal and his file, and my continuing to vehemently deny it, he said: "Very well, then; a regimental court-martial," and I was sent back to my quarters to await trial.

During the next two days I had ample time to reflect over my situation. For ten years I had honestly tried my best to act upon the advice Colonel T—— had impressed upon me in a few short soldierly words when I went before him as a recruit, and had successfully avoided drink and its evils. And now, after all, I was "high and dry," and on a level with any drunkard in the regiment, and not even through the paltry excuse of "having had a glass or two and being a bit fuddled," but solely for endeavouring to do my duty and induce others to do theirs. I certainly was excited on the day of the sports, but drunk I never was. I say it now calmly and deliberately when sixteen years have passed, and none of the bitterness of that disgrace remains. The excitement I laboured under was natural. I had just before ridden and won a race, and been disqualified over some technicality. Then I had joined in a tug of war, and a similar thing had occurred again. Following this came the riot. My anger was up, and I could not see men of the 14th Hussars being knocked about by half a hundred swaddies, and I may have used some such disparaging expression in the hearing of the Infantry picket as it came up. I think I did so, and that the corporal seized upon it as an excuse for including me in the mob, the charge of "drunk" being tacked on afterwards to justify his action. It is so easy to say a man is drunk, and so difficult to disprove it afterwards. Of course, in the hurly-burly I have described, there was not much time for discrimination, and when Infantry pickets are at work they will go for a cavalry man in preference to one belonging to their own arm of the service; nor are they sorry if they see a chance of running in a non-commissioned officer. But having once done so and committed themselves, whatever charge they first record they will stick to through thick and thin, as indeed they must do to save their own skins.

The court-martial came on, and I was tried and adjudged guilty, the witnesses repeating their first story, and the swearing being all on their side. However much the officers comprising a court-martial wish well to a prisoner, their duty is simply to find him guilty or not guilty; and if the former, to pass on him the sentence laid down by the Queen's regulations, which in the case of a non-commissioned officer convicted of drunkenness was in those days reduction to the ranks. And this was my sentence.

The colonel is placed in a different position to the officers of a regimental court martial, for it falls to him to approve and confirm the finding before it is carried into effect, or he can quash it, or approve it and yet remit a part or the whole of the sentence. The latter it is the custom to read out at a full parade, and keen was my pain and bitter my humiliation, as I stood facing my regiment, waiting my doom. It was the only time in twenty-five years of soldiering that I occupied that position, and it cut me to the quick. The adjutant began to read out the proceedings, and as I stood there with downcast eyes and listened, I thought how in a few minutes the stripes which had been on my arms so long would be stripped off. They were hanging on by a few threads, ready for the regimental-sergeant-major to remove them, for my wife had that morning, with many a sigh and many a sob, cut all but two or three stitches, so that the painful proceeding might be of as short duration as possible.

The adjutant read on till he came to the finding—"guilty"—and then the sentence, "reduction to the ranks." And then he paused for a moment, and a cold sweat burst out over my face as I felt that the dread time had arrived. But no; there was something more to read, and I thought to myself the pain of suspense was cruel long. But I was mistaken, for the words I heard were—

> I approve; but in consideration of the prisoner's former good conduct and of this being his first crime of 'drunk,' and of the care and attention he has bestowed on the young horses under his charge, I remit the sentence.
> W. A——
> Colonel

I cannot describe my sensations as I heard this. A great revulsion of feeling shook me, and when the adjutant turned and ordered me to join my troop, I did so, half dazed, and with the belief strong within me that I had been forgiven because I was not guilty, and that I might have been spared the disgrace of the conviction, since I was spared the punishment.

I returned to my quarters and was met at the door by my wife, to whom someone had conveyed the good news; and the first thing she did was to bring a needle and thread and sew on my stripes again. Her tears, which she had restrained before, came freely now, and they sealed those stripes upon that coat of mine. For as I thought of how she had silently suffered and worked at her sad task that morning, without a murmur at the punishment that would fall far harder on her than on myself, I made a resolve that there those stripes should stop so long as I kept a-soldiering.

Although I was pardoned and returned the next day to my duties in the riding-school, the court-martial long continued to rankle in my mind. And not without reason, for those forty-eight hours under arrest broke the continuity of my service as a sergeant, and when I came to leave the army some years later, was the cause of my losing fourpence a day, for life, of my pension. And so for a crime for which a private soldier could only have been admonished, and a civilian would most probably have been let off altogether, and of which I was not guilty, I am, to this day, mulct to the tune of £7. 12s. 4d. a year!

Misfortunes never come singly, and now one overtook me before which all that had happened before faded into insignificance. Ten days after my court-martial my wife presented me with another little daughter. Much against my wish she had been prevailed upon to go into the women's hospital for her confinement. As soon as they allowed me I went in and saw her, and both she and my child were doing well. After sitting with her a short time and cheering her up, I returned to my usual duties in the riding-school; but had not been there half-an-hour, when a native orderly from the hospital came to say I was wanted quickly. A misgiving smote my mind, and without dismounting from the charger I was schooling, I galloped off in a bead-line, taking all the walls and ditches on the way, in its stride.

But I was too late. The matron met me at the door, and a glance told me all. My wife was dead; her heart's action had suddenly failed. It is a subject I cannot trust myself to dwell on, and I shall do no more than record it.

The shock told upon me heavily, and following on the court-martial I had previously gone through, completely upset me. I felt I could not remain in the place, and the infant following its mother very soon afterwards, I sent my little daughter home to England, where I knew she would be happy and well cared for with her aunt, and set to work to obtain a transfer to some other branch of the Service, so as to get away from scenes and surroundings which had become so sad to me.

I received a great deal of sympathy from the officers, as well as from my comrades, and when they heard of my intention to leave the regiment, all joined in advising me not to do so. But nothing would satisfy me but a change, and I wanted it to be to an active life, which would leave me no time to brood over my troubles. An opportunity for promotion came which I should have jumped at had my wife been alive, for I was offered the post of sergeant-major to the Governor's Body Guard at Madras. This was not only a good rise, but held out the certainty of a lot of extra money, for it meant plenty of spare time for training the horses of wealthy natives at Madras. But I refused the offer, against the urgent and I have no doubt good advice of my superior officers, because I thought the life would be too quiet.

Soon afterwards another chance occurred, and this I at once accepted, as it promised all I wanted. The Afghan war had just broken out, and volunteers from the ranks of our senior non-commissioned officers were called for to go into the commissariat department. Having a good Hindustani certificate I had no difficulty in being accepted, and was appointed a probationer. My duties took me up to the Punjab, where I was posted to the line of communication. The change of life certainly served my purpose so far that I had plenty to do, and little time to dwell on my own troubles. But the work was not what I had anticipated. I had to look after a lot of camels, mules, and bullocks, which, though admirable animals in their way, are not the sort of beasts that a Hussar takes kindly to. Excitement there was none, whilst the majority of Europeans I was brought in contact with, and most of whom were my seniors, belonged to the Infantry. This did not suit me, and the opportunity occurring at the end of my period of probation of returning to the old corps, it was not in human nature to refuse. So back I went to the comrades I had so long soldiered with, and resumed my former appointment of rough-riding sergeant-major, which had not been permanently filled up.

I found on my return that although there had never been any chance of the 14th going to the front, Colonel A—— had not relaxed his drills and parades in the slightest, and that the regiment had been wound up to the highest pitch of efficiency and preparedness to start off at a moment's notice, if the happy order came for us to go to the front. But come it did not, and as the men read in the papers the chances of distinction enjoyed by other regiments engaged in Afghanistan, a feeling of gloomy disappointment came over them at being out of it.

For some time past I have not made mention of my old chum, Bill Thompson. His regiment had come out to India and was stationed at Meerut, and up to the time of my trouble I had kept up a regular, though not very frequent, correspondence with him. But when I went into the commissariat I dropped letter-writing altogether, for I was constantly moving about from place to place. Soon after my return to Bangalore I wrote to Bill, but receiving no answer, after a time, I wrote to another acquaintance in the 8th Hussars, asking him what had become of my old school chum, and to my great grief I heard he had been sent up invalided to some hill station in the Punjab, and the latest report received was that his death was merely a matter of a few hours, so that if my letter had not been answered, it was probably because he was dead.

Just about this time the 14th lost an officer who had been with them many years. This was Major K——, the same who was in command of my troop on the march from London to Edinburgh in 1867, when the gold watch was stolen from his friend at Grantham. He was very popular with the regiment, and the men were anxious to show their regard for him, but were hindered from doing so by the Queen's regulation forbidding a presentation to any officer whilst in the Service. However, our troop were not to be baulked, and a hunting saddle with silver stirrups and spurs was bought and sent up to his bungalow anonymously, just a few days before he left the station. This pleased "old Paddy" (as we called the major) very much, and not to be outdone in any way he gave a farewell ball, nominally to his troop, but in reality to the whole regiment. In the course of the evening he came up to three or four old hands, who were standing in one of the side rooms, and spoke a few kindly words to them. Whereupon they asked him to have a glass of wine with them for "auld lang syne's" sake, as it might be the last opportunity they would over have of drinking his health. Of course he assented and they filled their glasses and wished him good luck with a heartiness which showed how they meant it. Perhaps this encouraged Major K——, for turning round and looking significantly at two of the men, he said:

"There is one thing I *should* like to know, before I leave you for good, and I think one or two of you could satisfy my curiosity."

"What's that, sir?" asked one of the men, whom I will call Tayler. "If I can tell you, I will."

"Then I'll ask you. But before I do so, I want you to understand that there are only five of us here, and it will go no further. What I want to be told is: how was that watch stolen at Grantham in 1867, and who carried it out of the town?"

A queer laugh came from Tayler, a laugh more artificial than hilarious. "What makes you think I know anything about it, sir?" he asked sheepishly.

"Ah, well," answered the major, accepting this as a hint not to press the question, "if you won't tell me you won't; and I'm not going to urge you against your will."

"Dash it, sir," answered Tayler impulsively, "you shall know. Only give me your word you'll never bring it back on me."

"There's my hand," said the major, putting his out, "and now tell on."

"Well, Major," said Tayler, "you carried that watch in your own valise, and there it was all the time you were searching the troop so cunning When we found it was too valuable to be disposed of, one of us slipped down to the stable of the inn where your horse was put up, and shoved the watch inside your valise, knowing if it was found there you would not give yourself in charge. When we reached the next halt we watched our opportunity and recovered the ticker." To explain the safety of this hiding-place it should be mentioned that on the line of march officers' valises are often merely stuffed with straw, to save weight on the horses, their kit being carried in a trap that travels with the troop.

"What became of it?" asked the major, without any comment.

"We pawned it when we reached Edinburgh, and I gave the ticket to your batman, sir. But he always funked leaving it in your way, although we wanted you to have it so that you might redeem the watch."

"Well," said Major K——, "you had some good in you—but it was d——d little."

CHAPTER 15

Promoted to Troop-Sergeant-Major

When the first Afghan war was over and Sir Louis Cavagnari settled in Kabul, things in India quieted down, and Colonel A—— eased us a bit in the matter of drill, and we were not always exercising as though in the middle of an enemy's country. Then suddenly one day, like a thunderbolt from the blue, came a Service telegram which made our hearts leap, for it ran—

"Clear the line. Fourteenth Hussars proceed to the Front immediately."

"Clear the line" was, of course, only a telegraph office instruction, and meant: give the Government message priority on the wires. But we did not read it that way. "Clear the line," to us, was "Clear the railway line for the 14th Hussars" The enthusiasm of the men as they heard it was unbounded, and the only question that sobered some down a bit was who would be left behind, each dreading he might be one of the unfortunate individuals. Colonel A——, whose heart's desire seemed likely to be gratified at last, set to work to get ready instanter, carrying out all the details under his own supervision. In a wonderfully short space of time we were all supplied with new clothing suitable for the colder climate of Afghanistan, where we were going to revenge the cruel murder of Cavagnari. Our swords, scabbards, bits, and every piece of steel work, were sent to the armourer's shop to be blackened. All the men's kits were overhauled and replenished, and every invalid who could scrape through the medical examination was recalled to head-quarters from the sanatorium he had been sent to. In less than a week Colonel A——— was able to report to the general commanding, that the 14th Hussars were ready to proceed to the front.

Of course the men suffered a good deal of inconvenience and loss. Homes were broken up, and this especially in the case of married men. The men's boxes and all their surplus belongings were given into store, and pets of every description parted with. To accomplish all this within a week meant a sacrifice in most cases, for everyone was on the sell and no one on the buy.

Meanwhile the railway authorities were working day and night trying to get together the trucks required for the transport of our regiment, and we impatiently awaited the order to start, passing the time in singing jingo songs at the canteen, and talking of nothing but the war, whilst "Clear the line" became the regimental catch-word.

Unfortunately it was found the railway could not get together sufficient rolling-stock for our transport, and, to our grief and chagrin, we were ordered to stand fast. The delay was fatal to our hopes. With each week the pressure brought to bear on the railways throughout India grew greater and greater, and in the end Government discovered they could rail up another cavalry regiment from somewhere else with more expedition, and our order was countermanded!

I shall never forget the men's faces the morning this was made known to them. They were long and glum. Not a stave of song was heard after that, and the rash fellow who accidentally said, "Clear the line!" found it prudent to clear out of the way. All the things we had sent into store had to be drawn out again, and there was no alacrity this time. To complete our distress there was the new clothing to pay for, and the steel work to be re-polished, and the expense of both came out of our pockets, which we looked upon as worse than money thrown away.

I am afraid the disappointment had a bad effect upon the regiment, and I am certain it touched up our colonel. He had set his heart upon showing off the true mettle of his men, over whose training he had spent so much time and energy; and now the chance was gone. He was too good an officer to air his discontent, but he could not conceal it, and imperceptibly the former strict discipline was relaxed, and things allowed to fall into the slackish way that sometimes makes itself apparent in peace time.

This was soon reflected in the conduct of the non-commissioned officers with very sad results. It happened in this way. The sergeants' mess was allowed to remain open an hour and a half after watch-setting, but the colonel used to be very particular about its being closed and lights out at eleven o'clock. This rule was, however, gradually relaxed now, and the mess kept open, first half an hour after closing-time, then an hour, and so on, later and later, until finally it was not uncommon for some of the sergeants to sit up playing cards and drinking till they mounted their horses in the morning and rode off to parade.

A short time before this, our old regimental-sergeant-major was recommended for a commission, and whilst waiting for the papers was struck off duty, and a troop-sergeant-major, whom I will call Cairns, was appointed to act in his place. Cairns carried on the duties to the satisfaction of his superiors and the contentment of those below him, being most popular with all ranks, and would surely have been elected to the appointment permanently, had the choice lain with the regiment. But there are wheels within wheels in the Army, the same as everywhere else, and to our surprise, when the old regimental-sergeant-major received his commission, his place was not given to Cairns, but to another troop-sergeant-major, whom I will call Scotting, and who was far from popular.

One would have thought that a brand new regimental-sergeant-major would have stuck to the strict letter of duty, and, amongst other things, put a summary end to the system which had gradually crept in of keeping the mess open till all hours in the morning. But Scotting, to ingratiate himself, I think, with the sergeants, not only shut his eyes to this infraction of orders, but often stayed at the mess for an hour or two extra himself.

Presently the shoe began to pinch the wives of the sergeants, who felt both the loss of their husbands' society and the drain on their pay, for a deal of money was squandered during those long nights. At last two or three of them went to Colonel A—— and informed him of what was going on. He was astounded, and ordered the adjutant to enquire of the provosts if the report was true.

The provost-sergeant, for some reason best known to himself, had kept a private record of those non-commissioned officers who had been in the mess after hours. This he produced, and on this evidence Regimental-Sergeant-Major Scotting, three troop-sergeant-majors, including Cairns, and nearly a dozen sergeants were ordered under arrest.

It was a sad spectacle, and one very rarely seen, I fancy, in any regiment, when those senior non-commissioned officers were marched by sections as prisoners to the orderly-room. Colonel A——, calm, low-voiced, and white—they were dangerous symptoms with him—considered their crimes, and then sent the seniors up for trial by court-martial, and placed the juniors at the bottom of the roll for promotion.

The Court found the prisoners guilty of neglect of duty, and never shall I forget the parade of the regiment on the cold, wet morning when the findings and sentences on these unhappy men were read out. Scotting was reduced to the ranks, but we did not feel the same for him as for Cairns, who had been over twenty-one years in the Service, and would have gone home on a comfortable pension during the previous trooping season, had he not been led to expect promotion and waited on for it. This was the first crime ever recorded against him, and taking this into account, Colonel A—— reinstated him as a sergeant. But the mischief was done, for the pension of his rank was gone for ever. He was a good, fine, soldierly man, the picture of a smart Hussar. I think I see him now, in his familiar attitude, his elbow leaning on the mess-room bar, telling his droll stories, one after another, and keeping every one in spirits by his unfailing good comradeship. Never again was he to stand at the old place and hold forth in his jolly, kind-hearted way. For he had received a knock-down blow and was a broken man, and never lifted his head up after that fatal court-martial. He left us soon, and faded out of sight.

Cairns and Scotting were made the scapegoats, and the hand of punishment fell heavily on them alone. It was all pat according to the Articles of War, and it would not become me to criticise it; but this I will say, that the incident had a very grave and serious effect upon all the non-commissioned officers; for it showed that however smart and able a sergeant might be, however good his character, and however clean his defaulter's sheet, his welfare hung on a slender thread, and one slip—even the first— could in a moment deprive him of what had taken years and years of zeal and steady attention to duty to obtain. It created, moreover, a feeling of mutual distrust in the place of that good-fellowship which should exist amongst non-commissioned officers, and a seat at the sergeants' mess was no longer coveted as a prize, but regarded as something the advantages of which were questionable.

I can speak impartially for I was one of the few men who benefited by the event. Where there's breaking there's making, and another troop-sergeant-major being promoted to regimental, I fell in for his berth. And thus on the stepping-stone of a fallen comrade, and one whom I loved right well, I reached the summit of the ambition I had marked out for myself when I was a 'cruity. They say that everything comes to him who knows how to wait, and now after fourteen years, that which I wanted came to me. It was a fine position to find myself in, for a troop-sergeant-major who knew his duty and did it, was as well off as any man in the regiment. The post was one in which a knowledge of men and horses could be brought into play, and with it much power for good or evil. He who filled it was the right hand man of his captain, and each troop was almost as distinct in its way as one regiment from another. Every transaction appertaining to it—the food of the men and horses, the clothing accounts, the pay, and all the details connected with them, went through the troop-sergeant-major's hands, and if he used his power and influence with tact, and was trusted by his captain, and popular with the majority of his men, his position was one to be envied. Mine was a right good captain, and although I must admit my troop was a bit scorching in the bungalow, being extraordinary fond of their *pongelo,* they were second to none at stables or on parade.

This promotion not only carried with it a deal of extra gold lace and a good increase of pay, but several valuable perquisites, and comfortable separate quarters to live in. The horses of the troop I was appointed to had the reputation of being the best in the regiment, which was a source of great satisfaction to me; and I think I may say that as long as they remained under my charge I kept them up to the mark.

Soon after my promotion Colonel A—— went home on furlough, and in due time we received news that he was about to be married, and our officers determined to do honour to his wedding-day by giving a public entertainment, to begin with sports, and wind up with fireworks—the manufacture of which they undertook, assisted by some of the men. The day came, and the sports passed off very successfully; but through them all the men, as well as a large crowd of spectators from Bangalore, were eagerly and impatiently looking forward to the grand display of fireworks, which had been widely advertised, and which our amateur pyrotechnists had prepared with a view to surprising the simple minds of the natives.

The surprise was complete. The squibs and smaller fry went off all right, but when the more ambitious experiments were set alight, it was a case of "look out for Phil Garlic!" For the rockets, instead of soaring into the air and falling in graceful showers of stars and spangles, took a contrary course, and charged the crowd; the Catherine wheels declined to revolve on their pivots, preferring to whirl round and round in a sort of fire-fiend waltz amongst the truly astonished spectators; and that acme of ingenuity, the "devil amongst the tailors," which should have cracked merrily in mid-heaven, exploded prematurely amongst naked native legs, and close to the skirts of the ladies present, with the most disastrous consequences.

The second Afghan war of 1879-80 was over by this time, and the troops that had left Bangalore began to return from the front, and we did our best to give them all a hearty home-coming, making no distinction between any of them. Our men entertained the companies, and our sergeants' mess the non-commissioned officers, extending the welcome equally to those of the native corps of sappers and miners. What with these entertainments, and the reciprocal festivities that followed, the time passed with great jollity.

About a year or so before this there bad come out in one of our drafts from England a young soldier, who was now a lance-sergeant in my troop, Bingham (as I will call him) was a born athlete, and at any distance from a hundred yards to a mile, but especially as a sprinter, the fastest runner in Southern India, and had won every race of the many he had entered for.

Amongst the sapper sergeants was another fast runner, whom his comrades fancied a great deal, and who would doubtless have tried his speed with Bingham if it had not been for his absence at the front. One day Bingham and this runner happened to meet at our mess—which was often visited by the sapper sergeants after their return from the Afghan campaign, for they had plenty of *batta* and pay to draw, and spent it amongst us very freely. The meeting led to a lot of banter, and the ability of their crack to lower Bingham's colours was asserted; and in the end the sappers made an offer to back their man against ours for a thousand rupees, if Bingham would concede five yards start in a hundred.

Goodness knows we did not want the sappers to get rid of their money faster than they were already doing; but they were obstinate, and nothing would choke them off. Their challenge was therefore accepted, and it was agreed that the race should be run in a month on one of the station roads, half the stakes to be posted down, and the other half a week before the race. No sooner were these preliminaries settled than the betting began, and the sappers, noticing our men's eagerness and confidence, stood out for odds of two to one against their champion. But, nothing loth, the 14th plunged in, and at this price lots of money was laid in bets by both officers and men, until many thousands of rupees were dependent on the issue. But none went it so hot as the native sappers, to whom the chance of turning one rupee into two dangled an irresistible inducement.

But after a few days a reaction set in, and when the first glow of excitement had cooled down, and enquiries brought home to their calmer judgment the true capabilities of our man, the sappers grew less sanguine, and when the day grew near for completing the stakes, it would not have surprised us to find our money uncovered.

These anticipations were strengthened by an attempt made to get at Bingham, which he mentioned to me. I knew him well enough to feel sure that the race was safe, but I was a little taken aback the next day to find our second five hundred rupees covered by the sappers; and more so when one of them shouted: "I'll take seven to four about our man!" There was something suspicious in this; but when I questioned Bingham, all I could get out of him was:

"I'm going to win."

On the day of the match every available spot was taken up by spectators, the whole *élite* of Bangalore turning out, headed by the general commanding the station, and, of course, all the military, and a vast crowd of natives. Five o'clock was the hour fixed, and punctual to the minute the two competitors stripped. When the order was given to make ready, a hush fell upon the multitude, so that the dropping of a leaf might almost have been heard. As the starter stood holding the pistol in the air the spectators peered and craned forward with an eagerness that told not merely of interest in the sport, but of that far deeper anxiety which men display when they have "a bit on."

A hundred yards race can be quicker run than described. The report of the pistol was followed by a shout, "They're off!" but before it was taken up, the men were several yards on their way. Half-way down the course Bingham collared his man; they were breast and breast for the next forty yards, and then our champion surged forward and won by a couple of feet

At the end of the course was a road, which dissected it, and led right and left, and upon this three closed carriages had been drawn up, the two nearest with their horses' heads pointing one way, and the third pointing the other. Into the first of these, by a pre-arranged plan, Bingham and his trainer bolted, and the door was rapidly closed; then, without the crowd observing them, the two rapidly got out at the other door, passed through the middle carriage into the further one, which at once drove off, whilst the nearest one, wherein everyone believed Bingham was seated, made a great pretence of whipping up and starting in the opposite direction.

For a few seconds after the race there was an ominous pause, until Bingham's colours were run up. Then there burst a tremendous cheer from the throats of our men and the general public. It was instantly responded to by a storm of yells and execrations from the black sappers, and the men who had backed the beaten competitor. All in a moment the sappers, headed by their non-commissioned officers, made a rush for the carriage Bingham was seen to enter, and in less time than I can describe it, smashed it into matchwood. Baffled in this attempt to revenge themselves on the man who had sold them, these swarthy sappers now turned their rage against his European comrades. They were strong, brawny men, used to earth-work and road-making, in hard condition, well fed, and well paid, and very different to the ordinary Jack Sepoy. And they had lost their money; and nothing tickles up your true Hindoo like that. A stone came hurtling through the air, and that opened the ball. Then another, and another, and, by George! they could "whang it in," and no mistake. They had plenty of ammunition, for there happened to be several heaps of granite at their feet, piled there for the repairs of the road. The attack they made was indiscriminate. Ladies screamed, horses reared, and started off, and in three minutes there was a bloodthirsty battle raging between the maddened black sappers, backed up by the native Infantry, and our men, with whom the European Infantry and Artillery sided. But the sappers had all the advantage, being in a compact body, with stones to their hands, and their own lines just behind them. They did not give us a chance, but sent in volley after volley, and fairly pelted our men off the course.

Directly the race was over I had jumped into my trap and hurried off to the barracks, being anxious about Bingham. Glad I was to find him safe and sound, and dressing in his quarters. Very shortly afterwards our men began to return, several of them bleeding from cuts and gashes, others with broken heads or bruised limbs, and all in an angry and excited state. After a little while I left Bingham and went over to my troop-room, and there the first thing that caught my eye was the men's scabbards with no swords in them. That meant mischief. Running out, I seized a mounted horse, and galloped off in the direction of the sapper lines, and as good luck would have it, overtook my troop before they reached them. With many entreaties; and not a few threats, I succeeding in inducing them to return, and I think I averted something that might have turned out very seriously. But much had already been done, for a great number of men, both Europeans and natives, were injured, and three or four of the latter killed outright.

The sensation that this riot caused in Bangalore was immense. The news spread far and wide, and got into the Indian papers and soon everyone in the country was talking about it. A court of enquiry was ordered, and then the whole thing came out. Bingham, on the very day that the second half of the money was lodged, had agreed with the sapper and his trainer to sell the race for a thousand rupees, and the word being passed round to back their man, and never fear, the sappers had planked their last dib on what they thought was a moral, counting the anticipated winnings as so much cash in hand. It is a bad thing when men reckon on un-won money, as they discovered when they found themselves done; and they could not dissemble their feelings, but wanted to kick everybody downstairs. Bingham told the court openly and boldly what he had done, and why he had done it—"to teach the sappers a lesson for trying to corrupt him." But that was a bit of high falutin', and though he tried to argue that he had acted on the square, and won the race as the public expected, he was severely censured, and prohibited from giving or accepting any regimental challenges again, and, as a matter of fact, that was the last public race he ran in India.

The cantonment row had naturally a great effect upon the troops stationed at Bangalore, and led to a feeling of coldness between the different regiments, in place of the friendly feeling that had previously existed; and the Christmas which shortly followed, instead of being a festive and merry one, was the dullest ever spent by the 14th Hussars whilst I was in them.

Chapter 16
South Africa

Just before the foot-race which I have described in my last chapter, rumours of disturbances in South Africa reached us, but we did not take much note of them; for not only was it unlikely that troops would be sent from India to those parts, but our colonel was absent in England, and it was felt that if we could not get a turn of active service when he was with us, we should hardly tumble in for it when he was away.

I was getting on very well with my troop, and when the general's inspection came due in the early part of the year, was selected to take my men through the riding-school performance, on account of their efficient horsemanship. Early on the morning of the day fixed for the inspection I was parading them, when, in the half light of dawn, the adjutant dashed up on his well-known grey charger, Lorna Doone, and, without drawing rein, called out to me, "Turn your troop in, Sergeant-Major, and come to orderly-room at once."

To hear was, of course, to obey, though I wondered very much what was up, and if the general's inspection was postponed. Dismissing the men, I returned to my bungalow, and gave my horse to my "boy," intending to make my way to orderly-room on foot, when, just as I was passing through the garden gate, I almost ran over a man in civilian dress, and turning round to apologise found to my astonishment it was Colonel A——— He was the very last man in the world I expected to see, and I suppose I showed my surprise by the way I stood gazing at him, for he turned and said: "Well, Sergeant-Major, do you think you are looking at a ghost?"

Quickly bringing my hand up to the salute, I replied: "I must confess I did at first, sir, for I thought you were in England."

He said, laughingly, that I was mistaken, and then, giving me a few words of pleasant greeting, bade me come with him, as the regiment was ordered to proceed immediately to South Africa to take part in the Boer war, and my troop might be on the road that day.

This was great news indeed, and inspired with joy I followed Colonel A—— to the orderly-room, where, in a methodical yet quick way, he showed his complete grasp of all the numerous necessary details attendant on moving a regiment with expedition and well-equipped. Nothing could have demonstrated more thoroughly his administrative ability, for in a few minutes he had written out and made over to me complete instructions as to what I was to do. I found myself under orders to proceed with one hundred and fifty men and two hundred horses by train to Bombay, and there embark for South Africa, the officer in command being Captain G——.

Before dismissing me, Colonel A—— gave me a few words of advice and encouragement, pointing out that I stood high in his estimation, or he would not have selected me as the senior non-commissioned officer of the pioneer division of the 14th Hussars, and as this was the first time he had expressed this opinion of my merits I was not a little surprised. But I did not fail to realise the responsibility of the position and the honour done to me.

The first thing to do was to select a complement of men and horses, and it was not without difficulty that the choice was made, for of course every one wanted to go; but by two o'clock I was able to report all ready to start. We were delayed, however, till the next day, as the railway authorities required time to collect the necessary rolling-stock. At noon we left barracks, headed by the band, and marched down to the station, where we soon had our horses in the trucks, and the men in the carriages.

I shall not easily forget the farewell scene on the platform when the train steamed out. The general commanding the station was there, with his staff, and a great gathering of soldiers and civilians, who cheered us again and again with the utmost enthusiasm, whilst those of our comrades who were loft behind, envied our luck at being off first, and made us promise to leave a few Boers for them to kill!

Travelling by night and halting by day we reached Poonah, and de-training the horses, marched to a special camp fitted up for us, where we settled down for a halt of three days till the steamer was reported ready. The rest after our long journey was very grateful to both horses and men, and the general at Poonah, who came down to see us, took care we were comfortable. During these three days I was fully occupied drawing out stores, tents, and camp equipage for field work. At last the longed-for order came to proceed, and we were soon at the station and busy getting our horses into the trucks. We had almost finished when a messenger came running up and handed a telegram to Captain G———. He opened and read it, and then his face fell, and he looked at me blankly for a moment, as he handed me the paper to read. It ran as follows:

> Fourteenth Hussars de-train horses. Return to camp. Await further orders.

This was a knock-down blow and no mistake, for we feared it was another case of "Clear the line." In a moment all our bright hopes were shattered, and to the disgust and discontent of every one we were obliged to haul the horses out of the trucks. One of our young officers felt the disappointment so keenly that he drew his sword and snapped it across his knee, saying that he had done with the Army, for our regiment only seemed to be in India to be made fools of!

I cannot say very much in favour of the men's discipline that night. They were hard hit, one and all, for they took it for granted that our orders for South Africa would be countermanded in the same way as they had been for the Afghan war, and went about what they had to do in a listless don't-care manner. They could not stand being twice baulked of what is, and ought to be, a soldier's highest ambition: namely, to get a turn at active service.

But a gleam of sunshine came the next evening. As I was standing outside my tent, I saw the general driving rapidly in a dog-cart towards our camp—a mode of conveyance he had to adopt owing to a wound in his leg—and directly he caught sight of me he flourished a paper in his hand and called out, in the gleeful tones of an ensign: "Here you are, Sergeant-Major! To work at once! You are off to-night!"

There and then I got the men together, who quickly tumbled out of their tents, where they were having tea, as they heard my voice shouting to them. Most of them were eager and willing enough now, but a few gave vent to an opinion that we should be done again. However, all went to work with energy, and in a very short time we were at the station—men, horses, bag and baggage—and ready to start. But here another disappointment awaited us, for the railway people (how we blessed them!) said it was impossible to send us down the *ghauts* in the dark. But we made up our minds nothing should induce us to go back to camp, and so we got our horses into the trucks and settled down for the night at the railway station, determined not to budge an inch backwards. With the first glimmer of daylight the train, in various sections, went down the steep incline of the *ghauts*, or mountain passes, and by three o'clock in the afternoon we were all at the Princes Dock, Bombay.

The special drew up a short distance from a steamer flying the B. I. S. N. Company's flag and named the *Chupra*. The commander-in-chief of Bombay and his staff were present to receive us, and in a brisk and cheery voice the old general told us to hurry on, and we might be able to go out with the evening tide. His words acted on the spirits of the men, who now fairly believed there was no false alarm about it. The horses were brought out, and the work of embarking them began. It was hard and hot. Their novel surroundings and strange adventures and experiences since they left Bangalore had dazed most of our animals, and their old constitutional nervousness returned in its most pronounced form, and they lashed out and "played the goat" all round. But we were in no mood to stand any nonsense. With their leave, or without it, we fastened a broad band under their bellies, and then up they went and down again into the steamer's hold, wriggling and squealing like cats.

All this time the officers were encouraging the men by every means in their power, so that we might set sail that evening, and not be ordered back at the last moment. We seemed to feel that the open sea was the only safe place for us—the only haven where telegrams cease from troubling and the Hussar could feel at rest. My duty was, of course, to superintend, but a few minutes of standing by sufficed for me. I could not remain idle with so much at stake, so stripping off my uniform I went in with the men at work. Before long my shirt was in ribands, and five minutes later my flannel was hanging in strips, and last of all it was a case of bare down to the waist. But little I cared as horse after horse went down the hold, and if ever I worked with a will in my life I did so that afternoon. Before the sun had dipped I had the satisfaction of reporting to Captain G——: "Every horse on board."

I was pretty well exhausted, but there was still a lot to do in getting men, arms and baggage on board, and paying off the native followers who had to return to Bangalore. This finished I felt inclined for a moment's "easy," and seated myself on one of the stone pillars to which the steamer was made fast. I had scarcely done so when up came a very smart-looking man, with a bearded face, and wearing a sea uniform, who accosted me with: "Well, old man, you must be played out. I guess I've never seen a European in India go it like you have done to-day. Do you smoke, and will you accept this?" and he handed me a large cake of plug tobacco.

"I like a smoke," I said, " but I'm too dry."

"Well, what will you have to drink? Give it a name and it's yours! I'm steward of that ship over there, and you shall have the best aboard her," and he pointed to the steamer *Baltimore*, which was lying next the *Chupra*.

It seemed to surprise him much when I answered that a jug of hot tea was what I longed for most. "Tea it shall be," he cried, "and that in half a minute"; and he ran off, and almost as soon returned with a steaming jorum of it. I drank my fill, and then, as I drew a satisfied breath, remarked :

"You're the best Christian I have met for many a long day, and if ever I have the opportunity I'll return your kindness."

"Perhaps you'll have the chance some day," he said, off-hand; and then we had a few minutes' conversation, till I rose and wishing him good-bye went on board.

About nine o'clock the *Chupra* cast off her moorings and amidst the hearty cheers of the men steamed off But we had not proceeded far down the harbour when it was discovered that our lieutenant, Mr. M——, was not on board. He had been sent by Captain G—— to the treasury, to obtain the necessary draft for our pay when we reached Natal. We all felt sorry at this, and imagined his grief at being left behind, although we knew he could come on with the rest of the regiment. However, to our pleasure and satisfaction, as we dropped down abreast of the lighthouse, we were hailed by a small boat, which contained Lieutenant M——, who was soon clambering up the ship's side, followed by another European. Then the order was given "Full speed ahead," and we felt we were fairly on our way to the wars.

I am not going to describe the voyage, except to say it was a very pleasant one, and if it had not been for our anxiety to got to work with the Boers, no one would have grumbled if it had lasted double as long. Of course it was hot as we neared the Line, and for some days after crossing it, and something terrible down in the close hold where the horses were. But the men worked cheerily and well, everyone was in good humour, and we had not a single crime reported during the voyage. In the pleasant calm evenings we indulged in sing-songs on deck, the entertainment being much appreciated by the ship's officers, who kept the performers' throats from getting dry. The horses ate their food kindly, and considering the infernal regions they were in, kept their health remarkably well. What they looked forward to most was having the hose played on them at morning stables. There was, of course, no space for exercising them, but now and again when the sea was calm, we got a few out at a time, and walked them up and down the passage that ran between the rows of stalls. In one respect they suffered very strangely, for all their hair came off, and at the end of the voyage there was not enough between the two hundred to make a love-lock, and their skins being all much alike in colour we hardly knew one animal from another.

I must not omit to mention an incident which occurred the day after we left Bombay. I had mustered the men in the morning to see if all were present, and Captain G—— had given the word for the parade to dismiss, when I caught sight of a strange face peeping round one of the horse stalls, and noticed that the owner of it was wearing one of our regimental overalls. This surprised me, and after the men had gone, I took a quiet look round, when I found myself confronted by the stranger, who asked me:

"Is there anything I can do for you, Major?"

Somehow his voice sounded familiar, but who the man was I could not recollect. So I inquired:

"What troop do you belong to?"

"E troop," he replied.

"There you're wrong" said I, "for E troop is at home at the depôt. So out with it—who and what are you?"

"Don't you know me?" he asked.

"No," I answered, looking him up and down, and trying to remember where I had seen him. He was wearing one of our pattern overalls and jack-boots, and had on a fatigue cap, but no coat. Still, although in his shirt-sleeves, his military moustache and soldierly bearing made him look very much like the stuff a Hussar is made of.

"Let me come to your cabin and explain," he said, after a moment's pause; and as I fancied the look of the fellow, I signed to him to follow me.

"Now don't you remember me?" he asked, as we entered my cabin, and he removed his fatigue cap.

"No, I'm blowed if I do," I was obliged to confess.

"Well, when you last spoke to me—not so long ago either—you called me a Christian, and said you would do me a good turn if ever you had the chance. I want you to do it now, for I'm death on the Boers, and if you'll only enlist me, I'm the boy for the 14th Hussars."

"What?" I cried, beginning to see through him, 'you're never that——"

"Yes I am," he broke in, " the steward of the *Baltimore*—with his beard shaved off. I came on board with Mr. M——, got him on board I may say, for it was I who told him how to catch the steamer. And when we reached the *Chupra,* well—I just thought I'd stay on her."

He was, in fact, the man I had seen following Mr. M—— over the ship's side, and whom the ship's officers took to be that gentleman's servant, while I thought he was someone belonging to the steamer. Of course he could not be enlisted, but when I reported him I put in a good word for him, and so, although a stowaway on a Government steamer lays himself open to a very heavy punishment, it ended in everyone in authority winking the other eye; only it was intimated to him that when we reached Port Natal, it would be advisable for him to clear out as cleverly as he had cleared in, or it might be bad for him.

He thanked me very much for what I had done, and worked hard to show his appreciation. He soon made himself at home with the men, and I do not think there was anyone on board more active or willing to oblige. He helped to groom the horses, handed up the forage from the lower hold, washed and tailored clothes, and did everything and anything he was asked. By some means or other he rigged himself out in a complete kit of fatigue clothing, and almost passed for one of us. As he could sing a good song, tell a good story, and make himself thoroughly agreeable, he was soon accepted as a comrade. He often came to my cabin for a chat, and from casual remarks he let drop, I gathered he had at one time moved in very good society. At first I looked upon him with a certain amount of suspicion inseparable from his *rôle* of a gentleman-ranker, but his seemingly frank, open manners, soon inclined me to encourage his visits. He had knocked about the world a great deal, and though he never confessed it, I felt certain he had been in a cavalry regiment, for he knew everything about grooming and handling horses, and all the details of soldiering.

The voyage drew to a close, and one morning we were informed we should sight land the next day. As we neared Natal our attention was arrested by strange floating masses on the sea, which no one could distinguish at first; but one passing nearer than the others, we recognised the dead body of a horse, round which the sharks were swarming. Soon after this we caught sight of high land, and as we approached it, saw beautiful green hills with white houses and cultivated fields dotting their sides. In a short time the lighthouse came into view, guarding the entrance to Durban Harbour, whilst in the outer roadstead H.M.S. *Boadicea* and *Dido* were riding at anchor.

The *Chupra* drew too much water to cross the bar, so it was necessary to bring to outside. As she passed by the two men-of-war to take up her station, we were surprised at the coldness of our reception; for not a yard was manned, not a cheer given. But soon a boat put out, and the naval officer in command boarded us, and then the reason was explained. They had received no information of our expected arrival with troops, and when they saw a steamer coming from the north, they had been altogether fogged.

No preparations had been made for our disembarkation, and we had to lie at anchor whilst the shore authorities were getting ready. The rolling of the steamer was now terrific, and during this single day and night the horses suffered more discomfort than during all the previous voyage. Early next morning several barges were tugged out and laid alongside the *Chupra,* and the difficult and dangerous operation of unloading the horses began. It was exciting work to see the animals rapidly slung up out of the hold in the intervals between the rolling, and then dangling to and fro in mid-air, sometimes for several minutes, until a lull in the ship's motion and the exercise of the nicest judgment, enabled them to be rapidly lowered into one of the barges, the holds of which were half-filled with sawdust. Each barge held about two dozen horses with their complement of men, and as they were loaded up they were towed off by the tug over the bar into Durban Harbour, where the poor animals went through the final process of being slung out as they had been slung in.

Notwithstanding all this danger and risk, every man and horse that we had embarked in India was safely landed. The experiences of another cavalry regiment which arrived a short while before us were very different: they met with such stormy weather round the Cape, that a great proportion of their horses were irretrievably injured, and when they began to sling the poor brutes out of the hold in Natal roadstead, many had to be dropped overboard, and it was their dead carcases we saw floating out at sea.

There was a small ramshackle railway running from the Point to Durban, and into one of the trucks I clambered, after seeing everything ashore, and was soon followed by Surgeon Le M——, in medical charge of us. We had scarcely steamed a few yards, when, from under some baggage in one corner of the truck, who should pop his head out, like a fox from its hole, but the steward of the *Baltimore,* crying out as he did so:

"Hello, Major, here I am again! I told you I should turn up somehow."

As he crawled out I caught sight of a bundle he carried, and recognised two missing blankets, for which I had just been forced to pay as "ship's damages" on giving ours into store.

"I see you have," I replied, not over-pleased; "you and that couple of stolen blankets."

"Garn!" he laughed, as he drew a sovereign out of his pocket and tossed it over to me. "Don't make a song about it, Major; I want the rugs for up-country, so settle for them out of the quid, and drink the balance out in hot jugs of tea."

I couldn't feel angry with him, he was so merry over it all. And then he'd been a Christian to me once, as he was shrewd enough to hint. So I passed the matter and he kept Surgeon

Le M—— and myself in roars of laughter all the way with, his queer criticisms of the country and his situation in it. Just before we got into Durban station he coolly dropped off the train, and his last words to me were: "I'll see you again, Major, never fear! So long, old man!"

When the train pulled up I found my way to camp, where the men had preceded me, and had already picketed their horses in a couple of lines by head and heel ropes. The animals were fairly delighted at finding themselves on land again, rolling on the ground, nibbling at the grass, and as happy as schoolboys. We soon got the tents out of the train and had them pitched; they were light Indian palls, capable of sheltering sixteen men close packed together. Whilst some of the troop were employed in this work, others were told off to get dinner ready, and I busied myself receiving stores and taking over the bullock-wagons which were to accompany us on the line of march.

I was pretty well tired with my long day's exertions when I turned into my tent at dusk, after seeing the sentries posted, and lying down, soon fell asleep. But within a couple of hours a storm burst upon us, with terrific gusts of wind, and in a moment my tent was blown down. Extricating myself from its ruins, I rose to my feet, and found that most of the other tents had shared a similar fate, the soft sandy soil failing to hold the pegs. For the same reason most of the horses had got loose, and were galloping about in all directions, their heel-ropes flying after them, and the men shouting and swearing in their endeavours to stop them.

A nice night we had of it, hunting and recovering the runaways in the dark and in a strange locality. It was not until noon the next day that we had caught all, and I doubt if we should have done so by then, if it had not been for the assistance of some of the Natal mounted police, who showed us round, and helped us to find them. But all's well that ends well, and at two o'clock that afternoon we paraded, the muster was taken, and the detachment reported all present and ready for active service.

Chapter 17
To the Front!

It was a beautiful morning when we started from Durban on our march to Pietermaritzburg. But our manner of travelling was quite different to that which we were accustomed to, for we were ordered to send our saddles and valises on by train, and follow after on foot, leading our horses. Sure never did any cavalrymen feel so disgusted and humiliated as we. Here, after carefully tending our horses during the voyage, landing them without a casualty, mustering them safe and sound in camp, and, except for their loss of hair, in really rattling condition, as was proved by the spirit with which they stampeded their first night ashore—after all this we were not to be trusted to ride them for a ninety mile march, but ordered to tramp along like so many foot soldiers.

But for this we might have had a most enjoyable march. Our first halt was at Pinetown, where, following the custom of the country, we knee-haltered our animals with a thong of raw hide, and turned them loose. They did not know in the least what to make of this strange arrangement, and it was a truly comical sight to see them standing on three legs, wondering why their fourth, held up by their heads, stood straight out, and waiting for the grass to come up to their mouths. When they got tired of this attitude and put their fourth leg down, it puzzled them to observe that their heads went with it. However, they soon grew used to the system, and when they found the knee-halter was a fixture, adapted themselves to its peculiarities, and learnt to worry along as artfully as the Colonial horses.

The second day we started for a place called Boota's Hill. I should mention that all this time our men were wearing *kháki*, a light serge Indian clothing, and carried their arms. We had not got far on our march before the rain came down heavily, and with it the weather turned to cold. Soon the detachment began to tail off, as the roads grew steep, and the men were impeded by their riding boots getting wet and heavy. Some of them jumped on their horses' backs, but were quickly ordered down and threatened with a court-martial if they repeated it.

It was a long and weary journey for cavalry to tramp through mud and slush in jack boots, and four o'clock had passed before the head of the column reached the halting-place. This was a piece of sloping, sloppy ground beside the road, without a vestige of grass on it, and at the bottom a muddy stream. There were plenty of signs of the halt of regiments that had preceded us in the shape of half-buried carcases of horses which had died from the fatal "horse sickness" peculiar to the Colony, and the trampled and mucky surface of the encampment. Rain was still coming down in torrents, and pouring along the slope in an unbroken stream of water. It was almost dark before the last of the stragglers arrived, with the bullock wagons bringing up the rear.

Our first business was to unpack the horse-blankets and try to get some warmth into the hairless, shivering frames of the poor beasts. The men were drenched through and through, and their pinched faces and benumbed limbs showed how the cold and wet was telling on them. They were not fitted to stand such weather just after arriving from a tropical country, and clad in their lightest Indian garb, and we felt it was a bad beginning for our South African campaign. Our valises having gone on with our saddles, there was no chance of a change of uniform, and as for attempting to pick out a dry spot for the tents, such a thing was not to be found. So we plumped them down anywhere and anyhow in the dark, and very little use they were, for they had been intended to afford shelter from a hot sun in a dry climate, and were altogether unsuited for this work.

The next morning we could get no fire alight to make

anything hot for breakfast, and our meal consisted of damp biscuit, tinned meat, and muddy water. This was our fare and our experience for three days. The horses suffered more, for they would not touch the strange food supplied them, just sniffing at the Indian corn and rejecting it, and the pegs by which they were picketed not holding, they broke loose and huddled together for shelter and warmth; whilst the men, not a few of whom had been attacked by dysentery, did the same in their miserable tents.

On the fourth day the weather cleared, and we made another stage of our march; the horses tucked up and suffering from want of food, and the men from want of clothing. That evening we reached Camperdown, and the next, with similar experiences, only under a scorching sun now, marched into Pietermaritzburg.

Here we pitched camp on a plateau to the left of the town, the grass on which was up to our horses' knees. No sooner had we turned them loose than they began to eat it ravenously, for, excepting the little grass they had nibbled on the line of march, not a grain had they munched since leaving the *Chupra*. Nothing would tempt them as yet to look at the Indian corn, which was the only grain supplied by the commissariat, and in a few days the rejected food of two hundred horses mounted up to a great bulk.

On the second day, the grain contractor came to me, and said it seemed a pity to see good "mealies" wasted, and he would take over our rejections at three pounds a sack, mentioning that he had done this in the case of the regiment that preceded us, and I might as well have a few sovereigns in my pocket when they were going begging. But my heart was with my horses, and I did not care to grow fat while they grew lean; so I went to Captain G—— and suggested we should sell the mealies, and with the money so obtained purchase more suitable food, such as oat fodder, of which there was plenty to be bought, the oats being cut and stacked with the grain on them, and forming lovely forage which the horses would have fought for. But Captain

G—— would not sanction the proposal, saying that the horses must be taught to eat the grain of the country, and being a very particular officer, he ordered the mealies to be chucked on the manure heap, which was done. It grieved me to see the poor horses suffer, and I was sickened by the inconceivably stupid commissariat arrangements at Pietermaritzburg, for it seemed as though the horses were to be starved by regulation. They were showing signs of wanting something stronger than green grass, but orders had to be obeyed, and twenty sacks of mealies, which cost Government a hundred pounds, were heaved like so much muck on the dunghill, and the oat fodder the money would have bought was denied our horses.

The grass on which they now picked up their own food was swarming with horse-ticks, a minute animal in its natural state, but which, directly it fastens on a horse, begins to suck its blood and quickly becomes swollen and bloated out to an immense size. Our troopers were soon covered with these ticks, and what with the total want of grain and these bloodsucking pests, they soon fell into an impoverished condition. The men were not much better off; their feet were in a very bad condition after their journey, their jack-boots worn out, their clothing quite insufficient, and the water they had been obliged to drink brought on dysentery, and floored a great percentage of them.

We had now to incur the heavy expense of purchasing extra flannel underclothing, and various necessary articles of kit, as, through some mistake, the men's black bags, with most of their belongings in them, were left in store at Durban, and never forwarded on. So we had to launch out, and although credit was easily obtainable on an officer's signature, a day of reckoning, of course, had to come, and many a poor private, who could ill afford it, was mulct in what was to him a heavy sum to pay for articles made necessary by the climate of the place in which he was going to fight his country's battles.

Close beside us at Pietermaritzburg was encamped a battery of artillery; and there they seemed likely to stay, for they had lost all their horses from the dire scourge of horse-sickness, which was as fatal in its results as foot-and-mouth disease in England. There was no guarding against the visitation. A horse might be to all appearances in the best of health, eating his food with a relish, and looking fit and sound; suddenly he would stop munching, down would go his head, and then he would commence blowing, and within a short time it was all over with him. We tried many remedies, as well as preventatives, to save our horses, but they were of little avail; and though I only lost five of the horses under my immediate charge during the whole of the time I was in South Africa, I think my comparative immunity from the sickness was owing to good luck more than anything else.

So virulent was the horse-sickness in the colony, that the value of an animal was not determined by its good qualities, but by its power of resisting attack. If a horse once got over the sickness, he was supposed to be—and I believe was—safe from another attack, and was called salted; and if, in addition, he was an entire, the colonists would give almost any price for him.

Since leaving the service I have read a good many books, some of sober travel, others of sensational fiction, descriptive of Natal and the Boer war. In all of these the actual state of feeling in the colony is very grossly exaggerated. It has been printed that the colonists were in a panic, expecting the Boers to sweep down upon them at any moment and drive them into the sea, and that they lived in a state of perpetual scare and fright. Speaking from my own observation I saw nothing of this. On the contrary, what struck me most was the absolute apathy of the whites. One would have thought a Hussar regiment quartered in a one-horse town like Pietermaritzburg would have raised a little local enthusiasm; and especially as we had come to fight for them. But devil a bit of it was there displayed. Our horses were the only things that interested the colonists. At Durban a few of the townsfolk treated our men, but it was individually, not collectively; and from the time we entered the colony until the time we left it the stereotyped remark was that we were a fine body of horses! The only people who took the slightest interest in the rider without his horse were the camp-sutlers and contractors, who were on the bite like barbel. For the rest, the people whose homes we had come to defend did not chuck us a cheer, or squander a shout of greeting.

My time was pretty well taken up at Pietermaritzburg with my duties, for in my position of senior non-commissioned officer all the real hard work fell on my shoulders. But it was pleasant to be busy, for it was with the consciousness that we were going *To the Front;* and we could feel for the gunners who were stuck in camp alongside of us, like a steamer with its machinery broken down. Poor fellows! they suffered more loss than their horses, though that was bad enough; for one Sunday morning a terrible storm came up, and the lightning struck a single-poled tent at the end of their camp, and killed the majority of the sixteen men inside it, the few that escaped death being very seriously hurt.

At last we were all ready to proceed, and the night before we started, Sir Pomeroy Colley gave a dinner-party at Government House, to which the *élite* of the place were invited. It was followed by a grand dance—a sort of colonial parody of the ball at Brussels before Waterloo; for the general was going forward to assume command the next day, and sweep the Boers out of existence. Some of our non-commissioned officers formed the guard of honour for the dinner; and I was one of them. The general had taken a fancy to the 14th Hussars, for we were the only regiment that had landed in Natal with its horses intact, and in good condition; and I think this was the reason why twenty of us, under an officer, were ordered forward the next day to act as an escort, I believe, to Sir Pomeroy. We only accompanied him a single march, for after that he forged ahead with relays of horses, whilst we followed in the rear, our progress being much delayed by our baggage. This was carried in a mule-waggon; and although the mules, imported from South America, were very fast in comparison with bullocks, yet they could only do a certain limited distance a day. Pushing on by stages we sighted Ladysmith one evening, but found ourselves unable to enter the town on account of the swollen state of the Klip river, and had, in consequence, to encamp on its southern bank.

Whilst the men were busy pitching the tents, Lieutenant M——, who was in command of us, noticed an army-signaller trying to attract our attention from the opposite bank, and told me to call for Johnson, our trained signaller, who was a little way off. He soon came up, and was directed to read off the message, the lieutenant taking out his note-book, and preparing to write down the words as they were called out.

For a few moments I watched the flags twinkling and bobbing about, without taking any particular note of what Johnson kept reading; till suddenly Mr. M—— called out to me:

"Good God! Sergeant-Major, there has been the devil to pay up at the front, and the general has been killed."

"Killed, sir!" I cried. "Surely Johnson has misread that?"

"Get a repeat, Johnson," said Mr. M——, "and I'll check it". "No," he added in a gloomy tone, as he finished ticking off the words he had written down, "there is no mistake; and we are to return at once and join Captain G——."

It was no good trying to keep the bad news from the men, and they were told the message. After resting for an hour or two, the order was given to strike tents, and we reluctantly began our return march. At the Moie river we met Captain G——, who had been already apprised of the disaster by telegram, and whose first greeting to us was:

"It's the same old story over again. The 14th are a day too late for the fair!"

We now joined our main body, and encamped at Estcourt, where we received orders to await the arrival of the other two divisions of our regiment, which had just landed at Durban, and were marching up country. Our camp was pitched close to the district jail—a large, square stone building. Soon after our arrival, I was sitting in my tent doing some accounts, when I heard a voice outside, which I seemed to recognise, singing out: "Where's the major?" And a moment afterwards who should walk in but the steward of the *Baltimore!*

He was followed by a couple of setter dogs, and over his shoulders hung suspended a long string of vegetables, and these he threw down on the floor with the exclamation: "Here I am again, Major, and not empty-handed either!" And he asked my acceptance of the green stuff, which, as we had tasted nothing but tinned vegetables since we left India, was most welcome. Seating himself on my saddle, he began to account for his presence, telling me he was living in clover now, and close at hand.

"But there are no Boers here," I remarked. "The last time I saw you, you were going out scalp hunting."

"I have something better than Boers here" said he, jerking his thumb in the direction of the jail; "my brother is boss of the Tronk yonder and is putting me up."

"That's a nice new-laid yarn," I laughed, for I thought he was joking. "Have you got it dated? and when's your term up?"

"New-laid or stale," he answered, "hard or first-class misdemeanant, there's a special invite for you to come and dine with us to-night. And more than that, you'll meet two of the prettiest Europe girls out of old England. So, if you're disposed, come along!"

Seeing he was in earnest I made myself tidy, and accompanied him to a very comfortable house, surrounded by a large garden, which lay a little distance behind the jail, and was introduced as "his greatest benefactor" to a gentlemanly-looking man and two very handsome ladies, who really were his brother and sisters-in-law!

Three or four days after this our second division arrived from Durban, and was quickly followed by the third with the headquarters of the regiment. We were now all together again, and Colonel A——, in command, and it was a fine sight to see the lines, where the horses were picketed in two wings, the right consisting of animals of all colours, but chiefly bays, and the left entirely of greys. The hair which the horses had lost so rapidly on the voyage grew again almost as rapidly, and they soon had fine coats on them, though, curiously enough, of a much darker colour than those they had shed.

About this time we were joined by several officers who had

been on leave in England, and amongst them one whom we had all given up hope of seeing again, namely, Major K——, and I need hardly say they all received a very warm welcome from the men.

Of course everything was on real service footing now. Colonel A——, was here, there, and everywhere, inspecting all details himself, and he kept his non-commissioned officers on the alert. The most stringent discipline was enforced, and the men made to understand that they had come under the benefit of the Articles of War. We soon received orders to push on to Ladysmith, where the field base of operations was situated. We now marched as a regiment in an enemy's country, which was a new experience to us. After saddling our horses at daylight, we fed them, and whilst they were munching their mealies, which they had at last learnt to like, we struck our tents, loaded the waggons and had breakfast. The "boot and saddle" was then sounded, and we dressed and bitted up our horses preparatory to mounting. We travelled in field-service order, each man carrying only a change of linen, cloak and blanket.

It was a fine sight to see us march off, four hundred sabres strong, but as the majority of our waggons were now drawn by bullocks, we could not get along as expeditiously as when we had mule transport. After covering about six miles, we would be called to a halt, generally near a stream, and the bullocks out spanned and turned out to graze. Half of the regiment unsaddled, and knee-haltering their horses, turned them loose on the grass, whilst the other half remained mounted to guard them, with the usual pickets stationed some distance off to prevent a surprise. At the end of half-an-hour the dismounted horses were caught and re-saddled, and those that had been on guard turned out to graze, and when they had enjoyed their turn the parade was sounded, and woe to the man not smart in getting into his place.

The march would then be resumed, a service advance guard leading the way a quarter of a mile ahead of the main body, scouts out on the flanks, and the rear guard riding behind the long train of waggons bringing up the rear. There were no regular roads in the country we were traversing, but only wheel-tracks showing the route over the open *veldt,* as the vast plain was called. Occasionally the way would wind through a narrow gorge, where there was just room for a waggon to pass, and we were constantly crossing "drifts" or fords over rivers, there being no bridges north of Colenso.

It took us a week to reach Ladysmith, and this time there was no difficulty in crossing the Klip, and we entered what we hoped would prove to be the actual field of war. Colonel A――, selected the ground for our encampment, a small plateau on a hill on the further side of the town, and commanding the roads to Harrismith, in the Free State, and to Newcastle, on our frontier, where, just below the pass called Lang's Nek, the British army was massed. Our rear was protected by the Klip river, our right flank by Ladysmith, and our left by some perpendicular hills, whilst in front was plenty of level ground, suitable for cavalry to act upon, and at the same time providing excellent grazing.

Ladysmith itself was a poor little place of some fifty or sixty houses. Within the town was a large field hospital, and the wounded kept arriving in large batches from the front, chiefly men of the Rifles and Naval Brigade. We were soon settled in camp, and tour horses picketed in six lines in the centre. At the back stood the officers' tents and hospital; in front, the main guard, the quartermaster's store and forge and the sergeants' mess, whilst the men's tents were pitched on either side.

Of course we were all anxious to hear the news from the front, but such information as reached us was a medley of conflicting rumours and wild stories, one day's reports contradicting the previous day's version. News from India there was none, for not a letter had been received since we left Bangalore, which was hard on the married men.

An armistice was in force when we arrived, but it terminated on the fourth day, and a troop was then made up to proceed to the front, and I felt myself in heavy luck when I was chosen to accompany it, for there was endless emulation for the honour. It took us two days to reach Newcastle, riding hard, unencumbered by baggage, and bivouacking at night. Here we found the cavalry brigade under General Drury L——, consisting of the Inniskilling Dragoons and the 15th Hussars, both of which regiments had lost a great many horses from the sickness. In front of the cavalry encampment, and towards the direction of Lang's Nek, lay the Infantry and what was left of the Naval Brigade, in Laager.

We pitched beside the Inniskillings, who supplied us with tents and gave us the heartiest welcome. Our arrival was a surprise to the general, and I think we owed the privilege of our advance more to the enthusiasm of our own colonel than to any positive orders received for it. We were soon employed in scouting with the Inniskillings, but it was very different work to what I had expected, and devil a Boer did I get a run after.

For the Boers were conies of the rocks whom we could not get at. And how true this was will be gathered from the following story of Majuba Hill, which I have pieced together from accounts given me, not only by our men who took an active part in it, but by many of the Boers themselves, with whom I was brought in contact later on.

Chapter 18
The Story of Majuba

The natural barrier which divides Natal from the Transvaal is a range of high mountains known as the Drakensburg, impassable, except at two places: one opposite Harrismith, a town in the Orange Free State, and the other a narrow steep pass just outside Newcastle and known as Lang's Nek. The latter was formed by a natural cleft in the huge perpendicular rocks, and was just broad enough to admit the passage of a wagon to the high table-lands of the Transvaal, but the road leading to it was so steep that a few resolute men might defend it against thousands. Nor could it be flanked in any way, being protected by ravines and kloofs, or gorges, which had never felt the tread of human foot.

Before the disaster of Majuba, the British army was encamped in the open ground just below Lang's Nek, with the town of Newcastle for their base. The force consisted of several infantry regiments, two regiments of cavalry, three batteries of artillery, and a naval brigade under Commander Cameron. It was a compact little army, sufficient in every way for the task assigned to it; but in order to accomplish this it had to enter the Boer country, and its passage was barred by Lang's Nek, which could not be forced without an enormous sacrifice of life.

The Boers were in Laager, at the higher end of the Nek, having seized that position at the outbreak of the war. From their elevated station they had no difficulty in making themselves acquainted with the composition and strength of our army, for they could examine at their leisure the British encampment stretched below them, and with their field glasses note every movement going on within it and the reinforcements arriving. In addition to this they obtained correct information from the natives, and the knowledge thus acquired convinced them that if our men and especially the cavalry, once got through the pass, the Transvaal would be at our mercy. And so, they guarded the Nek for dear life and freedom, hoping vaguely that something would turn up to save them, and above all things determined to avoid a fight in the open.

Sir Pomeroy Colley and our leaders knew what was taking place in the Boer's Laager quite as well as the Boers knew what was going on in the British camp. Sickness and despondency were rife amongst the Butchers, and they were all longing to return to their farms and families. The depressed feelings which had been long growing up in their ranks was brought to a climax when they heard that the 14th Hussars had landed from India, with all their horses well and strong, and were daily expected at the front, and that another cavalry regiment, the 7th Hussars, was following on its heels. They now realised that England was in earnest. Their fear of cavalry was consistent with their boundless admiration of our horses, and the strength of Sir Drury Lowe's Brigade overawed them. To top all, they found that the Zulus, who had promised to help them, had no intention of keeping their words. Those three causes combined to complete their sense of despondency, and when Sir Pomeroy Colley arrived at the front to take over the command, the majority of the Boers at Lang's Nek were ready to disperse and break off to their own homes.

Their discontent was so pronounced that President Kruger hurried to Lang's Nek, where he arrived on the same day, I think, as General Colley reached the British camp. He at once assembled the Boers and harangued them, exhorting them as they loved and valued their independence, to hold out, and actually going so far as to say that France and Holland were sending troops to their aid. But even his great influence and rugged eloquence failed to rouse their former enthusiasm, and except for the wild, irresponsible, devil-may-care element in their camp, composed in no small degree of renegade Irishmen, and adventurers who had joined the Boers out of love of fighting, or hate of England, there was hardly a man who was not in favour of giving in and returning home.

General Colley was informed of this. He had come from India to make a name for himself. He was in command of a splendid and spirited force; all the elements of success were his. And now, at the eleventh hour, the enemy were on the point of dispersing, and there would be no fighting, no glory, no reputation. If anything was to be achieved, instantaneous action was necessary, and realising this he set about organising his fatal expedition.

Everything was kept a profound secret. This, indeed, was Sir Pomeroy's chief aim, and he succeeded so well that the majority of the men in camp did not even know of the expedition till long after it had started. The officers selected to accompany it received their orders under a bond of secrecy. They went to the men's tents in the dead of night, and waking them up, one by one, to the number each was ordered to bring, marched them silently to the *rendezvous*. The force thus chosen was composed of small parties from all the infantry regiments, so that every corps might have a share in the glorious surprise of the Boers, but the bulk was taken from the Rifles and the Naval Brigade. There was a mountain battery attached, and the whole expedition numbered six hundred. Each man received forty rounds of ammunition, and four days' rations of tinned beef and biscuits, and carried only a blanket and his great-coat.

At the *rendezvous* they found the general awaiting them, who led them forward without loss of time. Their march was directed towards a point in the mountains some miles to the left of Lang's Nek, where it was believed that a Kaffir footpath pierced the Drakensburg. They trudged along in silence over rough and broken ground, often stumbling and falling in the dark, till they came to a stream which debouched from the hills. Here they rested, and the men refilled their water-bottles, but they were not permitted to smoke or even converse, except in whispers. After a short halt the march was resumed, the officers being ordered to keep the men closed up, and in touch with one another. The column now entered one of the numerous kloofs in the side ot the mountains, and began the ascent. Soon the way became very steep, and frequently the head of the column had to halt to allow the rear to close up then all would proceed again. There was nothing but the stars to light them; now they were skirting a deep ravine, now toiling up a steep cliff, but ever in front of them hills rose on hills, higher and higher. Soon the quiet-voiced order had to be more constantly whispered down the column, "Close up! close up!" and laggards stumbled forward in haste. But with every furlong travelled the ground grew steeper and more difficult, till the men had to take to climbing in real earnest and use their hands as much as their feet. Then came the first check; it was impossible to get the mules any further. They were hardy, sure-footed animals, able to scramble over almost any ground, but they could not climb the Drakensburg. So the mountain battery was left behind, and the column continued to march on without it. And now the halts were more frequent, for not only were the men beginning to feel exhausted, but the general was in frequent consultation with his officers. There seemed to be some uncertainty about the route, and at last, an hour before dawn, a halt was called, and all ordered to lie down and snatch a brief rest.

General Colley seated himself on a boulder, with his senior officers round him. Near at hand lay a colour-sergeant of the 60th Rifles, from whom I subsequently learnt many of the particulars I am now relating. He overheard the general express an opinion that they were not in the position he had hoped to arrive at, and that it would be better to wait till daybreak and see exactly where they were.

Dawn came at length, and with it a dull, thick, cold mist, sweeping up from the valleys, and soaking the men to the skin. It drew a veil around the doomed column, hiding every object, except those a few yards distant, from view. Presently it lifted a little, and then was discovered, on the right, a deep ravine, with precipitous sides; and beyond, succeeding hills and ranges, and much broken ground. To the left uprose a great hill—Majuba itself. On its base the column had been resting; the summit was lost in clouds and mist.

The order was now given to move forward, and the little force resumed its march, skirting the deep ravine, the clear way between which and the base of Majuba frequently narrowed so that only two men could pass along abreast. This, perforce, broke up the column, till it became a long straggling line. The general's object was to cross the ravine, but it was soon apparent that if a place suitable for crossing it existed, the column had missed it, for the cliff below them was precipitous, and afforded no foothold for men to creep down.

Sir Pomeroy Colley now seemed to grow more anxious, as every officer he sent forward to reconnoitre came back with the same report that the ravine was impassable, and he frequently consulted a sketch map of the ground he held in his hand. By this time the mist had cleared a little, and the men could see in front a succession of hill tops, and to the right, at a considerably lower level, broken and rocky ground. To the left Majuba lifted its giant form sheer up, and along its base the column crawled. Some distance farther on the clear way widened a little, and the order was passed down to close up, as there was now room for several men abreast.

Suddenly "ping" went a bullet, and one of the Naval Brigade gave a bound in the air and fell dead to the ground. Then, before anyone could realise what had happened, or who were attacking them, the bullets came singing along, dropping men all along the length of the column in rapid succession.

It was a party of Boers actually on their retreat from the Laager at Lang's Nek. They were on the other side of the ravine, safely hidden from sight behind rocks and boulders, and were deliberately picking off our men, who had nothing to shelter them, and whose bodies stood distinctly outlined against the grassy slope of Majuba.

For a moment there was some confusion, as the officers gave

the word to get under cover; but it was an idle order, for there was no cover available. Between our men and their hidden enemy gaped the ravine, penning them in, and leaving them food for the bullets that sped across in a leaden shower, the white puffs of smoke alone indicating from whence the shots came.

The rear of the column hearing the firing on ahead now crowded up, but only to be shot down like so many trapped animals, as they came into sight round a bluff of the hill. And now the lamentable want of cohesion in the force was felt. Men and strange officers became mixed up together; no one seemed to know whom he was commanding, or whom to take orders from. Forty men had been selected from this regiment, sixty from that, a hundred from another, and so on. All were strangers to one another. There appeared to be no one to give definite orders, no plan laid down to follow in such an emergency, and no head to guide or direct. And all the while the deadly shots came pouring in from the unseen foe. Our poor fellows fell by scores. It was a massacre.

And so they were slaughtered; some in their death-leaps falling headlong over the precipice, others sinking backwards until their dead bodies blocked up the narrow clearway. The general had taken his stand on a spot where the level ground was a little broader, and here he rallied his men around him. From this open and exposed position they fired away in the direction of the white puffs of smoke. Sir Pomeroy himself seemed to bear a charmed life, for though officers and men fell thickly on either side, he remained untouched. At last not a cartridge was left, and then our men, in their impotent rage, hurled their tins of beef at the unseen foe below them. It was the audacity of despair, the last reckless sally of the British soldier.

Our fire had ceased, and our defenceless men stood to accept death. It came to Commander Cameron who was close beside the general. A bullet struck him, and he fell mortally wounded. Seeing the condition of affairs, Sir Pomeroy Colley took a white pocket-handkerchief out of his pocket, and waved it as a flag of truce.

The enemy ceased firing, and came crowding out from their places of concealment, shouting and hurling coarse abuse at, the Englishmen's cowardice. And then, to their eternal disgrace, one of their number advanced to within a few yards of their side of the ravine, and levelling his rifle, deliberately shot Sir Pomeroy Colley through the heart, and he fell, murdered with the flag of truce in his hand.

The rear of the column finding they could do nothing by pressing forward, now turned back for shelter behind the bluff, but the Boors opened upon them as they retreated, adding to their confusion, and turning the retreat into a rout.

Towards evening some of them reached camp at Newcastle, with the disastrous news, which was at first discredited; but when later on the wounded began to come in and confirmed it, the greatest anxiety prevailed, and saddles, stores, tents, and all available baggage were utilised to form a breastwork round the camp; and if the Boers had taken advantage of the panic, there is no saying how much or how little resistance they might have met with. For there was no commander left behind who appeared to know anything of Sir Pomeroy Colley's plans, and the whole force was wrapped up in uncertainty and doubt as to what to do.

But the precautions were superfluous, for the main body of the Boers at Lang's Nek were ignorant of what had happened at Majuba Hill, which was some miles distant. On the morning of the battle, about a hundred Boers had determined to trek home, and having proceeded some distance on their journey, the mist cleared, and to their surprise and dismay, they caught sight of the British column crawling along the base of Majuba Hill. Their first impulse was to fly. for they conjectured they were too late to escape, and that the British had taken them in the rear and cut off their retreat. But one or two amongst them, wiser and bolder than the rest, took a second look, and perceived that there were very few red-coats, and that they were so situated as to be attacked with safety, and the certainty of shooting them down. And so, although the majority of their party had actually begun to cut the bullocks loose and abandoned the waggons, these leaders pointed out that the British were delivered into their hands, and urged them to strike a blow for their independence. Their counsels prevailed, and the Boers were soon creeping up towards the column. Hidden by the mist they approached to within point blank range, and took up perfectly safe positions behind rooks and boulders, and then opened fire and inflicted on our men the defeat I have described.

I, myself, had many opportunities afterwards of questioning the Boers, and they told me that if General Colley had only waited a couple of days more, every Dutchman would have trekked away from Lang's Nek, and he might have marched through the pass without firing a shot. The small body of Boers who cut our column off, were the first to leave—the weak-hearted ones of the Laager—and within twenty-four hours would have been followed by all the others, who needed only this example to decide their wavering spirits. But the gallant and over-confident general, who believed it was feasible to invade Afghanistan with a single cavalry regiment, hesitated not in trying to win a reputation in South Africa by a method equally audacious and ill-considered, and Majuba Hill remains a monument to the most miserable and mismanaged undertaking that ever engulfed a British force.

Very soon after our arrival at Newcastle an armistice was concluded, and in March or April, 1881, we returned to Ladysmith, escorting a number of wounded men who were able to bear removal to the base hospital. On our return we found the 14th had shifted camp to a spot somewhat nearer the Klip river. We soon slid into a settled routine of life. We rose at five, and our first job was to search for ticks on our horses. It was an amusing sight to see the men scrutinising them, like so many monkeys over dogs, whilst the grateful animals lowered their heads and cringed down to enable their masters to reach them more easily, and rid them of the bloodthirsty pests. After this the horses were fed, and at half-past seven all hands went to breakfast. As soon as the sun gathered force, and the water, which had been frozen during the night, thawed, we performed our morning ablutions, and then the tents were struck and laid down flat, to enable the sun to dry the ground we had been sleeping on. The soil was a peculiar blue clay, so damp that it might almost be termed mud, and each man left a distinct impression on the spot on which he had been sleeping. Had it not been for our waterproof sheets, we should all assuredly have suffered from rheumatic fever.

Although our horses had become reconciled to the mealies, their chief food was the luxuriant grass which grew on the flat-topped hills around the camp. Soon after nine o'clock we watered them, and then rode them out about a couple of miles, to a suitable place, and after knee-haltering them, turned them out to graze, under charge of an officer and about half-a-dozen men. Not infrequently, in spite of every precaution on the part of the grazing guard, the horses, when they had got their bellies full, towards the afternoon, would stampede for the lines, led by some cunning old trooper who knew where the grain go-down was. But if they stayed out all day, the men marched out about five o'clock in the evening and took them down to the river to drink before riding them home. We had about half-a-dozen entire horses in the troop, and as they caused a good deal of agitation amongst the rest, they were taken out separately.

Such was the ordinary routine of our life at Ladysmith, but it was occasionally varied by instructive field days, when we practised the Boer mode of warfare. Riding out ten or twelve miles on the level plain which skirted the hills, the order would suddenly be given to "bunch" our horses, and, dismounting, we would fasten their heads together in batches, and then execute various foot manoeuvres, such as skirmishing in extended formation, or attacking an imaginary foe on the hills. This practice increased the steadiness and stamina of horses and men, and when Sir Evelyn Wood and Sir Redvers Buller arrived and put us through our facings, we showed we had learnt our lesson. Sir Evelyn was a dashing cavalry officer, and though Colonel A———, was in the habit of making us move briskly, we had to do all we knew to satisfy the general, who dusted us up hill and down dale, across rivers, ford or no ford, and over broken, lumpy ground, until it was astonishing to see what cavalry was really capable of doing, and what difficult country it could get over when fearlessly and resolutely handled.

The armistice with the Boers being renewed, and everything pointing to peace, we had an opportunity of taking stock of the district, and I travelled some scores of miles in nearly every direction to gain topographical information. The shooting was excellent, and included many species of deer and antelope, from a little animal not much bigger than a kid to the springbok, whose hind quarters were as large as a fat Smithfield ox. The river teemed with fish, and the cliffs with wild pigeons, and I never came home empty-handed.

As time wore on, we began to fear that all hope of fighting was over, for no sort of restriction was placed on people visiting our camp as often and when they liked. A great number of Boers took advantage of this to come and see our horses, which they greatly admired, and also to watch us at drill. On the Queen's birthday we had a grand parade, with some fine manoeuvring after it, and when they saw our two wings, one of bays and the other of greys, streaming out across the plain, and acting against each other, their expressions and gesticulations of delight showed how much they admired the animals.

On the afternoon of this clay we had some shooting matches, and by a tacit invitation several Boers competed, as well as a great number of colonists. Of course we were all anxious to see what the former would do with their long-barrelled Winchester rifles. The target was first set up at three hundred yards, and our crack shots started the ball, firing, of course, with our short-barrelled carbines. The Boers were a little shy of joining us at first, but their natural love of rifle-shooting, combined perhaps with a touch of pride and desire to show off their prowess, overcame this, and they were soon shooting man for man. At this range (it may surprise the reader to learn) our men were a trifle the best. The target was now shifted back to the five hundred yards range, and here the Boers were all at sea; for we wiped their eyes at every shot. This soon excited them, and they actually doubted the fairness of the marking, and sent some of their party forward to check it. They were soon satisfied that at the. longer range their accuracy was far behind ours. The truth was that not one in ten of them understood trajectory, or the real relation sights bear to any object at a distance of over two hundred yards or so, whilst our men shot straighter at the longer than at the shorter range, as it suits the Martini better. Some of the Boers now asked leave to change weapons, which only made our superiority more manifest than ever, for whilst we shot straight enough with their long Winchesters, they could do nothing whatever with our short carbines.

The afternoon's sport proved conclusively to my mind that the vaunted marksmanship of the Boers, of which so much has been heard, is vastly exaggerated. Their shooting is best described as close distance snap-shooting, and within the point blank range of their rifles they were perhaps dead shots; but they fell away directly they were called upon to fire at objects beyond their familiar range, and if we had ever met them in fair field, they would never have been able to come close enough to our infantry to do it any damage.

In June Colonel A———'s time expired, and he left us, and the command of the regiment devolved upon Major K———. I well remember the day when it sounded troop-sergeant-majors' call, and we all had to go up to Colonel Arbuthnot's tent. He spoke a few words to each of us, hoping we would do our best to support his successor as we had always supported him, and he sympathised with us in our disappointment in not having seen any active service. Then he gave us all a farewell shake of the hand, and mounting his horse, rode down the centre of the camp, past the main guard and away. And that was the last I saw of a commanding officer who certainly worked his hardest to make the 14th an efficient and smart Hussar regiment.

CHAPTER 19

A Stampede

Our new commanding officer, Colonel K——, was most popular with all ranks. If he had to do a sharp action, he had a considerate way which took the worst part of the sting out of it. He was a born horseman, knowing all the little ways and peculiarities of horses, and never so happy as when he was devising something for their benefit. Unfortunately his first attempt at improving the condition of those in the 14th Hussars resulted in worse than failure.

For some months past we had been obliged to go further and further afield for grazing, as the grass in the vicinity got eaten down; but we always kept to our side of the Klip River, although on the other side there were many splendid grazing plateaux on the flat-topped hills. But Colonel A——, for reasons of his own (which proved very sound ones, as events will show) expressly forbade us from taking the horses across. The ground there was different to that on our side, where the slope down to the river was a gentle one, whereas opposite there was a steep hill or cliff, which overlooked our encampment, and extended for some distance up and down stream. There was splendid grass on the top of this cliff, but to reach it we should have had to cross the river by a ford some three miles up stream.

There was this peculiarity about our horses when turned loose, that if they were in sight of camp, directly they had eaten their fill they would make for it, and sometimes in an excited stampede, which led to accidents. The morning after Colonel A—— left, Colonel K—— came round the lines, and observed in his pleasant Irish voice:

"There's a swate bit of grass across the river yonder, and the horses shall have their fill of it this day, I'm determined."

After breakfast the men were ordered to turn out, the left wing on the greys first, and the bay wing to follow half-an-hour later. Colonel K—— accompanied them to the ford, leaving in camp the few entire horses which always grazed alone. I remained behind that morning, and about half-past ten o'clock began looking across the river, expecting to see the men returning, which they could do by some rough stepping-stones just opposite our camp. As I stood smoking my pipe I saw the colonel's figure rise up against the sky on the brow of the hill, and he was followed in a few minutes by the men, who began to scramble down the face of the cliff to the river.

They had nearly reached the bottom, when suddenly another object appeared on the rim of the hill, outlined against the sky. It was a hobbled horse. The entires in our camp caught sight of it at once, and gave a shrill neigh of recognition. This was immediately answered by the hobbled horse, and then by several others, who quickly joined him, and who all seemed amazed at finding the camp lying at their feet. In less than five minutes the whole wing of bays was swarming up from the back to the brow of the cliff, and looking down on the camp, their heads erect, their ears cocked, and their knee-haltered legs held out in attitudes, like so many statues.

The entire horses in the lines now grew very excited, wanting to join their comrades, and began to neigh back louder than ever, while the shrill challenge was returned with interest from the heights across the river. Then the bays, led by old "A-12"—a big black trooper, with white legs—began to search for a path down the cliff to reach the camp. The men below were attracted by the neighing, and recognising the danger that threatened, hastily turned, and began to climb up again. Seeing this, the horses edged off, and then, still skirting the cliff, turned into the upstream direction, and from a walk the leader increased his pace to a trot, from a trot to a canter, and then it was a case of "They're off!"

Some distance further up the cliff trended down to the river, and this gave the bays an impetus, and soon forced them into a gallop, their hobbles, when they did not break, being of little use in stopping them, for they had learnt the way of using their legs when knee-haltered. Faster and faster they went, until they were fairly thundering down towards the river. It was a sight to see! On they tore recklessly, kicking, squealing, shouting, and now and then tumbling down and rolling over. All were bent on crossing the river, which they could now plainly see; and as they reached it, unable to stop their headlong course, a score of the leading horses plunged in.

The main body, however, pulled up short, and evidently frightened by this, turned off to the left— with artful old "A-12" still at their head—and made for an open plain known as the Ostrich Veldt, which was now jet-black, having been recently fired. To reach it they had to pass the shoulder of the hill, behind which Colonel K—— had left the grey wing to graze; these they did not notice as they swept by at their great speed; but the greys saw them, and throwing up their heads, stood staring for a minute. Then, in spite of the endeavours of the grazing guard to head them off, they started in mad pursuit of the runaways, who were now a good quarter of a mile ahead.

It was one of the finest spectacles I have ever witnessed, to see these two great bodies of unmounted horses thundering across the charred ostrich plain amid clouds of black dust, and in two wedge-shaped wings. It required no great stretch of imagination to fancy that they were going through their ordinary drill and evolutions. But they were wild horses now—camp, river, road, everything was forgotten in the mad excitement they laboured under, and which urged them aimlessly forward. As I realised what had happened, my first thought was to get a horse, and try and head them, for I felt sure they would follow anyone who gave them a lead. All they were doing on the vast veldt was careering and circling round and round, simply exulting in their freedom, their minds filled, no doubt, with dim memories of the Australian bush, where they had run wild in their youth.

As soon as I was satisfied of the direction they had taken I rushed to my horse, Neddy,—who was one of the entires in camp—and hastily putting a snaffle-bit into his mouth, jumped on his bare back, and started at a gallop for the ford. Unfortunately, not knowing it very well, I overshot it; and when I discovered my mistake, sooner than lose time by going back, I pressed on, hoping to find another drift higher up stream.

After a time I reached some broken ground leading up an ascent, which skirted the river, and pushing up it, reached the top, and was able to descry the greys and bays, some two or three miles away, on the ostrich plain, still wheeling and galloping about. This determined me to cross the river at all hazards, and leading my horse down a very steep incline, I reached the bank, but found, to my surprise, that it was not the Klip, but a tributary, which joined it a mile or so above the ford I had missed, and was known as the Sand River, from the nature of its bottom. It was about fifty yards wide, and contained only two feet of water, which flowed placidly along, so that its bed could easily be distinguished.

Such a gently-gliding, shallow stream appeared to oppose no obstacle, and, jumping on my horse, I was on the point of riding him into it, when I heard a voice calling out, and looking up saw a man on the other side violently gesticulating to me to keep off I halted, and sung out to him, asking what he wanted, and he replied that to ford the river there would be certain death, as it was one large quicksand, and that if I desired to cross I must go higher up. It is needless to say I backed away from the treacherous place, and following the direction the man indicated, as he kept up with me on the other side, came to a spot where he told me to halt, and look for a dark, narrow track, about two feet broad, which ran in a diagonal direction down stream. This, he said, was a ledge or shelf of hard marl or rock, and I must follow it to the opposite bank, remembering that a false step on either side would plunge me into quicksands from which there would be no escape.

I soon found the track, which could be easily distinguished by its dark colour, and urged Neddy into the river very gingerly. The man stood some distance off, watching me, and from time to time shouting out instructions. Neddy made no difficulty about it until we arrived within eight feet of the opposite bank, when the man warned me to be extra careful now, for the marl turned off sharp to the left, and ran parallel with the bank for some distance before joining it. But Neddy resented this, for he wanted to reach the grass, and, before I could stop him, gathered his legs together to make a bound. But just as he did so his hind feet slipped off the marl track, and, robbed of his impetus, he fell plump into the sand, his muzzle striking against the bank and the manner of his fall shooting me on to it.

I was on my legs in a moment, still grasping the reins, and tried to keep poor Neddy's head up and get him out. But he was already sinking fast, for his hind legs and quarters were below the surface of the quicksands, and only his head and shoulders, and part of his forelegs, visible; and with these he was struggling pitifully and wildly to extricate himself. I did all that lay in my power to drag him out, but he continued to sink deeper and deeper with each struggle, until at last only his head remained above the surface of the water, with great tears of agony and fright rolling out of his brown eyes. Then I could not bear the sight any longer, and turned my head away; and when I next looked down at the spot, poor old Neddy had been cast for good and all.

The man who had directed me now came up, and while expressing his concern for my loss, congratulated me on my own narrow escape from what would have been certain death, for if I had fallen in, no power on earth could have saved me, and I should have been keeping poor Neddy company beneath those yellow sands which were perfectly smooth again.

In reply to the man's enquiries I told him who I was and how I had come there. He then informed me his name was Field and he owned a large farm, of which this river was one of the boundaries. On my telling him that I was anxious to get back to camp, he said he would lend me a mount, and taking me to his house, he gave me a good meal and then accompanied me back by a short cut to Ladysmith, which I reached about two o'clock.

We had not seen a sign of the runaways on our way, which made me hope they had all been captured and brought back to camp; but this was not the case, for although many had been driven in, nearly a hundred were still missing, and parties of men were scouring the country in all directions after them. Several were brought in whilst I was there, some of them dreadfully cut about the legs by their knee-halters. I lost no time in getting hold of another horse, and taking two or three men to help me, joined the chase, and was fortunate enough, after two hours' ride, to come upon a drove of nearly twenty quietly grazing in the open, which we easily captured and led home.

A muster was now ordered, and it was found that there were still about forty bay horses, all Walers, not accounted for. There were several reported dead, and at one deep part of the river a small troop of fifteen were drowned; the action of one leg knee-haltered and the other free, sending them round and round in a circle, till the poor animals became exhausted and sank. Several of the horses were so injured by the cutting of the tendons of the leg that they had to be destroyed, and casualties from these and other sources reached a large total.

It was now determined to make a special effort to recover the forty missing horses, and parties were organised to scour the country. I was given charge of one, and taking four days' rations with us we started for the country almost due west of the camp. I spread my four men out in a great line so as to cover as great an extent of ground as possible, and in this way we searched every square mile along the base of the Drakensburg for four days. Whenever we saw a Kaffir kraal we made for it and instituted dumb-show enquiries. On the third day we came across a couple of our horses grazing in a kloof, and as soon as they saw us they evinced the greatest delight, and came cantering up, and thereafter followed us without being led or driven.

This was not enough to take home, so, being allowed a free hand, I determined to extend the search. On the fifth day we reached the borders of Basutoland, and now our rations were all finished. From this forward we lived on what we could get, which was chiefly goat's-milk and Indian-corn. Not knowing the language we could not converse with the natives, or find out where we were, and we lost all touch of direction and locality, wandering along, ignorant each morning where we should find ourselves at sunset, bivouacking in the open at night, and thoroughly enjoying the roaming holiday. About the tenth day we were riding through some scrub when we unexpectedly dropped on seven of our lost horses. They received us with the same tokens of delight that the first two had displayed. Four of them were very lame from the effects of the knee-haltering, but the others were in good condition, though covered with ticks.

Having recovered nine horses I felt I could show myself to Colonel K——, whose last words to me had been—"Go where you like, but don't come back empty-handed." So we headed south-east, and on the second day struck the road leading from Pietermaritzburg to Ladysmith, and reached camp on the fourteenth day after leaving it.

By this time almost every horse in the regiment had been accounted for, so we once more resumed our ordinary avocations; but never again were the horses sent out to graze in a body, each troop, in future, taking its own separately, and leaving a strong guard over them.

Not long after this the heroes of Potchefstroom and Wakkerstroom marched into Ladysmith and encamped near us. They had been cut off in the Transvaal on the breaking out of the war, and besieged in the two towns named, which they gallantly held till the convention was signed. Their bullet-riddled tents showed what they had gone through. A little later the cavalry regiments at Newcastle fell back on Ladysmith, on account of the scarcity of grass at the front, and two infantry regiments arrived from Durban, so we had quite a respectable force concentrated in the place. News was very conflicting: one day the men were cheered up with the prospects of avenging Majuba; stores and ammunition were served out, and preparations made for the renewal of hostilities. The next everything was countermanded, and it was "as you were" again.

With the increase of the military force at Ladysmith, sutlers and contractors began to throng into the camp, and amongst other things a canteen was started. Hearing of this I went down one day, half out of curiosity, to see it. On entering the tent whom should I see conducting the establishment but Mr. Howard (so, at least, I will call him), who had been governor of the jail at Estcourt. He did not recognise me until I jogged his memory by asking him where his brother, the steward of the *Baltimore,* was. It was an unfortunate question, and made Howard turn round with a gesture, half of passion, half of disgust; but recovering himself, he replied, "God alone knows where he is. It is all through that infernal scoundrel I lost my appointment at Estcourt." He then explained how this vagabond brother of his had not only robbed him of his money, but eloped with his wife, and had been the cause of all the trouble that followed. I apologised for broaching the subject, and offered him such sympathy as I could, but he said it was not my fault, and went on to tell me a good deal about that slippery customer, the steward of the *Baltimore.* It seems he belonged to a good family, but being very wild, and getting into a serious scrape, enlisted in a Lancer regiment and went out to India. There one day in a barrack-room, over a trifling dispute with a comrade, he shot his fellow-soldier, but fortunately without killing him. For this he was sentenced to a long term of imprisonment, but whilst going home as a prisoner on board a troopship, he managed to elude the guard whilst the ship was anchored in the Suez Canal, and dropping overboard, effected his escape. Ultimately he found his way to India as steward of the *Baltimore,* in which capacity I made his acquaintance.

The reader knows how he came to Natal and made his way up country. At Estcourt he was received with open arms by his brother, and he repaid him by running away with his wife and money. This obliged Howard to resign his post at the jail, and he had fallen into very low water, when some of our officers, who knew his family at home, interested themselves on his behalf, and procured him permission to open a canteen, in which he was doing very well now.

After he had been established about four weeks, I heard one morning there had been a rumpus at the canteen, caused by a civilian riding up and presenting a loaded revolver at Howard's head, and relieving him of his cash-box, under peril of his life. The dare-devil thief then made off, but was apprehended and lodged in an old stone prison in the town. That evening I went down to the canteen to hear the truth of the story, and I cannot say I was very much surprised when I learnt the robber was none other than the steward of the *Baltimore!*

That night he made a hole through the wall of his cell and escaped. Coming into the cavalry camp, he stole a salted horse belonging to a contractor in the commissariat, who was a native of the colony. No sooner did the owner find it gone than he hired three half-bred Boers to help him pursue the thief. The times were wild and lawless, and though a man might rob his brother and elope with his sister-in-law, to steal a salted horse was quite another thing. The thief made for the Orange Free State; his pursuers followed close at his heels. Just across the border they came up with him. Four rifles covered him, and he threw up his hands and surrendered. The horse was recovered, but he had to pay the penalty. A short shrift was his, for the contractor did not return till he had left the steward of the *Baltimore* swinging from a tree with four feet of daylight under him!

Some negotiations had now to be undertaken with the Zulu nation, and General Sir Evelyn Wood was entrusted with them. He took with him three squadrons of cavalry, each consisting of two troops from the three regiments at Ladysmith, and a full band. I was told off to accompany ours, and when we mustered I could not help observing that the squadrons illustrated two different theories of how a regiment should take the field for active service. We wore serge coats and *khâki* pants, with Indian *puttees,* or long strips of cloth, bound round and round the leg below the knee, in lieu of jack-boots: they were much more comfortable and supporting. Our helmets and belts were rubbed over with red clay to harmonise with the colour of the ground, and our steel work was all dulled. The squadrons from the Inniskillings and 15th Hussars adopted quite a different style; they were as spick and span as could be, helmets and gloves white and clean, and steel and brass work all sparkling in the sun. It was a queer contrast altogether, and represented two widely different schools of military opinion.

We marched in light field order, but with tents and baggage-waggons drawn by mules. Our route was almost the same as that followed by the army under Lord Chelmsford's command during the Zulu war, and we saw many evidences of the numerous fights that had taken place, especially at the fatal field of Isandlana, where some grim relics still strewed the ground, with here and there a few bleached bones, and human skulls half hidden in the grass.

Crossing a high range of hills, we encountered snow and intense cold, and several of the men suffered severely from frostbites. Our destination was Conference Hill, which we reached after a ten days' march. Here we found the Zulu army, or nation, formed up in a huge crescent, their chiefs at their head, ready for the palaver. A ragged tent was pitched, and in front of this we took up our station, with the assembled Zulus facing us. They were strangely apathetic at first, and remained squatting on the ground in their crescent formation, while Sir Evelyn Wood and his staff dismounted and entered the tent. For some time we sat at attention on our horses. Presently the general came out and ordered the band to play *God save the Queen*, and the men to give a cheer. As we did this, the Zulus half rose in an almost threatening way, but their head men remaining seated, they squatted down again. There seemed to be some hitch in the negotiations, for the chiefs remained very grave and quiet. At last an order came to the bandmaster to strike up something lively, and he, being an Irishman, treated them to *Patrick's Day in the Morning*.

Never have I seen any tune produce such a magical effect as this one did. First a few of the Zulus rose, then a few more, and then the whole lot, as if the Pied Piper of Hamelin was after them, and they could not help themselves. In less than five minutes the whole of that dusky host were swaying and dancing to the music. When it was over they swarmed round us, patting our horses, laughing and talking, all in the best of humours. Above all things they admired the big drummer, who could sit on his horse, and whack out such a fine tune. In the end the negotiations were successfully completed, and the Zulu army escorted us during the first day of our return march, and then left us with every token of amity.

At Ladysmith we settled down to work similar to that carried on at a camp of exercise, but, being conducted on foreign soil, we seemed to learn much more from it, especially as we often practised with ball cartridges at given marks during the operations. Camp life was much improved, for we were old campaigners now, and had learnt many little dodges of making ourselves comfortable, whilst the commissariat served out fresh meat, to which we added many luxuries in the shape of venison, fish, and wild fowl. What with field days, and what with plenty of sport, the time passed quickly enough, and the only drawback was that it was not *war*.

We had by this time become callous of rumours that seemed only born to be contradicted. But one day an official order reached us to prepare to sell our horses in the colony, and return to England dismounted. This caused great discontent in the regiment, until, following the usual course, the obnoxious order was so far cancelled that it was changed into another for our return to India, or "home," as the men delighted to call it, with our horses. When this was read out on parade, the intelligence was received with tremendous cheers, and we all broke off and hurried away to make preparations for our departure.

Everything was ready in a couple of days, including a good mule train for the baggage. Wishing our loss fortunate comrades in camp goodbye, our band struck up in front, and we marched out of Ladysmith, leaving only one regret behind, us—the unavenged graves on Majuba's lonely hill!

CHAPTER 20

Kálapoosh Again

Our march down country was very different to our toilsome journey up Natal. There were no halts to outspan and rest bullocks, for each light waggon with its team of twelve mules covered the ground almost as fast as we did. It was no longer war time, and often at places where we debouched into the open veldt, the order was given for the regiment to spread out in one line, and Colonel K——, on his big English charger, Temptation, placing himself at our head, would call out: "Go as you please, bhoys, but don't get in front of me!" Then there would be a good canter, quickening into a steady gallop, and although we often covered two days' march in one, it was surprising to see how fresh men and horses arrived at the halting-place. I sometimes used to think our horses knew they were going back to the land of soaked *gram,* and boiled *quilty,* for they picked up spirit in sympathy with the men, and never failed to respond to calls upon their endurance.

On reaching Pietermaritzburg I had to take over several boxes and bales marked with our regimental designation, and the distinctive letter of my troop, and these were forwarded on to India with our baggage. On opening them some months afterwards, at Secunderabad, they were found to contain books, men's jerseys, flannels, pocket filters (which would have been most invaluable to us in South Africa), and various other useful articles sent out by kind-hearted people in England for our use in the field. Owing to the difficulty of transport they had never got further than Pietermaritzburg, and there they had been stored till we picked them up on our return march. It all seemed a great waste of money, which was something, and of kindness, which was a great deal more; but although they did not reach us when we stood most in need of them, we none the less appreciated the intention of those who had done so much for us.

On reaching Pinetown, our last halting-place before Durban, we came across the 7th Hussars in camp, who gave us a hearty reception. We rested two days here, during which many good and well-trained soldiers were taken from us, for we now first experienced the action of the short service system. Every man within eighteen months of the completion of his long service, and all short service men of eight years standing, were debarred from returning with us to India, and ordered to sail direct from Natal to England to join the Depôt, and pass into the Reserve or obtain their discharge as the case might be. In this way we lost a great number, and although their places were partially filled by volunteers from the 7th Hussars, we were terribly broken up, and never again, whilst I was in it, did the 14th Hussars attain that standard of efficiency and matured experience which it could claim to possess in South Africa.

The weather had been very unsettled during the last month, and just before we embarked the rain came down in real earnest, and we marched into Durban under a tropical pour. There were a couple of steamers ready for us at the outer anchorage, and I accompanied one wing of the regiment and embarked on the *Cambria,* a fine roomy boat built for laying submarine cables, and superior in every way to the *Chupra* for transporting troops. We lost no time in getting on board, for in the evening of the day on which we left Pinetown, the anchor was raised, and we steamed away from Natal after nine months' rough and ready campaigning, which had tried our mettle, but as far as fighting was concerned proved quite barren.

We had a very comfortable voyage, the weather being so fine and calm that we were able to go through the Straits of Mozambique, a passage not often attempted by so large a steamer as the *Cambria*. Early in December we reached Bombay, where we heard with much regret that telegrams had been received from Natal reporting a great mortality amongst our friends of the 41st Foot at Ladysmith, and the 7th Hussars at Pinetown, from enteric fever, so that we could not but consider ourselves lucky in having left the colony just before the unhealthy season set in.

The *Cambria* was visited by a vast lot of people at Bombay before we disembarked, as we had to wait some little time for orders. Amongst other shore-folks who came aboard was a solicitor, who inquired if there was a soldier named Rivers in our regiment. I told him there was a trumpeter of that name in my troop, and it turned out that, through his wife who was at Bangalore, he was believed to have come in for a fortune of £80,000. I sent for Rivers, and took him and the lawyer before Colonel K——, who answered some necessary questions as to identity. The colonel was greatly taken at the idea of one of his "bhoys" coming in for such a fortune, and when a little later the order arrived to disembark, sent for Rivers (who was commanding officers' trumpeter) and bade him sound the parade, calling out in his pleasant, jovial Irish speech: "Blow up, trumpeter; blow up, me bhoy! It isn't ivry colonel of a cavalry rigimint that has a foine gintloman of fortune for trumpeter. So blow up, and let the bhoys hear ye!" I am sorry to add that subsequent investigation cut off the last three noughts from Rivers' £80,000, and in about two months he was glad of an excuse an accident gave him to be invalided home to a country where the "writs of the Secunderabad Small Cause Court, taken out by speculative money lenders, did not run.

We had no difficulty in disembarking at Bombay, for our horses were able to walk ashore by a broad gangway, and in a short space of time we were encamped on the esplanade. The men who left the *Cambria* were a very different looking lot to those who sailed away in the *Chupra,* for all of us who could raise them had grown beards, the order for shaving having been suspended during our service in South Africa. But now it was put into operation again, and the remorseless razor mowed down everything but our moustaches, leaving us all looking much younger, and the camp ringing with the remark that we were the "Young Jocks" once more—which was the name by which our regiment was known in the service.

We were permitted a week's rest at Bombay, and then began our journey by march route to Secunderabad. This was the longest march I ever made, and as I have described our order of marching in England and South Africa, I may as well complete the picture by a description of this. Our baggage was carried on elephants, camels, mules and bullocks, the two former conveying the tents, and the latter the men's kit. *Reveillé* sounded at 3 a.m., when we fed our horses, struck our tents, loaded the baggage animals, and started them off. By this time breakfast had been prepared by the native cooks, and we sat down to it in picnic fashion. Then came the order to "bit-up, dress, and mount," and in a few minutes we were formed into troops. It was always quite dark when we started, and tolerably cold. We rode easy at first, but as dawn broke began to brisk up a bit, and soon overtook the large train of baggage animals. About seven o'clock, or a little later, we reached the camping ground, and by the time we had unsaddled and groomed our horses, the baggage arrived, and we soon had the tents pitched. We were now free for the rest of the day, except for keeping an eye on the native grooms. Colonel K—— was very considerate with the men, and amongst other indulgences which he introduced was a travelling canteen to accompany us on the march, where the men might buy any amount of liquor, in reason, without any of the vexatious limitations and restrictions that had formerly been in vogue. This experiment proved a complete success, for when it was left to the men's good sense not to abuse the indulgence granted, they accepted it in the spirit in which it was conferred, and not a single case of drunkenness was reported on the march.

At a place called Carlee, about five days' march from Bombay, I struck up a friendship with an animal I had never been brought in contact with before. This was an elephant attached to our troop, who, on account of his enormous size, was christened Jumbo. It was part of his duty to carry the big tub in which the horses' grain was soaked, and amusing it was to see the scrupulous care with which he insisted on picking up the few grains that adhered to its corners and angles; and although otherwise obedient and docile, he would not budge an inch until allowed to do this. At Carlee the new-baked bread for the day's rations was, as usual, brought to my tent to be served out to the troop. There happened to be a loaf over, and as Jumbo was passing I called to his driver to bring him up, and gave him the spare ration, and thought no more about it. But the next day as I was waiting for the men to come up for their bread, and standing with my back to the door of my tent, I suddenly gave a start and yell at what I imagined to be a great snake crawling round my neck. It proved to be my friend Jumbo, giving me an insinuating bit of a fondle with his trunk. I gave him a pat and then motioned him to go on his way, but devil an inch would he budge, and there he stood, with his trunk at the salute, and his mouth wide open—the most comical-looking mountain on legs that ever I saw. I called to his driver, who was standing a little way off with an apologetic sort of smile on his face; he came up, and, with many a *salaam,* explained that as I had given Jumbo a loaf the day before I had let myself in for an established custom, and would have to keep it up or there would be "bobbery." So I made the best of it, and chucked the bread to the elephant, and thereafter every day, as regular as clockwork, he paraded in front of my tent for his ration, the same as the men, and Corporal Jumbo was soon a great and popular institution, physically and socially.

    I could write pages of this animal's sagacity and good temper, if I had the space. The order was that all elephants should be chained some distance outside the lines, for fear of their frightening the horses, but there was always a bit of a tussle with Jumbo, because he wanted to come up and chum at my tent, and before the march was out he would follow me about like a dog. I must mention one little matter which shows that he had a better memory than myself. After we reached Bolaram, where we were stationed, I lost sight of my big friend, not being aware that he still remained a near neighbour, for he went no further than the elephant lines at Secunderabad, where he belonged to the elephant battery. Happening to go over one day, some months after our arrival, to have a look round these lines, I was surprised at one of the elephants making overtures of great friendship towards me, and it was not until his driver came up that I discovered it was Jumbo. I at once sent to the bakery for a shilling's worth of bread, and think I left him with the same good opinion of me as when I came.

However, I must hark back to Carlee. Three days after leaving it we reached Poonah, and pitched our tents a mile or so from the usual rest-camp. There we were allowed a day's halt, and as I was bucking about some duty in the lines, a military-looking old gentleman came up to me and enquired what regiment ours was.

"The 14th Hussars," I answered.

"The 14th *Hussars?* I belonged to the 14th, but they were Light Dragoons."

"It was us you belonged to, sir," I replied, "for we were Light Dragoons till 1862."

He then informed me he had left the regiment long before that, and after some conversation I found he had been in the ranks once, but volunteering for the commissariat, had got on in life, gained a commission, and was now living in retirement at Poonah. I asked him if he would like to see our commanding-officer, and on his answering yes, took him to Colonel K———, and they had a long chat together. He then invited me to accompany him to his bungalow, where he insisted on broaching a bottle of champagne and drinking to the health of the old corps. Nor was this all, for after a time he said he must treat the regiment to its Christmas dinner, and carried me off with him to the best Europe shop in the station, and bought all the materials necessary for a feast. This he ordered to be packed in cases and sent forward to Mohl, where we expected to be on Christmas Day. Not satisfied with this, he purchased three fine fat humped bullocks, and sufficient bottled beer to give each man two quarts, and despatched them forward with us, and also a large supply of grain to keep the bullocks fat. I need not say that when he came to see us off in the morning, the men gave him a hearty cheer. It was amusing to see the care they took of the bullocks on the line of march, and hear the jokes passed on their condition at each halting-place, and the anxiety displayed that they should not over-fatigue themselves, but keep fattening up; and the day before they were slaughtered, the band played them into camp to the tune of *The Roast Beef of Old England*.

On our arrival at Bombay telegrams had been despatched to our friends at Bangalore, informing them that we had been ordered by march route to Secunderabad. This accounted for the arrival of my boy Harry at Poonah, the day we reached that place. He had heard a report of my death, which had obtained credence at Ladysmith when I was absent fourteen days hunting the lost horses, and this had actually found its way into print in the Bangalore papers. The news had nearly driven poor Harry crazy, and what must he do when he heard the 14th had reached Bombay but "beg, borrow, or steal" the money for his railway fare, and come to meet the regiment at Poonah, to hear tidings of me. I must say that his greeting, when he found I was alive and well, touched me very much. He did not lose much time, but just took charge of me at once, and never a thing did I want during the rest of the march, which Harry's forethought could provide.

From Poonah onwards the days brought us delightful variety in change of scene and country, and on Christmas Eve we reached Mohl, where great preparations were made to keep holiday next day. We were now in a wild country, and during the night the horses were much disturbed by the growling of leopards or panthers on the outskirts of the camp, and men were posted round to keep fires alight to scare them away. On Christmas morning extraordinary preparations were made for the pudding, and all went well enough till we came to a cloth to boil it in, when we found, to our dismay, we had provided none! Necessity is the mother of invention, and where civilised man wears shirts, a plum-pudding need not go a-begging for a bit of rag. When evening came, half the troop kept guard whilst the other half feasted, who in turn relieved their comrades, till all had enjoyed the Christmas cheer.

Up to now we had been singularly free from sickness, but before the year was out we were destined to experience it. Two days after Christmas, our camp party, which travelled a day in advance, came back to say that cholera was raging in a village near which we should have to halt. Of course the route was changed, and we began cholera dodging, by making a wide detour to windward of any place so infected. But in spite of our precautions we came in for it, and several men were attacked, of whom two or three died. The saddest case was that of Troop-Sergeant-Major Minnett. He had left his wife in England when he came out to join us at Bangalore, but during our absence in South Africa she had arrived in India with one of the drafts, and was waiting for her husband at Secunderabad. Poor Minnett was looking forward to seeing her, and could not conceal his joy as the time drew near. But it was not to be. As we marched out of camp one morning we saw a solitary tent left standing, the sure sign that someone was dead or dying within it; and that evening poor Minnett's corpse was brought on to the next halting-place. We could not manage a coffin, but we sewed him up in a blanket, and the colonel read the burial service over the remains. The spot selected for his grave was by the side of a stream, under a large tree, and on it we cut his name and date of death, and so left him sleeping his last long sleep out in the Indian jungle.

In about a week we marched out of the cholera zone, and the men began to recover their usual spirits. The mornings were not infrequently diversified by an impromptu pig hunt, many wild boars being disturbed by our approach, and often breaking cover close to the road. Headed by an officer, the men would draw their swords and give chase, and there was great emulation to draw first blood. The country teemed with game, and it was no unusual sight to see a herd of black buck on the crest of any rising ground near the camp, gazing with deer-like curiosity at the unusual sight of a British cavalry regiment under canvas. I was always keen for sport, and during the march bagged several black buck gazelle and spotted deer, besides one panther and two cheetahs, and any amount of wild duck, teal, partridge, jungle fowl, peacock and hare. Excellent fishing was also to be obtained in the numerous tanks and rivers we passed.

The march at last drew to an end, and we reached our destination, which turned out to be Bolaram, a cantonment some four miles north of Secunderabad. We were met a short distance out by the band of the 12th Lancers, whom we were relieving, and they played us into camp, and a week later evacuated the barracks which we entered.

There was an immense military force stationed at and around Secunderabad, and the barracks and military buildings stretched along continuously from Bolaram to Hyderabad, a distance of eleven miles, which no one could pass at night without being challenged at very short intervals by the sentries of the different regiments, both European and native, and those belonging to the Nizam, and known as the Hyderabad Reformed Troops. It was a grand sight to see the great force cantoned here formed up for parade, and the mixed regiments, composed of so many varying creeds, colours, and races, answering to one word of command on field days.

General Sir Frederick Roberts was the commander-in-chief at Madras at that time, and often visited Secunderabad. I shall never forget the first time I saw him, on the occasion of a parade of all arms being ordered for his inspection. The line extended nearly a mile, which will give some idea of the number of troops the cantonment hold. The general came cantering down, and every eye was fixed on the smart, soldierly, fresh-complexioned, white-haired man on the grey Arab charger, who had led the famous march from Kabul to Kandahar. He was in full uniform, the breast of his tunic covered with medals, and attended by a brilliant staff.

We soon settled down in our new quarters, and it was high time we got under substantial roofs, for the heat became excessive. Colonel K——, though keeping up discipline, and ordering frequent drills and parades, had great consideration for the men, and we were generally dismissed by seven o'clock, and, except the care of the horses, had nothing to do for the rest of the day. The canteen question was the first thing he investigated. He held the opinion that men should be allowed to get drink when they wanted it, and not be forced to swallow their liquor at certain arbitrary times or go without it. So he started the free system, and left it to the men's good sense not to abuse the indulgence granted them. The canteen was kept open from ten in the morning till watch-setting, and "pegging up" was abolished. The result was that men visited the place now to quench their thirst, and not to put down a regulated amount of liquor in a regulated time, and drunkenness decreased very much. Coincidentally with this, a very curious thing happened; for with the abolition of the restrictions on the issue of liquor, a temperance club was started in the regiment, and caught on so quickly that the receipts at the canteen diminished instead of increased. Within twelve months of our arrival at Secunderabad there were in my own troop—which I merely quote as an illustration—fifty abstainers out of a total of nearly eighty men; and the result was that the savings bank accounts increased enormously. In addition to this happy reform, another equally spontaneous one was introduced, and, as regards soldiering, a more important one. Every troop started a shooting club, and the men went in for regular practice, and this soon led to shooting competitions, which greatly increased the efficiency of the regiment.

And thus, without any parade of system, or hard and fast regulations, Colonel K—— improved the *morale* of the 14th Hussars, where other commanding officers—martinets for discipline, though earnest men in their way—had altogether failed in their attempts to bring about similar results by arbitrary methods.

CHAPTER 21

Harry

As the summer wore on, the heat became more and more intense, and the water supply becoming impure, typhoid fever broke out, and we lost several men one after another. About the same time another cause began to operate in reducing our ranks, for we had a smart experience of the working out of the short service system, and a great many time-expired men, but young soldiers, left us to join the Reserve. The result was the 14th became very short-handed, and there were considerably more horses in the stables than men in the barracks. In consequence of this, Government offered a bounty of one hundred and twenty *Halli Sicca* rupees to the time-expired men to extend their service in India for another year, and twelve months afterwards a further bounty of eighty rupees to extend for two years.

The mention of the *Halli Sicca* rupee reminds me of the peculiarity of the Hyderabad coinage, and the way my boy Harry worked it to my advantage. There were only two coins current at Bolaram, the *Halli Sicca* rupee (worth thirteen annas and eight pie, or about an eighth less than the ordinary East Indian rupee), and a copper coin called a *dub,* both bearing the Nizam's inscription. Each rupee was worth from seventy-six to ninety-six dubs, the exchange varying daily in the Hyderabad bazaar, but in the British cantonment the rate was fixed, and all payments made and accepted at the rate of seventy-nine dubs to the rupee.

Harry, who was as sharp as a knife, soon found out the fluctuations that ruled at Hyderabad, which was only nine miles distant, and coming to me one day, said, if I would trust him, he would make some money for me. Faith in the lad I always had, for he had long been in entire charge of my bungalow and effects, and so I had no hesitation in giving him a chance to exhibit his financial ability. It was worked in this way. I had large payments to make to native followers, whose wages were small, and exhausted a large amount of copper coin. Their money was drawn in silver, and directly I received it, I gave Harry five hundred rupees and sent him off in a palanquin to Hyderabad bazaar, where he changed the silver at the rate of the day which might be anything up to ninety-six dubs the rupee. Taking ninety as an example, I gained eleven dubs in each rupee, as I only paid out at the rate of seventy-nine, and thus, thanks to Harry, I made a profit of seventy rupees on my five hundred, without robbing anyone, and only the cost of a palanquin to defray.

Around my bungalow at Bolaram was a large piece of waste ground, and being fond of gardening, I obtained permission to take up an acre of it. Having plenty of native labour at my command, I soon had it encircled by a mud wall, and the ground dug up for cultivation, and when the rains burst it was green and beautiful with flowers and vegetables. In time I filled it with all sorts of strange pets, such as frogs, armadillos, chameleons, mungooses, and the like, and penned off a portion in which I kept ducks, rabbits, pigeons, and fowls. I also built a stable for a couple of ponies that drew my tonga or dog-cart. The verandah of my bungalow I turned into a sort of open-air conservatory, and soon had it filled with rare ferns, which I found amongst the rocky hills during my shooting expeditions. And it came to be a great joke against me whenever I returned from one of these excursions, to ask me, not what game I had bagged, but what "blooming green stuff" I had brought back. Harry was of great help to me in all this, for he always entered heart and soul into any hobby I took up, and made believe to appreciate every new botanical specimen with the air of a connoisseur in such things. My garden soon encouraged other men to go in for reclaiming ground, and in tune the road down to Moulali Rocks was turned into a veritable paradise in comparison to what it had been before.

I have mentioned my shooting expeditions, and I may here take the opportunity of describing them more particularly. I was now one of the oldest non-commissioned officers in the regiment, and except at the beginning or end of a month, could always depend upon a week or ten days' leave. I often went out for long trips with Harry, each of us mounted on a pony, and with a couple of coolies carrying the bedding and cooking-pots. We generally made for a place at the foot of some wild hills, about twenty-eight miles distant, where tiger, bear, panther, and sambar, and cheetul-deer abounded. Here I encamped out under a tree, slinging up a blanket in hammock fashion to sleep in, and making this my headquarters, I sallied out every day for sport. During these shooting expeditions I bagged at various times three tigers, several panthers and cheetahs, and I cannot record how many deer. In fact, I enjoyed sport that was fit for a prince.

There were a great number of Europeans in the Nizam's employ, and I made the acquaintance of many of them during my stay at Bolaram. The English coachman, who tooled the Nizam's team, came from Shepherd's Bush, and enjoyed an income of six hundred a year—with pickings. The head groom was a Frenchman, and had charge of the magnificent marble stables, containing a stud of horses it would be difficult to duplicate. Another Englishman was in charge of the kennels, which were filled with valuable dogs of every breed, notably some splendid greyhounds and bull-terriers. But the individual I was best acquainted with was a half-bred Italian, who had charge of the Nizam's palaces, and the hundreds of natives employed in them. He and I became very friendly, and through his kindness I was able to visit many parts of Hyderabad (often disguised in native dress) where Europeans of much higher position could never have penetrated except by favour of this Italian. The signor took me over several of the palaces, and it was remarkable to see the grandeur of the buildings and the luxury of the furniture, but, I think, even more remarkable to find, side by side with costly and beautiful objects of art, the most tawdry and common articles, such as no Englishman of the middle classes would have admitted into his house. Thus I remember observing in one grand reception room a fabulously large chandelier that might have hung side by side with the one in Covent Garden Theatre, and next to it a miserable trumpery gas pendant such as one would only expect to find in the bar-parlour of some common public-house.

The signor introduced me to the celebrated mines of Golconda, or, to be more literal in describing them, to the caves and vaults. Here were hoarded the enormous treasures of the Nizam; boxes filled to the brim with gold, jewels literally in heaps, and costly articles of every description, The caves were situated in a fortress, which was closely guarded, and I shall never forget his taking me up to a huge chest full of gold coins, and telling me to plunge my arms into it as deep as they could go, so that I might be able to say I had bathed in gold! Another remarkable place I saw was the courtyard of the Nizam's harem, guarded by women dressed and drilled like Sepoys, each carrying a musket, and conducting herself like a male soldier.

The European employees in the Nizam's service, the greater portion of whom were officers in his army, lived in a colony of their own at Chudderghat, a mile from Hyderabad. I cannot say very much for them, and they were considered outcasts from regular European society, many of them being cashiered officers and the like. The majority had intermarried with the natives, whilst others kept harems and adopted the native style of living. They seemed to have plenty of money, keeping carriages and living in luxuriously-furnished houses. But in spite of this there was something which warned a man off, and it was this feeling that influenced me in refusing a very good offer I received of the post of riding-master to the Nizam's cavalry. There were many of my friends who thought me foolish to let the chance pass, but its acceptance would have planted me in the Chudderghat colony, and I was not going there at any price.

When the cold weather came round there was a grand camp of exercise ordered by General Roberts, and in the sham fights which took place he frequently acted as umpire. One of these, an especially big affair, I shall long remember. The troops were divided into two forces, and the ground selected for the operations was about four days' march from Hyderabad, and in the middle of an open but well wooded country, which I knew very well from having shot over it. One army was supposed to be attacking Hyderabad, and the other trying to force its way through and take the town. Every morning at seven o'clock a gun was fired as a signal to commence operations, and neither party could begin work till it sounded.

On the particular occasion I am referring to, my troop was selected for scouting work with the attacking force, and plenty of galloping we had. After two or three days' marching and manoeuvring, the two armies drew up for the final issue, and the result depended entirely upon the defending division receiving or failing to receive (imaginary) reinforcements by rail from Hyderabad. Our object therefore was to cut the line of railway at the junction just outside the city. But this was thirty miles off, and the accomplishment of the task was not considered possible, although, as a sort of forlorn hope, my troop was ordered to attempt it.

Directly the seven o'clock gun sounded we started for the place, and as I had a knowledge of the country I was ordered to lead the way. I took the troop, by a short cut, straight across the country at a swinging canter, and soon after eleven o'clock we had accomplished our object and posted a written notice—"Line cut," on the telegraph pole.

It was now necessary to inform the umpire of this important factor in the day's fight, and I was ordered to carry the message, which was written and verified by my officer. I started at half-past eleven, and lost no time in making my way to the place where the battle was raging, guided by the firing. Galloping up to General Roberts, who was on an eminence overlooking the two armies, who had now come to close quarters, I handed him my captain's message at two o'clock. He was surprised at receiving the intelligence, and consulting his watch, reckoned the time. He then questioned me very closely, and could hardly believe that I had ridden over fifty miles since seven o'clock that morning. But he acted on the contents of the message (which was certified as correct by my captain when he made his report that evening), and sounded the order to "Cease fire," awarding the victory to the attacking force, on the grounds that the defending division had not been reinforced owing to the cutting of the railway line, and were in consequence numerically overpowered. He then called me up again and further questioned me as to how I had accomplished the ride. I explained that I had shot over the ground and knew every turn of the valleys and every bend of the hills, and had consequently been able to lead my troop the quickest way. This seemed to satisfy him, and he spoke to me very kindly, and when in reply to another question I assured him I had ridden the same horse the whole way, he was pleased to observe that if the 14th Hussars possessed many men and horses of the same calibre, he would take good care to have some about him in the future. Nor was this an idle remark, for I may mention that my troop had nearly always the good fortune to be detached as advanced scouts during the rest of the time the manoeuvres lasted; and we must have galloped many hundreds of miles under His Excellency's orders.

    The horse I rode was "C-3," a bay Waler about six years old, standing 15-2½, showing a deal of blood, and possessed of splendid stamina. He proved himself a worthy successor to poor old Neddy, who found his grave in the quicksands of the river near Ladysmith. I was often allowed to ride the horse out on survey work, which kept him in splendid training. and to this I attributed his powers of resisting an Indian sun, which affects the endurance of so many Walers. I think there were few horses of his class in India who could touch him. There was another horse in the regiment, which so resembled him in colour and build that I often thought that they must be own brothers. He was taken out of the ranks by Major H——, and made into his charger; and on his speed and jumping capabilities being discovered, put into training, and under the name of Dick Turpin became famous on the Indian turf, and showed a clean pair of heels to every steeplechaser in India between 1880 and 1883.

India at this time enjoyed a period of universal peace, and many officers, seeing no chance of active service, applied for furlough. Amongst them was Colonel K——, who went home to England, and the command of the regiment devolved upon Colonel M——. This officer was an enthusiastic lover of horses and a fine judge of them. He had scarce an equal as a cross-country rider, was passionately fond of sport of all description, and where horses were concerned, knew how to bring out their perfections in stables, on the parade ground, and on the steeplechase course. He was very popular with all ranks, and under him the regiment lost none of the good reputation it had previously gained.

Colonel M—— was always devising something interesting or amusing in which horses played a prominent part. For instance, he started a horse-show at Secunderabad, with classes for Walers, Arabs, and country-breds, the competition being open to all European and native regiments. On this occasion I had the proud satisfaction of leading up to the lady who distributed the awards a fine old Persian horse, No. "C-52," aged eighteen years, to be decorated with the red rosette, which denoted that he had won the first prize in his class for troop-horses.

Colonel M—— also organised several steeplechases, always riding in them himself; and in one of these, when mounted on his favourite black mare, Nora, she unaccountably blundered at the first obstacle and fell, rolling over her rider. He was up again in five seconds, and remounting without help, I pelted after the field, and won a slashing race by a head. As he was riding to the weighing-scales he fainted, and fell from his saddle into the arms of one of our men; and when the doctor came up to attend him, it was found his arm and collar-bone were broken. This gallant officer, when Colonel K—— rejoined us in 1884, carried away with him the good wishes of every man in the 14th Hussars.

I do not know that I have much to say about the rest of my soldiering at Bolaram, beyond what I have recorded. Nothing in any way exciting occurred, and I wish to avoid going over ground I have traversed before. The course of regimental history progressed smoothly. Old hands, time expired, bade us goodbye, and went home. Now drafts reached us, and had to be drilled into order. The hot weather, with its enforced idleness, consumed a slice of each year, and the colder months saw us busy in camps of exercise, or practising on the parade-ground our usual drills and field-day performances. The temperance movement made a great stride amongst the men, and in like ratio crime decreased and things went smoothly.

But now and again the drums were muffled, and the costly funeral-pall taken out of its linen wrapper, for Death tapped at the barrack-room door, and took away many a good soldier; and there are graves in that distant Indian cemetery, besides which I even now find my memory pausing, as I recall a dead comrade's face, and think of the merry smiles I saw upon it once, and the happy days we passed together! It was a sickly station, and there were many who lost the number of their mess, and passed away, feet foremost, from our midst. Here today and gone tomorrow, their eyes closed, and their ears dumb, never to open or listen again, until the last *reveillé* shall summon them to the Grand Review on the Judgement Day.

★ ★ ★ ★

Although I have not mentioned anything about my little daughter, it must not be imagined that I had in any way lost touch of her in England. She was living with her aunt, and the weekly letters I received constituted my greatest delight, as the old black postman knew who brought them to me, and got many a tip for it. As time went by, and I heard more and more about her, and her pretty, childish ways, and the little homely descriptions of her sayings and doings, a great longing came over me to see her again. This was brought to a crisis by a letter written by herself, enclosing a photograph. In this she reminded me that my answer would reach her within a few days of her seventh birthday; and this set me musing what a big girl she was growing. With this my longing to see her increased to such a degree that I almost wished I could get a go of fever, so that I might be invalided home; for, otherwise, there was no chance of my returning to England until the regiment went there in the ordinary course in about two years. Seeing it was no good wishing for what I could not have, I endeavoured, but with ill success, to put the longing from me.

It is strange how things happen, for now, just as I had overcome my feelings, and was beginning to get settled again, Colonel K—— sent for me one day, and startled me by asking if I would like to go to England. He then went on to explain that the sergeant-major at the depôt at Canterbury was going to leave the Service, and, if I desired, he would send me home to fill the post. But, he added, he knew how fond I was of my troop and my horses, and so he wished me to think the matter over well before deciding, and give him my answer the next day.

Now that the chance of going home was in my grasp, I found it much more difficult to accept it than I should have believed possible a month before. I loved my horses, every one of them, and so I did my troop; and then there were the dogs, and the pigeons, and the armadillos, and the mungooses, and the garden, and Harry! Somehow, I found I had sort of grown into this life I had lived so long; and as I sat in my bungalow that evening, pulling away desperately at my pipe, and trying to make up my mind, I was forced to confess it was not all joy going home. But when I drew out my little girl's letter and her photograph, the Indian life seemed to fade away like a passing dream, whose delight we are content to lose, and I could not but acknowledge there was only one thing that could sway my decision. Everything went tumbling down before the crooked lines and simple sentences of her letter, which conveyed to me my marching orders home

The next morning I told Colonel K—— I would gladly accept his kind offer, and my name was placed in orders to proceed with a battery of artillery which was about to start by rail for Bombay, to embark for England. But there was so much to be done in settling up, that I could not join it in time, and it left without me. Here again my old kind luck followed me, and that which I looked upon as an unfortunate and unhappy delay proved just the opposite. For on the way to Poonah, cholera broke out amongst the men of this battery, and they lost a cruel number by death. Who knows, if I had been with them, but that the call might have come to me?

I followed a week later. It does not become me to say much about my going away. But it was a hard thing bidding goodbye to my troop, and to the regiment I had spent the spring and summer of my life with. They were very kind to me, and Heaven is my witness that when the last moment came their goodness almost broke me down, and made me wish to change my mind, and stop with them. Of course the greater part of the regiment were new hands, but there were seventy-four left, old friends and tried, who had followed the big drum to the railway station at Colchester, eight years previously; and most, if not all of these, and many more, were at the railway station to bid me goodbye.

Of course, Harry was there too. Harry, with the tears streaming out of his big brown eyes, and his knees on the platform, and his:

"Master, master, take me! No food want. No pay want. Nothing want. Only Master take me with him."

But "Master" couldn't. And the last thing I saw through misty eyes, as I leant out of the carriage window, and waved my hand in sad farewell, was Harry, with his turban off and his long hair streaming in the wind, tearing down the line after the train!

Chapter 22

"Home, Sweet Home"

I had charge of a few details for the railway journey and we travelled in the usual way, halting by day and proceeding by night, until we reached Poonah. Here I found the battery of artillery which I was to have accompanied, isolated in a quarantine camp. They had lost a number of fine well-seasoned men who had completed their term of service, and were looking forward, poor fellows, to the "home, sweet home" they were never to see again. As I cast my eyes towards their tents in the distance, solitary and remote from all habitations, whither no man might go and whence no man might come, it suggested many grave and solemn thoughts to my mind. That afternoon I found my way to the cemetery which I had visited on my first arrival here from England, and, standing before the monument erected to those who had served in the 14th Hussars, reading the names upon it, my mind wandered to that isolated camp where Death had claimed so many victims, and the "Many a slip" was brought forcibly to my mind.

From Poonah we proceeded to Deolali, a name that stinks in many nostrils. Here there is a permanent resting-camp for all reliefs proceeding to Bengal and Upper India, and for details such as time-expired, invalids, prisoners, and insane, who have to collect here to get their accounts made up and all claims against the Indian Government adjusted before sailing for England.

I reported myself on arriving, and found I should have to wait a fortnight for a troopship. Of course I chafed at the delay, but my disappointment and trouble were light compared to those of many of the poor invalids, who, shattered with fever, or suffering from other dangerous complaints, counted the long hot hours, and wondered whether they could hold out for another fortnight. Nor was their anxiety idle, as the tombstones in the large Deolali cemetery could prove. For many and many a sick soldier, after days of agonising torture, jolting in a train to this depôt, has reached it with the hope that the sea-voyage which was to give him new life and health was within his grasp, but only to find there was a week or a fortnight to wait, and during that fatal period of delay, his bones, like those of countless other comrades, have been laid after all in Indian soil.

I paid a visit to the Deolali cemetery one day, and wandering round it came presently to some headstones erected to men of the 14th Hussars who had been buried here and whose graves I was in search of. Amongst them was one which affords a pathetic illustration of what I have written above. It bore two names: those of Michael Kelly and his wife Mary. Kelly was Colonel K——'s batman, and at Bangalore his wife's health had broken down, and she was ordered home by the doctor. But Kelly could not accompany her and so the poor woman had to go to Deolali by herself. Then came the fatal delay before embarking, and there she died and was buried. The next trooping season her husband, now time-expired, came to the camp on his way home. He had to wait too, and every day he paid a long visit to his wife's grave. One evening he failed to answer his name at roll-call A search party was sent out, and went first to the cemetery, which poor Kelly was known to haunt, and there they found him, lying dead across his wife's grave.

There were at Deolali men from almost every regiment in India, and amongst them some from the 8th Hussars, which naturally reminded me of my old chum, Bill Thompson. I made enquiries as to the exact place and date of his death, but the men I applied to for information were all short-service soldiers, and could not remember any non-commissioned officer dying about the time I referred to. But one of them remarked that there was an old troop-sergeant-major of the same name still living, who had left Deolali the day before I arrived, having sailed in the last troopship, and that "Old Bill," as they called him, was going home to take charge of the depôt of the 8th Hussars, at Canterbury. Hearing this, I questioned the men closely as to the sergeant-major's service and personal appearance, and their replies left not a doubt in my mind that it was my old chum, alive and well after all!

At last the fortnight drew to a close, and the troopship parade was ordered, when fifteen hundred men—time-expired and mostly short-service—and details of officers, ladies, women, children, insanes, and prisoners made up a total of two thousand souls. On this parade I was surprised to hear the commandant of the depôt call out my name and tell me I was appointed regimental-sergeant-major to this body of men till they reached England. This was an unexpected honour, and it not only carried extra pay, but, what was much better, warrant officer's accommodation on board, which ensured my comfort during the voyage.

All being ready we proceeded to Bombay in special trains, and embarked upon my old acquaintance, H.M.S. *Euphrates*. My hands were soon full of work attending to my multifarious duties, and only those who have seen a homeward-bound trooper fill up can form any idea of the medley of human beings that goes on board. Nor is there any lack of bird and animal life, for passes are freely granted for the men's pets, and dogs, monkeys, mungooses, and hundreds of birds, chiefly parrots, are shipped. We had but one horse on board, but he was a representative worthy of his race, for he had seen much active service, and been for twenty years the charger of the colonel in command of the troops. The old horse was now going home to enjoy a well-earned repose in a paddock on his master's estate, and I need hardly say, when the veteran's history became known he was at once made the principal pet on board.

We had a pleasant voyage home, with nothing exciting except a little false alarm at Suez that we were to be landed to join in the fighting that was then going on in Egypt. This was the result of a mistake, an over-zealous junior officer on board having volunteered the service of his men, by telegraph from Bombay, without consulting the colonel; he eventually suffered very severely for his indiscreet energy.

It is customary on all troopships for the captain to make an inspection round once a week, on which occasion he is accompanied by all the executive staff, naval and military, and every hole and corner of the ship is visited. It was my duty on these occasions to follow the colonel and adjutant, and I think a description of one of them will be interesting.

The captain began at the saloon, where every door entering the officers' and ladies' cabins was thrown wide open. He then proceeded along the troop decks to the sailors' quarters, the married women's quarters, the sick bay, the prisons, and the cells set apart for the insanes. In these latter were encountered some very sad sights. There were two or three raving madmen, who had to be kept in padded cells, and others who were dangerous to themselves and required to be closely watched. Of these the sad condition of two in particular had a great effect on me. One, a fine, handsome young soldier, suffered from a delusion that he could eat nothing, and refused all food. Two men were told off to look after him, and on the captain entering the cell he asked how their patient was getting on, and they answered there was no improvement. Whereupon the captain turned round and began to speak very kindly to the insane, who answered his questions rationally enough in a way, for he said he was offered plenty of everything, "But," putting his hand to his throat, "it won't go down here, sir."

"Oh, but you must force it to," observed the captain encouragingly. "If you don't eat you'll die, and Her Majesty cannot afford to loose a smart young soldier like you. Come now, don't you think you could fancy a little bit of chicken?"

"No, sir, thank you kindly; it wouldn't go down here," and the hand went up again to the throat with the usual gesture.

"Well, a glass of porter, then. You could slip that down, I'm sure."

"No, sir. Nothing will pass."

"Nonsense, nonsense!" answered the captain kindly. "Where there's a will there's a way. And I tell you what, I'll send you down a bottle of champagne, and you shall drink the Queen's health." And he turned round and gave orders to the master-at-arms to see that everything he had suggested was provided from the saloon table.

But all the patient said was, "Thank you kindly, sir; but it won't go down—it won't go down here." And we left him with his hand on his throat, and a look of hopeless resignation on his face.

As the captain entered the door of the next cell the insane inmate arose and stood at attention, more from force of military habit than from any intended respect. He was a tall, fine-looking infantryman, dressed in uniform kept spotlessly clean—an unusual thing with men mentally afflicted. His forehead was broad and lofty, and his face intellectual, but white and haggard, and he wore a long beard heavily streaked with grey. But for the vacant look of his large listless eyes one could not have suspected he was insane. He took no notice of the few kindly words addressed him by the captain, nor seemed to hear when the attendants explained that the religious melancholia he suffered from was no better, for he stood bolt upright, immovable and unmoved. But as we were about to pass out, suddenly his lips opened, and in a loud sonorous tone of voice he began to recite, "I am the Resurrection and the Life."

The sound of his voice in the quiet between decks, and the solemn words he spoke, had an extraordinary effect upon all. The captain stopped, and then, with the fine impulse of human sympathy, his hand moved to his cap and he uncovered his head. All followed his example. And there we stood, reverently listening while the poor mad soldier went through the burial service for the dead, and at its conclusion, delivered an extempore but eloquent homily on death. Then he gave the blessing, and bowing in a grave but dignified manner, turned round and retreated to the further corner of his cell.

Silently, and with his head still uncovered, the captain led the way out of the place, and we all followed with as reverent a mien as if we had been leaving a church. And oftentimes to this very day, when my thoughts chance to wander back to that strange service, spoken by the insane to the sane, the pathetic figure of that poor private in his padded cell rises before my eyes, and I seem to hear his deep sonorous voice crying out in tragic tones:

"I am the Resurrection and the Life."

In due time we had passed the Straits of Gibraltar and crossed the Bay of Biscay, and then came a period of expectation and impatience until, on the thirtieth day after leaving Bombay, we found ourselves late one clear, cold February evening gliding up the Solent.

They were English trees and meadows that we saw, and English homesteads and village steeples on either side. Glad sights for sore eyes! We who had been so long absent in foreign climes could scarcely realise that we were home at last! And just as the roofs of Portsmouth city reddened in the evening sun, the anchor dived down and the *Euphrates* took up her station at Spithead. It was too late that night to go into harbour, but a bag of letters came on board, amongst them one for me, conveying the news that my sister-in-law would bring my daughter to meet me on landing.

Early the next morning the anchor was weighed, and with a graceful sweep the huge white trooper entered the narrow harbour mouth and steamed slowly up to the jetty amidst the ringing cheers of all on board, and when the gates were opened the ship was regularly stormed by a crowd of people. I stood on the high deck anxiously scanning the stream of faces thronging up the gangway, hoping to see my daughter. But I was soon sent for by the adjutant to attend to the details of the landing of the troops, and dragged myself away to duty, with a feeling of keen disappointment, increased by seeing the happy reunions taking place on every side.

I set to work at once disembarking the women and children, and handing them over to Miss Robinson's agents, who took them to a shelter close by and warmed them with hot tea and coffee. Then came the turn of the colonel's charger, and hundreds of the men pressed forward to give him a parting pat, which the grand old warrior took quite unconcernedly, as he cocked his ears like a colt, and walked proudly down the gangway. Batches after batches of men followed and were marched in turn to the special trains waiting to convey them to their several destinations. As I was busy over this work a civilian came to me, and asking my name, told me there was a lady making inquiries for me.

"Has she a little girl with her?" I asked eagerly.

"She has; and a fine one, too," came the answer. With that he led me to the side of the ship and pointed out one of the shelters near which he had last seen her; "and there she stands now," he added, as he directed my attention to a particular spot.

Over the ship's side I went in a moment, and making my way more energetically than politely through the crowd, I soon heard my daughter calling out to me.

It wasn't long before I had her in my arms, and then, followed by her aunt, I made my way back to the ship, feeling prouder and happier at that moment than I had been for many a long day. As I carried May aboard, the master-at-arms came up to me with a kindly greeting, and I cried out to him, all a-joy, "See, what's come to meet me!" and it pleased me not a little to hear him answer, "Well, Sergeant-Major, you ought to be the proudest man that's come home aboard this ship!"

When I had got nearly all the troops ashore there came a hitch. Some gunners had been embarked at the last moment, and there had been some muddle over it, for no arrangements were made for their landing. There was nothing to do but to telegraph for instructions, which meant twelve hours' delay. As it was the ship-sergeant-major's duty to see all the troops clear, and the messing kit returned to store, I had to wait on board. But my sister-in-law was obliged to return home that evening, so I was reluctantly compelled to let my daughter go with her, though not without promising that as soon as I had reported myself at Canterbury, I would get a month's leave and spend the most of it with her.

I had heard a good deal of Miss Robinson's kindness and philanthropy to soldiers and their families, and I determined to experience it that evening myself. So I spent the night at her Home, and never was I more comfortably and cleanly housed, or better fed, than in this institution which owes its existence to the good, benevolent lady who is known throughout the British army as *The Soldier's Friend*.

By noon the next day I had settled all details and was free to leave the *Euphrates*. The colonel and adjutant wished me a pleasant good-bye, and gave me a souvenir to remind me of the voyage, which I value very highly. I then started by train for Canterbury, and after a bitterly cold journey arrived at the Cathedral city late in the afternoon, my mind full of pleasurable anticipation of meeting my old chum, Bill Thompson. But to my disappointment I found he was away on duty, and not expected back till the following day.

The next morning I went before Colonel Le Q———, the commandant at Canterbury, and then looked over the depôt of my regiment, and was pretty busy all day long. Towards evening I walked over to the sergeants' mess, and there the first man to meet me was old Bill Thompson. I need not say his greeting was a most hearty one, and right glad we were to renew the friendship of old days. We sat smoking and chatting till the early hours of the morning warned us to be off to bed. It turned out that after his recovery from his serious illness he had written me several letters, none of which reached me, probably owing to the black boys at the hospital destroying them in order to steal the stamps. Having received no reply from me, but only heard that I had left my regiment (when I joined the commissariat), he came to the conclusion that I was dead. But now, after all, we were both alive and well, and for the first time in our careers soldiering side by side, as we had intended doing twenty years previously, when we began together. Perhaps all things worked for the best, for had we been in the same regiment, one might have been up and the other down, whilst here we met on equal ground, each in a similar position and with equal rank; for Sergeant-Major Thompson was in charge of the depôt of the 8th Hussars, and I held the same post in connection with the 14th.

The sergeant-major whom I relieved being in no hurry to go away for a month, I obtained leave for that period, and went to the little village where my daughter resided with her aunt. Here I spent three happy weeks, and then went to Hammersmith to see my old mother. She was living in the same house, and I found her much aged, but as proud of me as ever, and delighted beyond words with all the things I had brought home from India for her. There were many of my old school-fellows, too—grown-up men now, with wives and families of their own—with whom I had pleasant meetings. But though they were much altered, Hammersmith itself was more so, for streets and streets of houses had swallowed up the green fields around St. John's church, and hardly a landmark remained to remind me of the scenes of my boyhood.

On the termination of my leave I returned to Canterbury to take up the duties of my new appointment. The barracks here covered nearly half a mile in length, a large portion being allotted to the cavalry. But owing to the short-service system and to the city being the depôt for all the cavalry regiments abroad, the number of recruits quartered in it was generally in excess of the accommodation, and we had to find room for some in the artillery and infantry barracks.

At this time there were ten cavalry depôts established there, and as each trooping season drew on, the recruits increased until they reached the total of between two and three thousand. There was, in addition, a large riding establishment, in which were collected representatives from every cavalry regiment in the Service, undergoing special instruction, and also a great number of senior non-commissioned officers perfecting themselves and awaiting commissions as riding-masters, for which they had been recommended.

The commandant of the cavalry depôt was Colonel Le Q——, who, in his fine Lancer uniform, looked what he was, one of the smartest cavalry officers in the army. He had great tact, and was kind and considerate to all, but none the less a strict disciplinarian, and it was wonderful to observe how he managed the enormous body of young lads who were collected here to be taught the first rudiments of soldiering, and drilled into shape before being sent to their various corps.

With each regimental depôt there were only two officers, and as they generally took leave turn and turn about during their service at Canterbury, the brunt of the work, in many instances, fell upon the sergeant-major, who had seldom more than two or three sergeants under him. Notwithstanding this, it was remarkable how smoothly everything went, and how little crime there was. The credit of this was due in the chief degree to Colonel Le Q—— and the system he adopted, which was to teach discipline by kindness, firmness, and example, and not to ram it down the throats of young lads, in the hope that it would do some good, like medicine, as soon as it was swallowed. To carry out this system a few old soldiers of proved good character were always kept at home at the depôt, and scattered amongst the recruits, being made to understand that their example was relied on to give a tone to the young hands; and these nearly always proved worthy of the trust, and conducted themselves in a way that conduced to the result desired.

When I took over charge I found my depôt contained three hundred and ten men, and if fifteen non-commissioned officers and old soldiers had been taken out, the average service of the remainder would have been under four months. For as soon as a recruit got knocked into shape a bit, he was shipped out each trooping season to join the regiment in India, and it was a very rare case if any individual remained twelve months at the depôt. My first work on joining, was to get together a draft of one hundred and fifty men to send out to Bolaram by the last trooper of the season.

There was a great deal to be done, for every man's kit had to be made up and his accounts settled before he left the depôt. Moreover, during the last few days in England, there used to be some rare games going on amongst the lads, who held it a duty to indulge in a final spree, knowing there was not much danger of punishment. The wrecking of the barrack rooms was not infrequent, and their destructive propensities would occasionally find an object in some public-house in the town, whose proprietor had made himself obnoxious. The draft I was sending out behaved themselves rather better than the average, and did not give much trouble. In due course they were paraded in the barrack-square to receive a few last words from Colonel Le Q——. They then marched to the railway station, headed by the band, and for my part I must say I was thankful to get them all off safely; for I was not yet settled down to my post, and a stranger at such a work is at a disadvantage. With their departure I felt my regular experience of depôt life was beginning.

Chapter 23
Depôt Life

After the despatch of my first draft, I began to look about me and see what sort of material I had left, and make preparations to receive new recruits. These shortly arrived in such numbers at Canterbury that it was found necessary to increase the barrack accommodation, and the splendid green was cut up by the erection of new permanent buildings and temporary huts, and later on by many tents pitched during the summer.

The sergeants' mess at Canterbury was a very fine one. The members consisted of the sergeant-majors and sergeants of the depôt and riding establishment, most of the latter being men awaiting commissions as riding masters, and it not infrequently happened that one of them took his breakfast in our mess as a non-commissioned officer, and then, the *Gazette* having come to hand, found himself in orders and lunched in the officers' mess. On such occasions, Colonel Le Q—— made it a point to be the first to publicly congratulate the new officer, whom he invited to be his guest at lunch. But if the lucky individual had got into comfortable quarters, he left equally comfortable ones behind, for the cavalry sergeants' mess at Canterbury is, perhaps, the finest in the Service. It is most luxuriously fitted, and on its walls and in its plate-chest are several very handsome presentation articles from non-commissioned officers who have passed through it on their way to a commission.

And so I found the place where I expected to finish my soldiering a very pleasant one, and, in addition to its own advantages, I had my old chum, Sergeant-Major Thompson next to me, and my daughter within easy distance; whilst the sights and amusements of London could be reached in an hour, and leave and money were plentiful.

The soldiering itself was very different to what it had been in the regiment. The ranks were filled with boys—not the "bhoys" Colonel K—— was fond of apostrophising, but smooth-faced, thoughtless lads, who wanted a schoolmaster rather than a sergeant-instructor. As for the horses, in India we often had spare ones in the stables, but here there were some four recruits to each horse's leg, for the entire stud at our depôt only numbered twenty-two. Whatever other duty was shirked, it was more difficulty to keep the lads out of the stables than in them, and I had to quell more squabbles over grooming kit than anything else.

It might be considered with such a lot of young, thoughtless lads collected together the canteen would thrive. But this was not the case; although the majority of the recruits had each four or five shillings to draw every week. As a fact, the crime of *drunk* was a rare one, and instead of looking in the canteen for a "schemer," I would seek for him in the library, where he was generally to be found assuaging his thirst for knowledge and liquor with magazines and coffee.

In short, the lads were sober, eager, willing, and, take them for all in all, good stuff for soldiers. And, moreover, there were lots of them. So popular was the 14th, that we never suffered from a lack of recruits, and were often obliged, though sorely against our will, to transfer batches of newly-joined men to other regimental depôts. But this was regarded as a great hardship by those who had enlisted for the "Young Jocks," and already learnt what *esprit-de-corps* meant. For it often surprised me to discover that youngsters, who had only been three months at Canterbury, knew everything about the regiment and its traditions, and could quote you, not only the Peninsular battles inscribed upon its colours, but also the Persian, Punjab, and Central Indian victories; aye, and Chillianwallah, too, about which they were not only ready to argue, but double their fists and fight if any recruit of another depôt, in the heat of discussion, attempted to throw the old unjust slur in their teeth.

After my first draft had sailed, I had upwards of one hundred and fifty men left. There were two officers in command, but one or the other was always away on leave. Sergeants I had four on paper, but one was in the riding establishment, a second detached to the school of musketry at Hythe, a third at Aldershot, and only the fourth remained for duty at the depôt. But he was a rattling good one, and after making a few of the smartest recruits lance-jacks, we were able to rub along very well.

There were about four or five field-days a year, generally inspections, and these were the only occasions on which I was mounted, and with a foot parade now and again, comprised all that was to be done in the way of drill. My chief duties were to receive the recruits as they arrived, look after their discipline off parade, keep an eye on the condition of their arms, clothes, and quarters, and see that they received proper food, and that their accounts were in order. This, with the supervision of the horses, kept my time fully occupied. The horses, however, had their share of soldiering, for being ridden by successive batches of recruits every day, they could go through the rides much better without their riders than with them.

The recruits might be, broadly speaking, divided into three classes. The first, which I will call Class A, consisted of young fellows, who enlisted for the pure love of soldiering, and certainly made the best soldiers. Those who were driven by their necessities, or force of circumstances, composed Class B. They were much older, as a body, than the recruits in the former class, and many were dissatisfied fellows who had a sort of general grudge against the army because they had drifted into it; but not infrequently there were good men to be found amongst them. Class C was the least numerous, and was made up of men who looked upon enlisting as a sort of trade. It was their profession to enter a regiment, get their kit, sell it, and then desert, and carry on the same game over and over again until caught. I have heard such men boast that they had been in eight or nine regiments before their fraudulent career was cut short. But even in Class C there were some honourable exceptions, for some were men who fraudulently enlisted and yet without disgrace. These were short-service soldiers, who had completed their eight years' service with the colours, and been sent against their will to the Reserve; and young fellows invalided but who, loving the Service, managed after a bit to scrape through the medical, and joined another regiment under an assumed name. The re-enlistment, or attempted re-enlistment of men from the reserve is, I think, one of the greatest arguments against the short service system. For by the very nature of their act, and the risk which they know it involves, these men prove their real love for a soldiering life. They are, indeed, in my humble opinion, the very men who ought to be encouraged to serve on, instead of being forced to retire into inactivity before they have reached the early prime of life, and just when they have become efficient cavalry soldiers. Nor could any other employer of labour, except Government, command the services of a man in a particular profession for twelve years and then dismiss him with a prohibition from following it again.

On the whole, the class of recruits I received at the 14th Hussar depôt was very good, and I had little or no trouble with them. There was a leaven of educated young fellows, whose parents were well off, and whose one idea in enlisting was to obtain a commission—a phantom prize dangled before their eyes in the vast majority of cases. Then there were a few wild and erratic individuals, who now and then startled the depôt by some devilment more daring than usual. But the great bulk of the recruits were steady, well-conducted lads, who needed leading, not driving, to make into good soldiers.

I have mentioned how little they were addicted to drinking, and the following incident will bear this out. Every regiment in the British army has an honorary colonel, and ours was a fine old retired cavalry officer, named General Thompson. He took a great deal of interest in the doings of the 14th Hussars, and whilst they were in India always visited their depôt at Canterbury once a year. In conformity with this custom, he came down to see us one day, soon after I had taken charge, and when he had walked round the stables, came to a halt close to the barrack-room, where the men were at dinner. He was a kindly officer of the old school, upwards of eighty years of age, and expressed himself very much pleased at all he had seen. Then he said there was something he wished to do, namely, to give the men a little treat to remember his visit. And he asked me what I suggested. I thought for a moment, and then remembering that Canterbury fair was in full swing, and the lads had thoroughly enjoyed a half-holiday the day before, I said that I thought nothing would please them better than another.

"Pooh-pooh, Sergeant-Major!" cried the old general, cutting me short. "It is the soldiers I am speaking of—not the children."

"Well, sir," I answered, "you asked me what would please the soldiers best, and I have told you."

"What!" he cried, "do you mean to say it is the *soldiers* who would like a half-holiday to go to the fair?"

"That's it, sir—the soldiers."

"Dear me!" he answered, all taken aback; "in my time they have looked for a quart of beer each, and that was what I made sure you would ask for."

"Well, sir," I said, "it's for you to give whatever you choose. But if you give the lads a quart of beer each, nine out of ten won't drink it, and the remainder will be in the guard-room for *drunk*."

General Thompson looked fairly surprised, until I ventured to say:

"Here is Colonel Le Q—— coming across the green, sir. If you will get the afternoon's leave granted, I am sure you will be satisfied by hearing how the men receive the news."

The request was immediately made, and, of course, granted, and the barrack being quite close, I took a few steps forward, and called out:

"No drill this afternoon, and leave for all, on account of the general's visit."

In an instant the lads responded with a loud shout of pleasure, which increased into three cheers for the general. The old gentleman was thoroughly satisfied, and smiled and nodded with delight; and yet could not altogether make out how British soldiers preferred a half-holiday to a quart of beer. He said the times were changed since his day; and with that he slipped a bank-note into my hand, and went off, his thoughts, I feel sure, contrasting the present with the past.

Shortly after General Thompson's visit, I had to appear on parade again, and this time in front of all the men of the entire depôt. But it was with far different feelings to those I laboured under when last performing the principal part in a public function of this sort at Bangalore. For on the present occasion I was presented with a silver medal, bearing on it the words—"For Long Service and Good Conduct," with my name, rank, and regimental number engraved on the rim. As Colonel Le Q—— pinned it on my breast he spoke a few words of kindly praise, wishing me long life to wear it; and I am not above confessing that I felt proud of myself when he shook hands with me in front of the whole parade, and dismissed me to my troop.

Time passed pleasantly enough at Canterbury, though the life was not exactly what I could have wished. Often at morning stables Bill Thompson and I used to talk about our past days, and contrast them with our present ones. And then we would discuss the future, and I learnt from him that his ideas tended towards the yeomanry. This led me to think about the same, and we got on to imagining how pleasant it would be if we were settled within reach of each other. But I was not so keen as he upon leaving Canterbury, my wish being to work up the depôt, and hand it over to my regiment in a high state of efficiency on their return to England.

Early in September, 1885, we sent out eighty-eight men to India, and they were accompanied by our two officers. No others being posted to take their places, I was left without any superior for three months, which threw a great deal of responsibility on my shoulders, until the end of November, when

Captain T——, who had been our adjutant for many years, arrived from India, and took over charge. It was very pleasant meeting again an officer with whom I had been brought into much contact in South Africa and at Bolaram, and hearing all the news of the regiment.

Very soon after he joined it was decided by the authorities that the depôt of the 14th should be transferred to the provisional cavalry depôt at Colchester, as owing to our large muster we took up too much room at Canterbury. Before we left, Colonel Le Q—— addressed us briefly, telling us that we had earned a good name, and that he was sorry to lose us. We then marched to the station, where, of course, Bill Thompson turned up to wish me good-bye, and his last words were I was not to be surprised if I heard soon of his joining the yeomanry.

The provisional cavalry depôt at Colchester was under the command of Colonel G——, and consisted of the depôt s of the 19th and 20th Hussars, who were in Egypt, and the Inniskillings, who were still in South Africa. The system and arrangements were very different to those in vogue at Canterbury. There were a greater number of horses for the lads to ride, but fewer instructors; and although there was much more mounted drill, I do not think the recruits learnt so much of the ordinary duties of soldiering as they did at their last station. Colchester itself was not such a pleasant place, and the system new to us; but we were able to hold our own, and I think Colonel G—— was soon as fond of us as Colonel Le Q—— had been.

Depôt work, however, did not suit Captain T——, for here he had hardly anything to do with his men on parade. For many years he had been the active adjutant of a smart cavalry regiment on foreign service, often in sole charge of it at both mounted and foot parade. The transition to depôt life, with only recruits to superintend in the stables and barrack rooms, was very different work, and altogether too idle for him, and I soon began to suspect he had had enough of it.

Nothing particular occurred at Colchester until midsummer, when all the depôts received orders to move to Shorncliffe to make room for an entire cavalry regiment. Sir Evelyn Wood had received command of the Eastern district, and he was not the man to have one of the finest cavalry barracks under his command without a good regiment in it; so off we had to pack. I had made up my mind that my marching days were over, but here was a pretty little march to accomplish, for we went by road to Shorncliffe. I need not say that the time-honoured institution of the White Jug was kept up, and that Captain T—— gave our lads as pleasant a ride as they could wish for, through the garden county of England, including taking our horses over the Thames from Tilbury to Gravesend, in batches of a dozen at a time, by penny steamboat.

This chopping and changing about which we had undergone during the last six months, made things very uncomfortable, but nevertheless Captain T—— put his shoulder to the wheel, and I did my utmost to second his endeavours to prepare a good body of recruits against the arrival of the regiment from India, for we knew it would reach home very short-handed. We got together a fine body of two hundred smart young lads, and it is no exaggeration to say we were at it night and day. And although we often found ourselves comparing this tame enough life with that which we had led in the old days, we were cheered by the knowledge that the regiment would reap the benefit of our efforts.

Judge then our feelings of dismay when one Sunday, about four months before the 14th was expected home, on returning from church parade, every man of our depôt was ordered to parade in front of orderly-room. Colonel G—— then called the troop to attention, and to the surprise and mortification of both Captain T—— and myself, read out an order that all our men under three months' service were to be forthwith transferred to the 7th Hussars, and that all over that service might volunteer for the same regiment, which was just proceeding to India to relieve the 14th. To make matters worse, he pointed out to those who desired to see foreign service, that now was their time, for as the 14th was coming home and would remain in England for some years, unless they accepted this chance all their soldiering would be in the United Kingdom. The argument was irresistible, for *Kálapoosh* was every young fellow's ambition. Before evening our depôt had lost more than half its muster.

I should have mentioned that just previous to this, news reached us of the death of Colonel K——at Bolaram. I need not say how deeply I felt it, for the kind old officer had always been a good friend to me. Captain T——, too, was very much attached to him, and when on the top of this came the transfer of half our depôt, which we had worked so hard to bring to efficiency, I could see that he was working up his mind to carry out his often expressed resolve of sending in his paper.

And so I was not surprised when two days later I took him the documents connected with the transfer of our men, for his signature, to learn from him that his mind was made up, and he was going to leave the Service. It seemed to me that we were defeated in trying to accomplish that which we had been sent home to do, and that we had now no time left to remedy the matter. We talked of this a little time, and I expressed the opinion that I, too, felt inclined to give it up as an impossible job.

"I can't blame you," was all he said.

Then I told him that my ambition was to serve out two years more, so as to complete my twenty-five years, and that was the only thing that kept me hanging on.

"Would you like to go as sergeant-major to a troop of yeomanry?" he asked, as if the idea had just struck him.

I thought of Bill Thompson, and at once answered, "I should, sir."

"Then I'll see what I can do for you," was Captain T——'s reply.

I knew him well enough to feel sure that when he said he would "see about" a thing, it was as good as done if he could do it, and I realised that the days of my soldiering in the 14th Hussars were drawing to a close. But, as it turned out, I had one more military function to attend in my capacity of sergeant-major of the old regiment, and it is one the memory of which I shall always cherish.

His Royal Highness the late Duke of Clarence and Avondale came down to Dover to present colours to an infantry regiment, and the cavalry depôt at Shorncliffe was ordered to furnish an escort. For this honour Colonel G—— selected the 14th Hussars, and a non-commissioned officer and four men were told off to meet the Prince at the railway station at Dover, and escort him to the Shaft barracks. I accompanied the escort, both to see the work properly carried out, and in order that my charger might be placed at His Royal Highness's disposal. On arriving at Dover, I would have no help, but groomed the horse with my own hands—the first time I had done so (except in active service) for many years—and made his coat shine like satin. When the Prince arrived, his saddle was put on the animal, and I had the honour of holding it while he mounted.

On my return to Shorncliffe I received a message from Captain T—— asking me to come up to his quarters at once, when he told me he had been making enquiries about the yeomanry, and found there was a troop vacant, for which many applications had been made, but there was yet time to send in mine. He added that he had resigned the Service, and this was the last time he would speak to me as my captain. More than sorry I was to hear it, for it broke the last link between me and the 14th Hussars as I had known them, and it decided me to make my application for the yeomanry. Thanks to recommendations from Colonel G—— and Captain T——, I was successful in obtaining the appointment, and a notification to that effect reached me within a fortnight.

There was of course some delay before the papers were made out, but having friends in the headquarters' office of the South-Eastern Division at Dover, I paid them a visit with a view to finding out the probable date of my transfer. I was allowed to look at the official letter-book, and there by a curious coincidence, I found two letters on consecutive pages, and both dated the same day. One relating to my transfer to a troop of yeomanry in the eastern counties, and the other to my old chum Bill Thompson's appointment to a similar post in Oxfordshire!

And so it came to pass that we two old friends and old soldiers, who had joined the army within a month of each other twenty-three years before, had soldiered, sometimes together, but more often apart, in England, Ireland, and India, and finally side by side at Canterbury, by a strange chance left the depôts of our respective regiments on the same day to take over similar appointments in the yeomanry of England.

CHAPTER 24

The Queen's Shilling is Worked Out

On receiving my final orders for transfer to the yeomanry, I wrote to the adjutant of the corps to which I was posted, asking him where and to whom I should report myself. His answer surprised me not a little, for he said there was nothing particular going on just at present, and I had better take two or three months' leave, and report myself when convenient! This did not suit my ideas, for my wish was to get settled. So after spending a week with my daughter, and arranging for her to come and live with me, I made my way to the town where the head-quarters of my new troop were located.

I soon began to make inquiries about it, and I must confess I was a good deal disappointed at what I had learnt. The troop I had to take over, although it had once been in a flourishing condition, was now far from that, having dwindled down to about a dozen men; and all I heard and saw of the state of affairs made me wish myself back at the depôt.

The captain of the troop was a barrister and the son of a well-known landed proprietor in the district. He had hitherto lived in London, but having recently purchased a large estate in the neighbourhood, was coming to reside on it; and the adjutant informed me that things would be very different when he came, but he was not expected for two months and nothing much could be done in the interim. Luckily I had work to employ me during this period, for I was shortly ordered to proceed to Aldershot to undergo a month's instruction to qualify me for my new duties At the end of it I passed my examination with credit, and returned to the country town, where I rented a nice little cottage, with a garden attached, and furnished it very comfortably. When all was ready, my daughter, who was now eleven years old, came to live with me, and although she did not exactly keep house, she went near doing it with a little help.

When the captain of the troop arrived I met him by appointment at the principal hotel in the town to receive his instructions. He told me he wished to bring the troop into its old state of efficiency, though he feared it would be a difficult task, as, owing to the agricultural depression a great number of farms were without tenants, which deprived the yeomanry of the services of a great many men. He asked me to use my best endeavours to raise recruits, and if possible from amongst the better classes, such as those who could afford to provide their own horses, but failing this, to raise a respectable muster by any means in my power, so that at the annual training the troop might do credit to himself and me. I soon saw I was dealing with a liberal and public-spirited gentleman; for the upkeep of the yeomanry devolves almost entirely upon the captains of the troops, who are put to considerable expense if they are ambitious of showing up well.

Knowing now exactly what I was required to do I set to work to shake the troop up. First of all I got rid of the "Boozers" who were not fit for the work, socially or physically, and ought never to have been enlisted. Then I began recruiting, keeping my eyes purling on market days, noting the smartest young farmers and not overlooking the town's folks. A civil word here, a cheery nod there, and a smile for everyone soon got me into touch with them, and then I worked on their soft sides. But what did more than all the blarney was the improvement that I suggested and the adjutant effected in the uniform, making it altogether much smarter and more becoming, so that all the young sparks fancied they would look a treat in it. In this way, working steadily and with one purpose in my mind, I was successful in getting together about thirty young fellows, all well mounted and well set up, and looking fine and soldierly in their new uniforms.

The various troops in the corps had to meet for their annual training at a county town about thirty miles distant, and in order to give the town's people a touch of our quality I persuaded the captain to ride by march route to the *rendezvous* instead of going by rail as had been the custom before. This little incident, trifling as it was, brought us a good deal of credit, which was increased by the workmanlike way in which the men conducted themselves during the training. The consequence was, people began talking about us, and on my return I had no difficulty in increasing our strength to a number which the captain thought enough.

My life was a very pleasant one, the only drawback being that I had not enough to do. My duties were too easy, for I had only two foot drills a month, four or five mounted drills in the year, and the ten days' annual training. Before I took over charge, the foot drills used to be conducted in a large room in a public-house and were regarded more as an excuse for enjoying a jovial evening than an occasion for learning drill. This I soon altered by obtaining a room in the town museum, where no liquor was to be had, and where the surroundings were of an austere nature, with long Latin names, calculated to promote steadiness of thought and sobriety of discipline. I also visited the men at their private residences or farms to give them a little individual instruction, and these occasions were made very pleasant for me, always ensuring plenty of fishing and shooting in the proper season and hospitality and welcome all the year round.

But, counting everything, I had certainly less than two months' work in the year, and ten months of leisure. The idleness of the life began to pall upon me soon, for although I had my cottage and my garden and indulged to the full my hobby for keeping pets, still I never felt able to settle down to civilian pursuits so long as I remained a soldier, and what I did in my garden and in poultry and rabbit-rearing was pastime, not business. I always had a liking for farming which was born in me, I think, and now, mixing with farming folk the ruling passion came out strong and I began little by little to turn my thoughts to it as an occupation for the future. And soon I determined in my mind that when I had put in my full twenty-five years' service and completed the work I had been engaged for, namely to raise and train a full troop for my captain, I would buy a bit of a farm and settle down to country life.

During these lazy days I had much time for reflection and retrospect, and often whilst sitting in my garden, smoking my pipe, and watching my little girl flitting about among her flowers, or attending to her pets, my thoughts would travel back to the past, and I lived again in recollection through many of the incidents recorded in these pages,

And they were pleasant thoughts which wandered back to the old regiment, and the years I had spent in it; to the officers I had served under; the horses I had handled; the comrades I had soldiered with. What changes there had been! My first comrades had been men who enlisted for a life-time, whilst the lads I recently had to deal with served what was, in comparison, merely an apprenticeship to the profession of arms, and left the army just as they had become trained and serviceable cavalrymen. Then there were the great strides education had made, whether for good or evil remains to be seen, and the change in the class of recruits. As far as irksome restrictions are concerned, the young soldier now begins his career where many of the hardy veterans of my younger days left off; and, indeed, he is in many ways infinitely better off, both as regards food and clothing, and the money he can earn. A private Hussar in the early sixties was a clever man if he was "on" threepence a day for the last half of each month, and I can remember a spell of six months when my own pay, after deductions, was sixpence a week; but now any decently-behaved recruit can walk up to the pay-table once a week and take off three to five shillings certain. The modern Hussar has no uniform to replace, as his predecessor had, nor is the circle of his recreation restricted to the letters that spell "canteen." Libraries and recreation rooms in barracks open their doors to him, and institutes and soldiers' homes outside remind him that there are many people who think kindly of him and wish him well. These reforms have done good. Drunkenness in the army is the exception now, and not the rule, and crime has greatly diminished. The Service is a good service—short and sweet, perhaps, where it might be long and sweet—and compares favourably as a profession with many civilian ones. Think of the thousands and thousands of lads starting life without a trade in their hands, living from hand to mouth, shunted from pillar to post, in an uncertain struggle for existence, who, when their day's work is done, have no comfortable home to return to, and no facilities for improving themselves. Compare this to the benefits a soldier enjoys in the present day. A young fellow who has learnt a good trade, or has fair business prospects, may be wise to remain where he is; but those whom I have described, the pickers-up of promiscuous livelihoods, would do well to take the Queen's shilling. And, having taken it, let them make up their minds to work it out, which they can only do in these days of short service by becoming non-commissioned officers. Let them start with a good heart, determined to make soldiering the business of their lives; to take their chances as they come, always bearing in mind the eleventh commandment, and to keep clean, obedient and steady. Having once enlisted, always look forward and work away for the sergeant's stripes. These gained, I most emphatically assert they will never regret the step they took, for a sergeant in Her Majesty's army lives a life that is worth living, and while still in the prime of it can leave the service with a pension sufficient for his old age.

 I must not forget to mention the off-chance of a commission, but this really is an off-chance, and not, as is often set forth, something in everyone's power to obtain. It should be left out of all practical calculations, for during my twenty years' service I only remember seven men in my regiment who gained one.

 Many young gentlemen, unable to pass the examinations, join the ranks with a view to becoming officers. I could mention a great number who enlisted, full of spirit and determination, and worked hard. But from three to six months seemed to satisfy them, for they nearly always found the game different to what they expected, and purchased their discharges. To give them their due, whilst they were at it they shirked no duty, nor the petty fatigues which were far more irksome; but they were not born for the life. Whilst they were in the ranks their influence was for good, and they were always able to take care of themselves; but they soon recognised that without interest at their backs they could hope for nothing, and that in peace time only about one non-commissioned officer in a hundred gets his commission, and then very often by a fluke. This may sound strange, but I will relate the actual experiences of three men who, under my own observation, rose from the ranks to a commission, and whose cases, I believe, are fairly representative ones.

A—— was a gentlemanly, well-educated young fellow, and proved himself a steady soldier, but, in a military point of view, he was a very indifferent rider. He was sergeant for five years, but never distinguished himself, most of his fellow-sergeants being superior to him in smartness and drill. But he had interest (his father being a general officer) and money, and the consequence was he gained a lieutenancy in a Lancer regiment, on the apparent grounds of seven years' peace service, and a nice quiet style of behaviour.

B—— came from the lower middle classes. Whilst a recruit he had the misfortune (or good fortune ?) to receive a wound in his hand from the instructor's sword, and went to hospital for some time. When cured he was sent as a waiter to the officers' mess, and in time rose to be mess-sergeant. Being a well-conducted man he became popular with the officers, and this led to his obtaining his commission when a vacancy occurred for quartermaster, although he had never been on guard, or done a single day's sergeant's duty.

C—— was another soldier drawn from the same class in life as B——. He was invalided home from India, as a sergeant, and sent to Canterbury, where he was employed on odd jobs about the riding-school

Being a good rider, he was placed on the riding establishment, and eventually gained a commission as riding-master in one of the crack cavalry corps of the Service.

These are not special instances, but are quoted as showing promotion to the combatants' branch, a quarter-mastership, and the rank of riding-master. Against the three officers I have nothing to urge, and it is far from my desire to hint that they were not deserving of their commissions. They were all right good fellows, and popular members of their sergeants' mess; but I think their promotion shows that a commission in their cases was not gained by any extra smartness or particularly fine soldierly qualities, but by sheer good luck.

And so I repeat to all young fellows entering the army, regard a commission only as an off-chance. And my advice would be to make for the sergeants' mess, and when you get there, stop there. I speak from the experience of many years, and have grounds for my opinion. A commission from the ranks is not always an unmixed blessing, as I could prove by some sad instances I have seen.

Before closing my last chapter I must say a word or two about horses, for most of my service was spent in looking after their welfare. They varied as much in disposition as the men did. Some were always gentle and docile; others, when they first joined, wild and nervous; but all, with very few exceptions, were amenable to kindness and eager to learn. Their colours gave a very fair idea of their constitutions or characteristics. Bright chestnuts and light bays were invariably high-spirited animals, but of nervous unsettled temperament and delicate constitution. Dark chestnuts and glossy blacks were hardy, and, as a rule, good-tempered. Rich bays possessed great spirit, but -were, at the same time, docile. Dark greys and iron greys were hardy and of good constitution, whilst light greys were just the reverse. The hardest and best working horses of all were roans, either strawberry or blue, which were always even tempered, the easiest to train, and took kindly to everything. They were, in fact, just the opposite to a rusty black, which gains the palm for pigheadedness. Another curious indication of a horse's character could be gleaned from its white stockings. A horse with one white leg is a bad one; with two white legs, you may "sell it to a friend;" with four white legs, you may trust it for a spell; but with three white legs, you may safely lay your life on it.

Horses very often display a particular affection for one another, as old Will and Balaclava did, and I always found it a good thing to expend a little patience and observation in discovering such friendships, and then stabling the horses next each other, and keeping them as much together as possible on the parade-ground or in the field. They looked better, and did better, and brought more credit on all concerned. With very few exceptions all horses like to have a chum, and in several instances in Ireland I was able to trace the friendship of two animals to their having been bred on the same farm, and though brought to market at different seasons, on meeting afterwards in the Service, they remembered each other, and renewed their old intimacy.

Of the affection of horses for their riders I could tell many a story, but must confine myself to a single instance. "H-36" was a splendid black Irish horse, and with a man on his back there was no handsomer or quieter trooper in the regiment. But in the stable he was a perfect devil, especially with his teeth, and would savage man or horse who came within his reach. In spite of being placed in a loose box in the sick lines, and many precautions taken, so greatly was he dreaded that I have known a man desert when told to look after him, rather than run the risk it involved.

At last a wild, drunken old soldier, known as "Larry," took over charge of Black Jack, and somehow or other completely mastered him, until he was able to do as he liked with the animal, grooming him without a muzzle on, and going about the stable as he would with the quietest horse in the troop. But Larry was a thirsty soul, and it often happened he would get drunk, and whenever this was the case, he would roll from the canteen to Black Jack's box and throw himself on the straw. The horse would immediately take up his stand in front of his prostrate master, and defy the whole guard to take Larry to the clink, till he chose to go of his own accord.

When Larry's soldiering days were over, and he was discharged, Black Jack soon followed. He missed his old rider, and grew more and more savage, and one day tore the breast out of a soldier named Scotland, and was cast for vice.

But I must now return to my story and bring it to a conclusion. In 1888, Sir Evelyn Wood, the general commanding the Eastern Division, signified his intention of inspecting our corps of yeomanry, and on the last day of our annual training came down for that purpose. We were encamped near the sea-shore in this year, and the expansive level sands afforded fine ground for manoeuvring. General Wood put us through our facings in fine style, and as he shook us up, my thoughts went back to the field days at Ladysmith, when the same officer made the old regiment move in a way that was brisk even for it. Here he practised us in those sorts of movements which yeomanry are specially fitted for, and fond as my troop had become of galloping and drilling, they had their fill of it. But when it was over they felt themselves amply repaid by the liberal praise General Wood gave them, for he expressed a very high opinion of their efficiency, their smartness, and their horse-flesh.

It is often the case that on the last day of the yeomanry training an officer from the Army Remount Department attends, in order to see if there are any horses for sale, suitable for Government purposes. In pursuance of this custom one came down to attend our last parade. When it was over the word was passed down for me to present myself, and galloping up to the front our colonel told me that a gentleman, in civilian clothes, riding next him, wanted to speak to me. On turning my eyes to see who it was, I recognised Colonel M———, who had commanded the 14th Hussars in India, when Colonel K——— went home on furlough, and again after that officer's death. Colonel M——— was now head of the Army Remount Department, and proud I was when he shook hands with me, and applying many kindly words of praise to my troop, said he was delighted to find they had been worked up to their state of proficiency by an old non-commissioned officer of his.

For some weeks before this I had made up my mind to leave the Service, having fixed on a nice little bit of a farm, which seemed likely to suit me, and I only deferred sending in my papers till I had completed my twenty-fifth year in the army. The time was now up, and the opportunity seemed a suitable one. I felt I had done my task, having recruited a full troop for the captain, and drilled them into an efficient state, and that I might tender my resignation with a free conscience.

So the next day, after I had paid the men, received back their arms, and settled all details with the captain, I handed him a written request for my discharge from the Service, and on the 27th July, 1888, I passed out of the profession into civilian life, feeling I might fairly claim I had worked out the Queen's shilling.

With the record of a sergeant's and a sergeant-major's rank for seventeen years; with a discharge bearing against the word *character* the description *very good;* with a good-conduct medal on my breast, a pension of upwards of forty pounds a year to draw, and a balance of several hundred pounds in the savings' bank, in perfect health and strength, and indeed feeling fit to do another quarter of a century of soldiering, I left the army. And I thought that day, and think still, that had I my life in front of me instead of behind, I would start again, just as I did when I was a lad of eighteen, and desire nothing better than to live those happy twenty-five years over again in the ranks of the Old 14th as a King's Hussar.

ALSO FROM LEONAUR

AVAILABLE IN SOFTCOVER OR HARDCOVER WITH DUST JACKET

A JOURNAL OF THE SECOND SIKH WAR by *Daniel A. Sandford*—The Experiences of an Ensign of the 2nd Bengal European Regiment During the Campaign in the Punjab, India, 1848-49.

LAKE'S CAMPAIGNS IN INDIA by *Hugh Pearse*—The Second Anglo Maratha War, 1803-1807. Often neglected by historians and students alike, Lake's Indian campaign was fought against a resourceful and ruthless enemy-almost always superior in numbers to his own forces.

BRITAIN IN AFGHANISTAN 1: THE FIRST AFGHAN WAR 1839-42 by *Archibald Forbes*—Following over a century of the gradual assumption of sovereignty of the Indian Sub-Continent, the British Empire, in the form of the Honourable East India Company, supported by troops of the new Queen Victoria's army, found itself inevitably at the natural boundaries that surround Afghanistan. There it set in motion a series of disastrous events-the first of which was to march into the country at all.

BRITAIN IN AFGHANISTAN 2: THE SECOND AFGHAN WAR 1878-80 by *Archibald Forbes*—This the history of the Second Afghan War-another episode of British military history typified by savagery, massacre, siege and battles.

UP AMONG THE PANDIES by *Vivian Dering Majendie*—An outstanding account of the campaign for the fall of Lucknow. *This is a vital book of war as fought by the British Army of the mid-nineteenth century, but in truth it is also an essential book of war that will enthral military historians and general readers alike.*

BLOW THE BUGLE, DRAW THE SWORD by *W. H. G. Kingston*—The Wars, Campaigns, Regiments and Soldiers of the British & Indian Armies During the Victorian Era, 1839-1898.

INDIAN MUTINY 150th ANNIVERSARY: A LEONAUR ORIGINAL

MUTINY: 1857 by *James Humphries*—It is now 150 years since the 'Indian Mutiny' burst like an engulfing flame on the British soldiers, their families and the civilians of the Empire in North East India. The Bengal Native army arose in violent rebellion, and the once peaceful countryside became a battleground as Native sepoys and elements of the Indian population massacred their British masters and defeated them in open battle. As the tide turned, a vengeful army of British and loyal Indian troops repressed the insurgency with a savagery that knew no mercy. It was a time of fear and slaughter. James Humphries has drawn together the voices of those dreadful days for this commemorative book.

AVAILABLE ONLINE AT
www.leonaur.com
AND OTHER GOOD BOOK STORES

ALSO FROM LEONAUR
AVAILABLE IN SOFTCOVER OR HARDCOVER WITH DUST JACKET

WAR BEYOND THE DRAGON PAGODA by *J. J. Snodgrass*—A Personal Narrative of the First Anglo-Burmese War 1824 - 1826.

ALL FOR A SHILLING A DAY by *Donald F. Featherstone*—The story of H.M. 16th, the Queen's Lancers During the first Sikh War 1845-1846.

AT THEM WITH THE BAYONET by *Donald F. Featherstone*—The first Anglo-Sikh War 1845-1846.

A LEONAUR ORIGINAL

THE HERO OF ALIWAL by *James Humphries*—The days when young Harry Smith wore the green jacket of the 95th-Wellington's famous riflemen-campaigning in Spain against Napoleon's French with his beautiful young bride Juana have long gone. Now, Sir Harry Smith is in his fifties approaching the end of a long career. His position in the Cape colony ends with an appointment as Deputy Adjutant-General to the army in India. There he joins the staff of Sir Hugh Gough to experience an Indian battlefield in the Gwalior War of 1843 as the power of the Marathas is finally crushed. Smith has little time for his superior's 'bull at a gate' style of battlefield tactics, but independent command is denied him. Little does he realise that the greatest opportunity of his military life is close at hand.

THE GURKHA WAR by *H. T. Prinsep*—The Anglo-Nepalese Conflict in North East India 1814-1816.

SOUND ADVANCE! by *Joseph Anderson*—Experiences of an officer of HM 50th regiment in Australia, Burma & the Gwalior war.

THE CAMPAIGN OF THE INDUS by *Thomas Holdsworth*—Experiences of a British Officer of the 2nd (Queen's Royal) Regiment in the Campaign to Place Shah Shuja on the Throne of Afghanistan 1838 - 1840.

WITH THE MADRAS EUROPEAN REGIMENT IN BURMA by *John Butler*—The Experiences of an Officer of the Honourable East India Company's Army During the First Anglo-Burmese War 1824 - 1826.

BESIEGED IN LUCKNOW by *Martin Richard Gubbins*—The Experiences of the Defender of 'Gubbins Post' before & during the sige of the residency at Lucknow, Indian Mutiny, 1857.

THE STORY OF THE GUIDES by *G.J. Younghusband*—The Exploits of the famous Indian Army Regiment from the northwest frontier 1847 - 1900.

AVAILABLE ONLINE AT
www.leonaur.com
AND OTHER GOOD BOOK STORES